Awkward Politics

Technologies of Popfeminist Activism

CARRIE SMITH-PREI

AND

MARIA STEHLE

McGill-Queen's University Press

Montreal & Kingston · London · Chicago

© McGill-Queen's University Press 2016

ISBN 978-0-7735-4746-9 (cloth)
ISBN 978-0-7735-4747-6 (paper)
ISBN 978-0-7735-9896-6 (ePDF)
ISBN 978-0-7735-9897-3 (ePUB)

Legal deposit second quarter 2016 Bibliothèque nationale du Québec

Printed in Canada on acid-free paper that is 100% ancient forest free
(100% post-consumer recycled), processed chlorine free

This book has been published with the help of a grant from the
Canadian Federation for the Humanities and Social Sciences, through
the Awards to Scholarly Publications Program, using funds provided by
the Social Sciences and Humanities Research Council of Canada.

McGill-Queen's University Press acknowledges the support of the
Canada Council for the Arts for our publishing program. We also
acknowledge the financial support of the Government of Canada
through the Canada Book Fund for our publishing activities.

Library and Archives Canada Cataloguing in Publication

Smith-Prei, Carrie, 1975-, author
  Awkward politics : technologies of popfeminist activism /
Carrie Smith-Prei and Maria Stehle.

Includes bibliographical references and index.
Issued in print and electronic formats.
ISBN 978-0-7735-4746-9 (cloth). – ISBN 978-0-7735-4747-6 (paper). –
ISBN 978-0-7735-9896-6 (PDF). – ISBN 978-0-7735-9897-3 (ePUB)

  1. Feminism – Political aspects. 2. Feminism – Social aspects. 3.
Technology – Political aspects. I. Stehle, Maria, author II.
Title.

HQ1233.S65 2016   305.42   C2015-908593-4
                                 C2015-908594-2

Typeset by New Leaf Publication Design in 10.5/13 Sabon

For our future popfeminists –
Adeline and Leopold, Emily and Rebecca

Contents

Illustrations

Acknowledgments

This book is a collaboration that goes beyond its two co-authors. In so many ways, writing this book was not a pristine, solitary act but, instead, an embedded process. As we wrote, we thought through ideas by and with other academics, activists, artists, friends, family, and students. We wrote and thought together on- and offline while we collaborated with our families and friends on other life-tasks. We shared ideas and had ideas while we showered, washed dishes, played with our children, or held our babies. We listened to news stories and read commentaries. We travelled, we gave talks, we published, and we discussed. In the following, we name but a few of the people who made this book possible and of the institutions that supported us during the process of writing it.

Awkward Politics is part of a larger project – "Technologies of Pop-feminist Activism" – funded by an Insight Grant from the Social Sciences and Humanities Research Council of Canada (SSHRC). We thank the anonymous reviewers of the proposal as well as the committee members who recommended that our project be supported. The grant supported us throughout the research phase of this book, including fieldwork in Germany, conference travel, and graduate and technical assistance, all essential to making *Awkward Politics* what it is now. We also thank the numerous research assistants and technical support staff who have helped us along the way: Ruslan Bergenov, Mary Catherine Lawler, Daria Polianska, Lars Richter, Kay Rollans, and Emma Tunney as well as Clare Peters and Kamal Ranaweera. Very special and heart-felt thanks goes out to Olena Hlazkova, our research assistant who has been with the project since its very inception, reading drafts of the project proposal, collecting research on Pussy Riot and Femen in particular, translating texts from Russian and Ukrainian into English, compiling our bibliography, and assisting in other related projects. Without her dedicated collaboration with us, this book would not have been possible.

In the process of conceiving of *Awkward Politics*, we have also communicated and worked with many colleagues in North America and Europe. An important component of this project was a digital lecture series, co-organized with Christina Scharff, Hester Baer, and Pinar Tuzcu. A special thanks goes to Beverly Weber, who engaged with, tweeted about, and commented on our lectures. We also want to thank all the contributors, the journal editors, and our issue co-editor Christina Scharff for the special issue of *Feminist Media Studies*. A special thanks goes to Hester Baer and Alexandra M. Hill, co-editors of *German Women's Writing in the 21st Century* (Camden House, 2015), for their insightful comments on our contribution to this volume – comments that helped us to refine our arguments at a crucial stage in the writing process. We also thank the co-editors of the *Women in German Yearbook*, volume 30, for inviting us to contribute to the special section "Provocations for the Future," in which our thoughts on the academy offered here germinated.

Awkward Politics was inspired by our opportunities to give talks at various venues in Canada, the United States, Germany, and Ireland. A special thanks goes to the organization Women in German, which enabled our first meeting and the initial discussions that led to this project. In the following years, we presented parts of this work at Women in German conferences, discussed drafts during the conference, and shared some of our ideas in the *Women in German Yearbook*. We also had the opportunity to talk through some of our ideas on popfeminist awkwardness with colleagues and students at the University of Bremen (Germany), the University of Münster (Germany), Maynooth University (Ireland), Reed College and Portland State University (Portland, Oregon), the Monnet Center for European Studies (Gainesville, Florida), and at our home institutions in Edmonton (Alberta) and Knoxville (Tennessee). In conjunction with these invited talks and other collaborations, we thank the following people: Katja Garloff, Harrell Fletcher, Valerie Heffernan, Britta Herrmann, Marion Schulz, and Michael Thomas Taylor. We thank our colleagues and students at all these institutions and places for their interest, input, and support!

Further, we especially thank Reyhan Şahin for her input and enthusiasm – and really, for getting this whole thing started, for it was her work that brought us together – as well as her willingness to join us on future endeavours. We also thank Fiona Garden, epa, and Credo film for sharing image rights with us; Ralf Schweimeier for being our on-site photographer in Berlin; and Elysia Mann for related art. An important thank you goes out to the team at McGill-Queen's University Press. Thank you to Jacqueline Mason, who initially showed interest in the project and whose enthusiasm and advice has been invaluable. We thank you for the courage to support our work. We further thank the three anonymous reviewers of the manuscript for their thoughtful comments, careful reading, and positive responses. Finally, we thank the rest of the editorial team at the press, including Ryan Van Huijstee, managing editor; Joanne Richardson, copy editor; and others for seeing this project through the publication process.

We thank our families who have supported us throughout this work, at home and in our travels, and especially our partners, Doreen Prei and Matthew Brown. Final thanks is reserved for the reader who is willing to pick up this book, to think through the importance of feminism with us, and to embrace our thoughts and methodologies.

AWKWARD POLITICS

Awkward Activism in the Digital Age

THIS IS A CALL TO ALL PUSSY RIOT SUPPORTERS Whether you are in Berlin or anywhere in the world. Peaches and Simonne Jones are writing a FREE PUSSY RIOT SONG tomorrow and shooting a video for it on Wednesday. If you are in Berlin, show up dress as your best bad self and march down the streets and in the park with us singing FREE PUSSY RIOT: The more the better so big supporter with you. we will meet at 5pm outside GLory Whole cafe at Oderberger Straße 13, 10435 Berlin not far from Eberswalder u bahn If you are not in Berlin or can't make it. please send a 30 second video of yourself showing support by dancing, jumping on your bed, breaking shit, laughing, holding a free pussy riot sign etc. send a link to your video to my e mail address peachesnisker@gmail.com we will edit this on the weekend and get it out into the world by Monday. We have to do this!!!!!! Thxxx to you all and FREE PUSSY RIOT. (Riot Grrrl Berlin on FB; spelling and grammar in original)

In August 2012, Canadian Berlin-based feminist punk musician Peaches put out a call on the Facebook page of the group Riot Grrrl Berlin, inviting all Pussy Riot supporters to join in creative action. Such immediate Western cries of support for the then imprisoned members of Pussy Riot were only possible because the group's own protest actions; the documentation of their arrest, ensuing trial, and imprisonment; their songs and manifestos; and their image – dominated by the now-ubiquitous colourful balaclavas – were geared towards transnational digital dissemination. The very evening following Pussy Riot's performance in Moscow's Cathedral of Christ the Saviour, which led to the

0.1   Peaches "Free Pussy Riot" video shoot (Berlin), 2012

arrest of three members of the group and thus to the beginning of their international recognisability, a video of the performance entitled "Punk Prayer – Mother of God, Chase Putin Away" had been produced and distributed via online platforms. A similar process of instant dissemination enabled the creative responses in Western feminist communities to Pussy Riot's arrests, such as the wearing of balaclavas in solidarity, the printing of posters and making of statues, the compiling of the digital poetry collection *Poems for Pussy Riot*, and, as the call for contributions above illustrates, the making of music videos. "Free Pussy Riot," therefore, not only became a political catchphrase but also symbolized the acknowledgment of and participation in the global force of popfeminist protest art in the age of digital technology.

The call for submissions and participants distributed by Peaches exhibits a number of features. In its grammatical and lexical missteps, its running together of sentences, its text messaging-like shortening of words or preference for lower case, and its excessive use of exclamation marks, the call communicates a sense of immediate urgency pushed forward by emotion. The mistakes combined with the use of slang further indicate the message's intended audience: a specific demographic of young people whose first language might not be English. When the appearance of this call on the Facebook page of Riot Grrrl Berlin is taken into account, additional dimensions of feminist solidarity, digital community building, musical historical lineage, transnational influence (United States as the origin of the riot grrrl movement), and place specificity (Berlin) are added to the mix.

These features of the call are also found in the responses submitted and the other footage that comprise the video, which itself is legible as protest, creative action, and participatory event. *Rolling Stone* (2012) reported that the call garnered four hundred "participating activists" and seventy video submissions. In addition, like the video of Pussy Riot's original protest, the Peaches *Free Pussy Riot* video is also clearly made for transnational dissemination while remaining locally recognizable. The video oscillates between scenes from a rally-performance on Oderbergerstrasse and Mauerpark in the Prenzlauer Berg neighbourhood of former East Berlin and brief clips of people who filmed themselves in various poses and actions, following the call above. The video thus offers visuals that suggest the simultaneity of two localities. The first, the street protest, forms one continuous narrative thread that takes place in a clearly marked space of a specific quarter of Berlin, known for its combination of former artist squats, high-end tourist spots, and gentrified shops and restaurants selling local and organic products to the large influx of anglophone new-resident hipsters. In this manner, the choice of this location for the video speaks specifically to a range of transformations around the city of Berlin, especially with regard to the relationship between capitalism and resistance, creativity and commodity, in digital and performance art activism. Further, this is replicated in the demographics of the protestors, who, despite their hooded appearance, are clearly young, hip, overwhelmingly white, and, it can be assumed, feminist-minded. As the video comes to an end, police officers mix with the crowd in Berlin, but the gathering ends peacefully with what is deliberately filmed to look like a large crowd cheering and chanting together in Berlin's Mauerpark.

Scenes filmed in mainly unidentified locations from possibly anywhere in the world and sent in digitally by supporting activists repeatedly interrupt the street protest. The scenes in Berlin are local and public in their recognisability, but they also reference the material base for protest cultures in the form of the street protest. In contrast, the interspersed scenes taken from the submitted videos are private (sometimes solitary) and transnational or, better yet, de-nationalized. They therefore suggest the conflicting nature of the digital protest action – that is, its often individual and private creation paired with its broad reach across multiple global spaces. The footage includes scenes of people partying, destroying things, undressing, and dancing, all located primarily in bedrooms or unidentified enclosed rooms, with many scenes, such as a person on the toilet or a toddler on a playground, humorous in their staging. Most of the people in the frames are wearing balaclavas and some have painted "Free Pussy Riot" on parts of their bodies. The poses range from sexy (with lewd references to cunnilingus being the most prominent gesture) to defiant to embarrassing. What unifies these disparate scenes, including the street scenes in Berlin, is the palpable sense of joy of the participants. The colour of the frames is also distinctly pop, beginning already with the "Free Pussy Riot" opening titles that flicker orange, red, green, and yellow like neon lights. These title colours transform into the brightly tinted balaclavas of the protesters, balaclavas that multiply in a material match to digital code. The song that accompanies the visuals is composed as a rally chant, thereby replicating the tenor standard to protest songs with punk flair. It ends with the line "we are all Pussy Riot," yelled in increasing speed as the pace of the visual cuts increases to keep up with the speed of the music.

The final product was posted on the official YouTube channel of Peaches on 14 August 2012 and includes a link for viewers to sign the Change.org petition to free the remaining two imprisoned Pussy Riot members, thereby making a direct connection to traditional activism. At the same time, the comment section is left open, which leaves the video and its intention open to participatory, supportive, critical, or even virulent voices that are given a forum long after the imprisoned members of Pussy Riot were freed in December 2013. Thus, while freeing the members of the punk-performance group Pussy Riot from prison in Putin's Russia is the clearly stated political aim of this video project and song, the performance of solidarity also conveys a more general political message about feminist solidarity, joyful protest, and the intersection between art and activism in a digital age. It is difficult, though, to identify exactly where these politics are located, what their implied global aim might be, and how they are articulated beyond the colourful spectacle of a catchy song, the party atmosphere, and the participatory hype of social media. And while the images and music work together, they also clash and point to multiple directions of possible political intervention. The DIY (Do It Yourself) videos, the scenes of obviously staged street protest, the clearly recognizable activist gestures, the digital dissemination of the video, a global branding of Pussy Riot, and the fact that a professional musician (who herself appears, if only marginally, in the video) produced what is also clearly a commercial product clash in awkward ways.

In our initial attempts to tackle the question of feminist politics in the twenty-first century, we stumbled upon the term "awkwardness," and it stuck with us. The word, a combination of "ward" as a term to describe directionality and of "awk" as a term to describe a misdirected motion, even a motion that can be neither initiated nor controlled, that is non-chronological and multi-directional. Awkwardness messes with timing and with the timeline, it messes with space and location. It is very much of the body and its hormonal secretions, but it is also social and ephemeral, moving in and out of visibility, gone in an instant though leaving its emotional traces. Awkwardness can be coincidental, unintentional, or even an externally given label demarcating the upsetting of social norms, but it can also be intentionally provoked or engaged. Looking at the awkward allows us to approach popfeminist performances with a playful self-consciousness and a sense of agency. The digital becomes a means of capturing, archiving, and transmitting awkwardness. Digital spaces underscore the simultaneously public and private experience of the awkward while also intensifying the materiality, aesthetics, and affects of the awkward position.

The unclear political position seen in Peaches's *Free Pussy Riot* video that we describe as awkward is fostered – even enabled – by the fleeting and slippery nature of the digital as a medium, material, or means of circulation and by the performative. Integral to these two modes is the complex over-emphasis and marginalization of the body as gendered and racialized (Fleig 2000, 10). Both of these aspects of the body are crucial for a political understanding of awkward moments in popfeminist activism. The allusion to Teresa de Lauretis's groundbreaking text *Technologies of Gender* in the subtitle of our book – *Technologies of Popfeminist Activism* – is intentional. In *Technologies of Gender*, de Lauretis (1987, ix) sees gender as a product of "various social technologies" (ix), with reference to academic discussions and social and culture practice. According to de Lauretis, "the representation of gender *is* its construction," which "goes on as busily today as it did in earlier times" (3, emphasis in original). If gender is defined as a discursive construction via a flurry of representations, then gender categories are also defined by their deconstructions, by feminist discourses that question what they see as gender norms, and by any excess of its representation, by ruptures, destabilizations, or potential trauma (3). Technologies refer to that mechanism of construction, which facilitates a crossing of the theoretical with the practical. Both material bodies and the digital work as technologies that communicate the place where practice and theory collide.

These material and digital bodies are gendered and are also always communicated as racial. As Wendy Chun (2009, 8, emphasis in original) postulates in the introduction to a special issue on "Race and/ as Technology" of the journal *Camera Obscura*, "race as technology shifts the focus from the *what* of race to the *how* of race, from *knowing* race to *doing* race by emphasizing the similarities between race and technology. Indeed, *race as technology* is a simile that posits a comparative equality or substitutability – but not identity – between the two terms."[1] Thinking of gender and race as technologies, to follow Chun's argument further, means to displace the gendered or racialized body as purely cultural or purely biological because, as Chun posits, "technological mediation … is always already a mix of science, art, and culture" (8). If thinking about race as technology allows for the possibility of "mak[ing] race do different things" (28) as a way to fight racism, then, in the context of our discussions in the following chapters, this can be related directly to the ways in which digital feminisms and feminist activisms in the digital age attempt to create a different kind of body politics, to make both gendered and racialized bodies "do different things." This is where we locate new forms of agency in the interface of digital and analogue activisms, where words, images, and narratives matter. The aim of this book is to describe aspects of what these "different things" might be and to explore the messy – and awkward – ways in which we can read these "things" politically.

While discussions of the body and new technologies have long been standard to feminist theoretical vocabulary, little headway has been made in assessing the theoretical and practical impact digital mobility has had on transnational and local feminist body politics in protest performance art. This is a result, in part, of the difficulty of articulating the political in popfeminist activism and the attendant affective appearance of awkwardness. The moment we are describing in this book is one of realization that (maybe because of digital proliferations of the body) irony and playfulness no longer create a way of distancing ourselves from normative body politics; rather, such playful performativity illustrates over and over again the close connection between digital representations of the gendered and racialized body and the physical body in the digital age. Reading for awkwardness erases this distancing (the conscious decision to engage or disengage was always only a privilege for some people) and emphasizes connection.

In popfeminist activism, questions of the digital as a political space and of the body or the physical and material in that same space come together in a visibly troubling manner. It is precisely the awkward location of the body in feminist activism based in or inspired by digital technology and embedded securely within neoliberalism that is of interest to us. Contrary to what some branches of cyberfeminism suggested in the early 1990s,[2] digital space is not automatically a space where differences vanish, where borders dissolve, and where physical bodies take on new meanings. Pinar Tuzcu (2015, 1) suggests that, instead, "the true reason for feminist excitement about the expansion of virtual reality space is not the sudden, redemptive abolishment of all interfering differences, but rather, the opening up of new possibilities of politics of difference." Tuzcu argues against any overly optimistic *or* pessimistic approaches to the possibilities of digital spaces, but she suggests we understand the interface between digital and geographic locations as a place that allows for the production of shifting understandings of borders and locations. In the digital age, "locations become slippery, ungrounded, and regrounded" (ibid.). In a digital feminist understanding, locations, and along with them the differences therein, are open, shifting, and redirected: they are awkward.

Since we have arrived at the historic moment "when narratives of disembodiment are becoming normative" (Tuzcu 2015, 2), we face the challenge of developing a new kind of politics to address questions of difference found in or generated by such spaces. Minh-Ha Pham (2011, 2) echoes Tuzcu's perspective when she critiques what she calls "cyber-democratic perspectives" as "rooted in and reproduce[ing] neoliberal assumptions about bodily transcendence and freedom." In her analyses of race and body politics in fashion blogs, Pham shows that "the rhetoric of digital disembodiment" assumes that social markings, hierarchies, and passions would be negated by scientifically rationalized network systems (such a belief is connected to the neoliberal racial agenda of colour blindness) and that "the disappearance of the body in cyberspace would effect the disappearance of the desire to consume difference" (3). Her analyses prove that these cyberdemocratic assumptions about digital disembodiments are too simplistic and that they, in turn, merely replicate the neoliberal agenda that suggests we already live in a post-gender, post-racial world. She argues, though, that "technologies, which must now be understood as everyday technologies, show how cultural practices and technological innovations are not only framed by the global dynamics of the political economy and of state power but can also reframe the terms and conditions in which culture, technology, and capitalism intersect" (28). In short, Pham describes the question of political change and of the location of political moments within technologies in general as caught in a circular motion of framing and reframing. What we describe as awkward has a mis- and redirected motion found within this circularity, consistently knocking around inside of and bumping up against these moving frames. In the following chapters, we describe awkwardness as a political disturbance that is firmly part of this circularity but that also creates potential for disruptions.

The example of Peaches's call to Pussy Riot supporters and the resulting video introduces a number of elements essential to these discussions and that are at the heart of *Awkward Politics*: not only collaboration, protest performance art, digital communities, participatory politics, urgency, and joy but also circulation, local and transnational cultures, simultaneity, transformation, consumption, event culture, mistakes, and mishaps. Many forms of large-scale feminist activism today depend on popular culture in the form of digital culture, becoming as much a consumer-based participatory event as a political action. The digital is part of the activist performance – even in or as critique of that performance – but is never separate from the material. At the same time as these events or actions are decidedly contemporary, they reference historical roots by replicating the form and content of pre-digital feminist protest movements, including the political valuation of bodies, an emphasis on a DIY aesthetic, and the dissemination of messages through writing texts and taking to the streets. Further, the transnational reach of feminist activism through digital circulation does not mean that the local is drained from the protest; instead, the local continues to appear as context or content, though it is often reformulated in a manner sometimes strange and uncomfortable.

Related to these complex entanglements and their murky political effects is the question of "success," or of how one should evaluate the effects of these actions. For example, because of the viral global spread of Pussy Riot's videos, protest aesthetics, and the associated political messages, the makers of the award-winning documentary film *Pussy Riot: A Punk Prayer* (2013, HBO, dir. Mike Lerner and Maxim Pozdorovkin) claim that Pussy Riot is the most successful art performance in history.[3] As a result of this "success," which is defined by Pussy Riot's ability to inspire and motivate other people to "protest" on a global scale, a range of issues arise. The exact points of political intervention of Pussy Riot–feminism remain murky. The group members themselves insist that Pussy Riot's art is anti-capitalist, but it might be difficult to uphold this claim in the context of the global consumption of their image. What further complicates any analysis of the political context of Pussy Riot's feminist protest performance are the global travels and inevitable transformation of the nationally specific message of their political activism: their original critique of what they see as a patriarchal Putin dictatorship in alliance with the Russian Orthodox Church. Finally, the most recent conflict in the group's unity around an understanding of feminism following the circuit of two of its members – Nadezhda (Nadia) Tolokonnikova and Maria (Masha) Alyokhina – to discuss their experience of imprisonment and to advocate for change in prison conditions resulted in further political ambiguity, not least because the disagreement led to the fracturing of the group.[4] Thus, the phenomenon of Pussy Riot is an example of a shift in the economy of global circulation of art and protest movements. The moment Alyokhina and Tolokonnikova play themselves as Pussy Riot (despite the rest of group's explicit distancing from the two women) on the third season (2015) of the Netflix original series *House of Cards* marks but a further stage in this circulation. Their political messages travel through digital spaces, urban streets, local media, and different national contexts, while the content of that message is unstable. This is true for all of the popfeminist actions we discuss in the following. Uncovering what is at stake politically at the different moments in this circulation is what inspired us to write this book.

In *Awkward Politics*, we not only think through the way feminist performance, protest, and activism work in the digital age and how they, in turn, rewrite the digital economy, but also how our own research process is bound up with this story and, along with this, how contemporary feminism as an ethos must be rethought for the twenty-first century. We explore the urgency of feminist politics today, but not in a matter that is measurable by its success or failure on numerous issues standard to feminist analysis. Instead, we identify circularities in current feminist creative work and activism that we describe as creating awkward moments. Awkwardness does not necessarily or only radiate from a single performance or protest event; rather, it emerges in new forms of dissemination and reception, particularly in the multi-media circulation of such events. It thus also includes audience, medium, and form. Such political moments are awkward not only because a neoliberal digital economy enables them but also because these activisms, which doggedly persist in their political actions in spite of this enabling, simultaneously reveal the false promises of neoliberal capitalism. They do not or cannot detach from the economy that enables them; rather, they stick to that economy in an uncomfortable, awkward manner. This stickiness contains the suggestion that there must be different modes of life, connection, and community outside of the consumption patterns and identity stylings that drive neoliberal economies. Awkwardness, therefore, also describes politics as an aesthetic form of becoming, of defiance, and of disruption. In this sense, our readings of popfeminist protest events in the digital age propose that exploiting, using, and keeping with the awkward – instead of smoothing it over or explaining it away – is a mode of politics.

In this book we develop the concept of awkwardness and a pop-feminist methodology, unfolding our theoretical and methodological approaches through interwoven examples. Our methodology is formed by our own histories of feminist activism and academic feminist engagement, by our struggle with and thinking about new forms of political activism, and it is grounded primarily in recent feminist and affect theory. In our personal histories and in our theoretical engagements, awkwardness is simultaneously coincidental and intentional, conscious and unconscious. We utilize the primary examples in a manner that is illustrative and that allows for theoretical exploration, breaking down a division between object and its analysis. These objects in a sense pre-empt and in some cases already include their analysis, highlighting the fact that theoretical feminist work is a process that is always intertwined with practice. Thus, disciplines and discourses are mixed together to form a unique story. The examples we use throughout *Awkward Politics* come from local contexts, specifically (though not solely) from the German-speaking countries that are familiar to us personally and as researchers. By reading, watching, and tracing the digital and analogue representations of such activism, through close readings of our examples, and through connections to feminist and queer theory – theories about technology and activism, neoliberalism, and aesthetics and affect – we develop a specific narrative of contemporary feminist politics in Germany, one that, in its specificity, is also wide reaching. While we focus on Germany in many parts of the book, we do so not to reduce the analysis to the forced parameters of nation but, rather, to best illustrate how the transnational circulations and reverberations of contemporary activism gain complexity and texture when examined with a specific historical and cultural context in mind. We thus invite our readers to utilize such considerations and approaches and to apply them to other national contexts and transnational flows.

The way in which each example is embedded in our personal lives and in a local context but circulates transnationally in digital and material form is an essential aspect of feminist activism and scholarship in the twenty-first century, one that we trace and theorize in *Awkward*

Politics. We therefore suggest that, by starting with the personal and by looking locally – whatever that local context might be – we gain a better understanding of global processes central to feminist politics today. In our readings, Germany becomes a point of confluence for the urgent questions now facing global feminisms. The category of the national remains, albeit rather complexly, affectively charged. Gabriele Griffin (2012, 13) writes: "National sentiment, in so far as it has affective foundations beyond its media construction, is not only a curious but also a complex thing, taxing and testing even the pluralised 'transnational feminisms' that have taken hold in our current imaginaries, both theoretical and activist." Germany allows us to trace the process in which a locality or a nationally coded space becomes, to reiterate Tuzcu (2015, 2), "slippery, ungrounded, and regrounded." Our conclusions shed light on how digital feminisms pose new challenges to locality and on the potential impact of global feminist activism on national, transnational, and digital contexts.

Beyond the fact that many of our examples have a German facet, they all share some kind of connection to feminist and digital activism, and are in some manner performative, thus legible for their utility as protest performance art. Kristine Stiles (1996, 694) defines performance art as "often uncommodifiable, difficult to preserve and exhibit, and defiant of social mores and morals while upholding the highest ethical principles."[5] Performance art, she concludes, "render[s] palpable the anxious corporal, physic, and social conditions of global cultures in the radically changing electronic and nuclear age" (ibid.). While not all of the protest performance art actions we discuss can be seen as uncommodifiable, since the branding of such groups as Pussy Riot and Femen would suggest the potential for commodification, their reverberations reach beyond the art gift shop; the process of their commodification is a complicated and messy one, but it also has the potential for self-empowerment. Performer and activist Lady Bitch Ray, as one example, designs and distributes her own merchandise (T-shirts, stickers, CDs, books) through her own label. Further, the effects of such actions are fleeting and temporary, as are many of their objects. Finally, they display the impulse to be defiant, whether that defiance is directed at broader social morals or undoes the very definition of feminism itself. In that defiance, they reflect back on us the anxieties of a global age as well as the urgency of political action in the face of its sensed impossibility.

The commonalities in our examples as contemporary (primarily spanning the years from roughly 2007 to 2015), somehow Germany-related, and feminist-performative offer a deliberately vague definition since one of the red threads in this book concerns tackling questions of temporality, location, and form in the digital age. In digital immediacy, form often takes precedence over content; however, when we describe "technologies" of activism, we propose a redefinition of what "form" means, how it can be understood in analysis, and how it can be implemented in action. Feminist activisms do not take similar forms in contemporary examples. Our examples range from feminist blogs (e.g., *maedchenmannschaft.net*) to global feminist actions (including SlutWalks and One Billion Rising) to protest groups and their global travels (such as Pussy Riot and Femen) to local protest events (e.g., the feminist protest against the Barbie Dreamhouse Experience in Berlin or the hashtag activism of #aufschrei). They reach from individual feminist pop activists and performers (Lady Bitch Ray and Chicks on Speed) and theorist-artists (Hito Steyerl and Sonja Eismann) to author-performers (Helene Hegemann and Charlotte Roche). Political messages, especially the ones that might appear as side effects of the initial content or goal of the protest events, can be tackled by analyzing the various forms that describe the awkward paths of protests, processes, and disseminations.

The examples (both theoretical and primary) we offer illustrate, roughly, four main points: first, that the political in popfeminist activism is a moving target because awkwardness emerges at the most inopportune and uncalculated moments; second, that the digital and corporeal are not at odds but intertwined; third, that the local context (whether of origin or of re-embedding) is central to understanding the transnational implications of activism; and fourth, that the form the activism takes dominates the content, often becoming the implicit or explicit "message." Our chapters demonstrate these points not in any particular order but, rather, throughout, in a manner that is intended to provide a collective sense of political urgency and our own attempts to address this urgency. Our engagement, however, does not display the smoothness of a new and easily adopted theoretical position – that is, we offer no new "-ism" with which academic feminists might newly tackle old subject matter – but, rather, our search for an entirely new subject matter beyond categorical pigeon-holing.

In *Awkward Politics*, we utilize primary examples to engage with larger questions related to political value and feminist work today while also inserting ourselves into the narrative. In chapter 1 we set the stage by depicting our process and those questions informing the study. We begin with our personal pasts in order to unfold the historical trajectory of feminist concerns that have an impact on feminist theory and action today. We then engage in positioning ourselves, and this book, within German and transnational feminist thinking since the new millennium, with particular focus on circularity, belonging, collaboration, and activism. Our voices and collaborative processes are essential to the form and content of *Awkward Politics*. We have written it in concert, thereby engaging with the collaborative spirit of feminist academic work (exemplified by scholar-pairs such as Hélène Cixous and Catherine Clément, Sandra M. Gilbert and Susan Gubar, and Lauren Berlant and Lee Edelman, to name a few) that suggests our personal experiences as feminists and as scholars – including our affective, intimate, and libidinal ones – are bound up in our research positioning and in our political framing. Instead of burying the researcher in an ostensibly objective view of the subject matter, we place ourselves, subjectively, at the forefront of these discussions. By exploring our voices, histories, and experiences at the outset of this study, we simultaneously set up, while trying to avoid, the trap of commanding authority, consistently undoing any claim to objectivity or infallibility in the research process. We do this in order to display a politically engaged form of scholarship that is as awkward and as slippery as is its subject matter. Our own histories intersect with feminist theory and the development of new politically oriented performance cultures in the digital age. Chapter 1 therefore traces the shift from how feminist performances created meaning and politics in the 1970s to the contemporary moment of awkwardness.

Chapter 2 explores the larger context of popular forms of feminist activism in the current political moment, the history of German feminism, and feminist activism in the digital economy. It offers a discussion of the specific context of Germany and illustrates, via a range of contemporary examples, how national histories and global dissemination intersect in feminist-political meaning making in the present day. It thus provides the groundwork for the development of contemporary feminism as rooted in historical forms, including street protest, dissemination of zines or pamphlets, and the foregrounding of the female, queer, racialized, or trans body as simultaneously a tool for protest and a corpus delicti of the structures of inequity. However, when these historical forms meet digital circularity, their stories of progress and linear return – upon which feminism's waves depend – are upended, though not in a manner that suggests ahistoricity but, rather, in a manner that highlights the circularity in genealogy. This chapter therefore develops an understanding of awkwardness that uncovers contemporary feminism as being categorically beyond the waves.

In chapter 3, we engage in close readings of two examples to explore
the implications of reading for awkwardness and to develop a popfeminist methodology. We begin by expanding our analysis of circularity
to a broader context, drawing on Lauren Berlant's theory of cruel optimism and Sara Ahmed's concept of "willfulness,"[6] among others. We
apply these perspectives to two main examples: the performance group
Chicks on Speed and performer, musician, and sex activist Lady Bitch
Ray. Through these two examples we explore the entanglement of theory and practice as popfeminist method or craft – our own and that of
our examples – and further trace the historical development from feminist performativity to (digital) feminist awkwardness. Both examples
also generate a range of questions around sexual politics, the body and
representation, race, visibility, and excess that we address in subsequent
chapters. Awkwardness as a political perspective allows us to position
ourselves politically among these and other examples. By identifying
both our perspective as researchers and our objects of study as "willful," we enmesh our own political perspectives with the perspectives of
the artists and objects we examine. Our methodology suggests that theory and artistic practice can be brought into conversation in ways that
help us to trace and uncover political trajectories.

Chapters 4, 5, and 6 take up the perspectives developed in chapter
3 to address specific aspects of political awkwardness – its circulation
and movement, its process-based adolescent aesthetics and affect, and
its virality and contemporaneity – across a variety of examples, ending with awkwardness in the academy. Chapter 4 traces the different
kinds of politics of awkwardness in digital circulations that are triggered by hyper-visibilities and acts of virtual disappearance in a neoliberal economy. Circulation, the key concept of this chapter, allows us
to describe specific features of neoliberalism as creating moments for
awkward interruptions that expose the sticky relations between neoliberalism and popfeminist activism. Among other examples, we return
at length to Pussy Riot and trace the features of the group's global
digital circulations.

Chapter 5 returns to technologies, specifically in terms of affect and
the aesthetics of the technologies of the body and the material-digital: it
is through the relations and connections, the senses and the social con-
noted by affect and aesthetics that awkwardness reaches its audience.
Grounded in an understanding of aesthetics as process-based, we further
examine the term "awkwardness" as it evokes the figure of the adolescent – in our examples the adolescent girl or young woman – through

select examples from literature and film that are part of (also always digital) popfeminist event cultures. The state of adolescent becoming, of not yet having arrived at a complete form or of having found a position in a socially normative role, open up new ways of reading for the political and of doing politics that are inherently driven by emotions and connections (affect) as well as bound to the social aspects of the senses (aesthetics). In many ways the protagonists that the texts and films describe and the forms the authors choose each refuse to grow up. Theorizing such adolescent aesthetics highlights the affective and aesthetic features of awkwardness as political and emphasizes that awkwardness is not a fixed concept but, rather, something that is in a constant "state of emergence." Further, this chapter allows us to illustrate our expansive understanding of the digital as inherently part of analogue or material creative forms.

In chapter 6, we take up the notion of process evoked by the adolescent to think through awkwardness as emerging from, perhaps even defining, the contemporary as a category as well as its viral nature, both of which are key features of digital feminism and feminist activism. Our examples in this chapter range from references to Chicks on Speed's current work to our popfeminist readings of the Barbie Dreamhouse Experience, an exhibit that sparked protest while it was in Berlin in 2013. We then turn to examples from the academy and to our own position as (popfeminist) academics. Certain feminist actions have reached the mainstream by spreading virally and sparking discussions in mainstream media, which, in our reading, does not make them void of politics. By reading for the willful in the viral and in the contemporary, we insist that creating awkwardness is a political intervention. This allows us to conclude *Awkward Politics* by thinking about new forms of community, trouble, and joyful solidarity, and puts out a call for an awkward ethos across feminist work, including work that takes place within structures of the academy. Joy, as "the increase of our power to think and act" (in opposition to sadness as the "decrease" in that power), is not to be confused with happiness (which might lead to complacency) but, instead, describes an alternative vision for energetic feminist interruptions and disruptions (Hardt 2014, 219).

Formulating our thoughts and theories in a book, a material object that presents a linear narrative and that cannot ever be immediate and contemporary, clashes with our (mainly digital) collaboration and process-driven methodology as well as with the form and circulation of the objects of our study. At the same time, the book form produces exactly the kind of awkwardness that we are searching for and that we are trying to describe. We might even suggest that, by writing a book, we model our academic engagement on some of our examples. Artist-activists such as Lady Bitch Ray and Chicks on Speed published material books well after beginning their digital engagement, and the boundaries between art and theory blur when we include discussions of the academic work of Lady Bitch Ray's creator, Reyhan Şahin, and of video artist and theorist Hito Steyerl.[7] Various collections – of poetry, of court records – and documentation relating to Pussy Riot have been published in print and translated into different languages.[8] The instigator of the German Twitter campaign #aufschrei, Anne Wizorek, published a "manifesto" based on the hashtag debates in traditional book form with Fischer Verlag, a respected German publishing house. These examples show that print remains an important part of what we describe as – digital and non-digital – circulations. Print materials document, archive, and capture a certain moment within this process; they may spur it on, react to it, or reflect on it, or they may interrupt and redirect the process. They certainly do not, and are not meant to, offer a conclusion to the issues at hand but, rather, need to be understood as a (possibly intentionally awkward and decelerating) part of a process.

By the time *Awkward Politics* is published, things might have moved on, or they might have already circled back to meet up with the beginning. Because the form of the book attempts to freeze or take a snapshot of something that is in motion, it conveys a sense of authority, helped along by the continuing reification of the monograph as a publishing model in the academy. In that sense, as authors of this book, we search for a position of authority from which to speak about this subject. At the same time, by pressing our unwieldy thoughts and subjects into this form, we undermine our own authority – only to reclaim it willfully. This is the awkward process for which we are mining, and which we mirror and harness in the chapters that follow. The conclusion to *Awkward Politics* takes on this aspect of our position and our voice as well as our investment in the feminisms we describe as academics and as politically engaged feminists in the academy. By infusing the results of our study, the forms and activisms we examine, with the notion of trouble and joy, we add further dimensions of agency and solidarity to these new forms of political intervention that are happening in spite of it all.

1

Process as a Politics: Collaborative Research, Political Urgency, and Feminist Histories

The collaborative form in the humanities and social sciences is one that is, at least philosophically, both democratic and feminist.[1] In *Rethinking Women's Collaborative Writing: Power, Difference, Property*, Lorraine York (2002, 3) maintains that the "act of collaborating on texts does not in itself determine a specific or consistent ideological stance, feminist or any other." She then goes on to theorize "women's collaborations as ideological projects ... some more hierarchical, some more liberatory and subversive" (4). She speaks of collaborations not only as grating and uncomfortable but also as pleasurable, and she rightly underscores the problematic and idealizing narrative given to women's collaborations that fall back on essentialist and maternalist viewpoints of women's natural ethics of care, nurture, and community (6).[2] Collaborations, of course, can also be disagreeable, uncomfortable, and fractured (15). Recognized at times as subversive, at times as revolutionary, collaborating as a form of writing pushes back against paradigmatic notions of single-authorship and destabilizes the canon, whether intentionally or not, though it does not necessarily do so in a manner that connotes anti-power or anti-property, as York warns. Collaboration becomes "miscegenated, monstrous, messy" to those individuals or institutions whose model remains that of the single author (14). This applies in her readings to both critical (academic) and creative (non-academic or artistic) work.[3] In her assessment of critical work in particular, York is concerned with those partnerships that engage in disagreements and that allow the rough edges of the collaboration to show (50). She uses Gilbert and Gubar as an example, though here content-based disagreements are displaced into composition and writing.

While the displacement of difference does not apply to our work specifically, what York's thoughts underscore is the importance of mess and the essential integration of the awkwardness of process into the collaborative work. As Berlant and Edelman (2014, x) write in the preface to their conversation in *Sex, or the Unbearable*: "our own conversation includes and exceeds us at once." The possibilities opened up by the digital medium to capture precisely this awkwardness of collaborative work is exemplified in an article by Danya McLeod, Jasmine Rault, and T.L. Cowan published in *Ada: A Journal of Gender, New Media, and Technology*. In "Speculative Praxis Towards a Queer Feminist Digital Archive: A Collaborative Research-Creation Project," the authors "chronicle[] the challenges of creating digital spaces that can house and encourage trans-feminist and queer affective and cultural archives [in the form of a] collaborative process document" (McLeod, Rault, and Cowan 2014). They utilize the capabilities of the online publishing platform to also include their collaborative comments, writing that they wish to "document [their] thinking towards designing digital space that does not collapse, or render invisible, the complexities and contradictions of both the digitizing process itself and of the feminist and queer performances that [they] seek to 'preserve.'" The resulting document makes "transparent the polyvocal nature of collaboration" and "tracks" how the researchers engage with the project itself, just as it reflects on the trans-, feminist, and queer possibilities of the digital space as an object of study.

Our collaboration, of which this book is a part, began in a shared sense of academic and feminist political urgency, driven by a desire to integrate our own process of exploration and theorization into research that would uncover the importance of new theoretical approaches for feminist German Studies while also remaining interested in the manner in which our research may or may not be motivated by political possibilities. We started our partnership after a session on academic collaboration at the 2009 conference of the North American organization Women in German, which was held in Michigan. Since that first meeting, in e-mail conversations, articles, and academic presentations, we have grappled with how to counter both the relative invisibility of politically charged feminist work in German Studies proper and the constant drive to evaluate this work regarding whether it is good or bad for politics, whether it "works" or not, and whether it is, in fact, "feminist" or not. While our concerns germinated in the reception accorded our individual analyses of creative works and the debates around artist-performers such as Lady Bitch Ray and Charlotte Roche – a reception

that most often asked us to somehow defend (or decry) their works as
feminist – these concerns mirror much of where popular culture roots
feminist discussions today. The academic reception of our work and
our thinking around the continued critical evaluation of contemporary
feminist actions, performances, and politics today forms the starting
point for *Awkward Politics* – an evaluation that is, we suggest, located
in a desire to cling to methods of analysis and critique based in linear
constructions of feminist "waves."

Examples for this struggle with evaluation of feminist work have
been building in frequency over the past few years and are found across
a wide range of media and formats, stretching from popular culture
to activist communities in multiple cultural contexts. Such media discussions appear and disappear quickly, go viral and vanish from the
scene. For example, despite her continued status as a queer icon, pop
superstar Lady Gaga has sparked numerous blog headlines, such as
"Is Lady Gaga a Feminist or Isn't She?" and "Is Lady Gaga a Feminist? A Discussion,"[4] thus seemingly satisfying the public perception
of feminism as shameful, outdated, and/or unseemly. Similarly, often
short-lived discussions about the validity of Emma Watson's 2014
appearance in front of the United Nations to plea for gender equality
and of Beyoncé's (2014b) performance at the 2014 MTV Video Music
Awards,[5] which utilized Nigerian author Chimamanda Ngozi Adichie's
TED talk "We Should All Be Feminists" – a performance that brought
up the crucial question of race and that reached Germany via a highly
problematic "pro-and-con" discussion of Beyoncé's position in the feminist magazine *Emma*[6] – engage in such viral media wars over what
"real" feminism is and if feminism is still "needed."

· Of course, not only superstars receive such evaluative scrutiny; the
ongoing, or perhaps continually resurging, debates around motherhood
in North America, particularly, but also in Germany and France, are
ultimately debates about the political validity of feminism and wom-
en's appropriate roles in home and career. The public response to *Time
Magazine*'s May 2012 sexploitative cover story on attachment parent-
ing entitled "Are You Mom Enough?" or to the April 2012 release of the
English translation of popular academic Elisabeth Badinter's book *The
Conflict: How Modern Motherhood Undermines the Status of Women*
have, at their core, the question of whether, or what type of, feminism
has been effective – or even too effective. Moreover, digital media and
social networks allow for the immediate popularization of such discourses across national-cultural borders. For example, the July/August
2012 *Atlantic* article by Anne-Marie Slaughter, "Why Women Still

Can't Have It All," written for the US context, was almost immediately answered by Claudia Voigt in an August 2012 edition of the German magazine *Der Spiegel* entitled "Frauen können alles haben" (Women can have it all). That this latter article is obviously written for the German context is apparent in the subtitle – placed below the digital fold – "Sie sollten nur viel früher Kinder bekommen" (They just should have children much earlier in life), which makes a clear reference to the demography debate that has dominated much of the family-political discourse in Germany since 2000 (Smith-Prei 2009; Hill 2004; McCarthy n.d.).

It is not just mainstream popular media that perpetuates the drive to evaluate feminist effectivity and women's political roles. Feminist media engages with this evaluation as well, as is seen in the discussions surrounding the Ukrainian sextremist group Femen. *Bitch Media* responded negatively, for example, to the controversy over the revelation in the film *Ukraine Is Not a Brothel* (2013) that Femen was founded by a man (see Paul 2014), and *Feminist Wire* published discussions following the arrest of Tunisian feminist Amina Sboui, known as Amina Tyler, in 2013 that saw Femen's protest of this arrest as wrong (see Najumi 2013).[7] In 2012, on *Feminist Current*, one blogger claimed: "There is a wrong way to do feminism. And Femen is doing it wrong" (Murphy 2012). More, international digital campaigns such as the Tumblr "I am a feminist because," which invites women and men to post images of themselves holding signs that explain their reasons for thinking that feminism is necessary, spark a form of reactionary backlash, as was seen in 2014 when the German neoconservative party Junge Alternative für Deutschland (Young alternative for Germany) used this format to protest the institution of a women's quota in upper-level management.[8] By explicitly replicating the form of a feminist digital action, the group intends to undermine and question the utility of feminist protest. The content of its protest matters less than the recognition of and match to identical form.

Such pop-culturally specific additions to the evaluation of feminism in the form of popular icons, the mommy wars, sextremist activism, and social media highlight the global universality of the discussion around women's roles and feminist effectivity. Indeed, the ever-increasing digital media presence of feminism throughout 2014 led to claims that it had been a "historic year" (Solnit 2014) for feminism, the year that "culture became a feminist issue" (Vincent 2014). Rebecca Solnit (2014) writes in the *Guardian*: "I have been waiting all my life for what 2014 has brought." After listing a series of actions in which women spoke out about gender-based violence, Solnit closes her article with the following: "The ... North American stories I'm telling here are about a shift in power that is partly a shift in whose story gets told and believed, and who does the telling ... Women are coming out of a silence that lasted so long no one can name a beginning for it. This noisy year is not the end – but perhaps it is the beginning of the end." What is beginning to end, however, is unclear. With the word "feminism" now a pop cultural cipher, it is only fitting, perhaps, that *Time Magazine* placed it on its list of words that should be banned in 2015, alongside "I can't even," "om nom nom nom," and "kale." They later apologized and removed it from the list, claiming they wished to "invite debate about how the word was used this year" but that the "nuance was lost" (Steinmetz 2014).

In all of these examples there is an expectation of success or failure of "the" feminist cause. Our affective reaction against the expectation that we, as feminist scholars, should pass evaluative judgment on the political effectivity of popfeminist activism turned into our attempt to ask not if, but *how*, such protest works politically. Our assumption, of course, is feminist to begin with: that we do not live in a world where feminist activism is not needed anymore and where all is well. On the contrary, examples of such actions and protests, and, equally important, the questions and reactions generated by them, point to the fact that gender (thought in an intersectional way) remains a key category in the play for political power.[9] The consistent drive to evaluate the effectiveness of feminist work (creative, activist, or academic), the circularity of the representation and reception process, and the ambiguity and necessity of the feminist-political have become ever more visible in the marked rise of the digitally transnational reach of local political activism (Occupy),[10] including feminist activism (SlutWalks, Pussy Riot, Femen). Awkwardness allows us to address precisely the stickiness of the political in this discussion; it does not describe provocations but, rather, searches for forms of disruption.

This search suggests that it is not only the two of us who are collaborating here by writing and thinking through awkwardness in book form: the materials about which we write and the historical lineage of our thinking collaborate with us. In York's discussion of collaboration, she draws on Raymond Williams's concept of socialized authorship, which he presented in *Marxism and Literature* in 1977. He writes that, through overt collaborations, we develop a "sense of a collective subject ... This goes beyond conscious co-operation – collaboration – to effective social relations in which, even while individual projects are being pursued, what is being drawn on is trans-individual" (Williams

1977, 195, quoted in York 2002, 24). This sense of a collective subject describes the work with which we engage in what follows. York extrapolates this idea of the trans-individual to digital work, such as hypertexts. We might take this further and suggest that now, firmly in the second decade of the twenty-first century, the question of authorship and what constitutes the digital is messier than ever.[11]

York (2002, 32) also underscores the subject position that collaborators take as "performed, as thoroughly socialized sites of fluid and complex power exchanges." Messiness and fluidity, performance and power, describe our work, particularly by foregrounding the manner in which we engage with the notion of our own and the material's lineage. In order to capture this messiness, our personal stories become part of the story of contemporary feminisms. Researchers are neither objective nor devoid of power; even if we suggest from the outset that our position itself is feminist, and that feminism is – philosophically, ethically, hopefully – necessarily democratic, issues of power and authority emerge, if not between us as collaborators then among our positions vis-à-vis the work at hand and our imagined reader. However, personal histories, national histories, and feminist histories (defined by space and time) inform our engagement with these questions of authority, power, performance, and mess. Our own stories suggest feminisms and politics that are also often happening in places we do not expect, where bodies and representations are entangled, where national and activist history, local and global issues, merge. In what follows this chapter engages with the historical trajectories of two terms central to this study: performance and feminism. These trajectories include our personal experiences with performance and feminism, feminist performance art of the 1970s and 1980s and its DIY reconfiguration in the 1990s, and feminism as waves and feminisms beyond the waves.

PERSONAL STORIES AND FEMINIST HISTORIES: GIRLS AND RIOTS

Anne Cvetkovich (Staiger, Cvetkovich, and Reynolds 2010, 6) has put out the call to do the work of critique differently, and to "formulate new ways of thinking the relations between the emotional, the cultural, and the political for those who are tired of reading cultural objects in order to decide if they (or the emotions they produce) are good or bad for politics." One way of doing this critique differently involves starting with the personal and the intimate. We borrow very liberally from Lauren Berlant and Michael Warner (1998, 547), who, in their collaborative essay "Sex in Public," outline "sex as it is mediated by publics." While their analysis goes in a radically different direction than does our topic – the manner in which institutions of public intimacy maintain heterosexual culture – their claim that "intimacy is itself publicly mediated" (553) is useful here. In the confinement of intimacy, and sex more specifically, to the private, the "heteronormative conventions of intimacy block the building of nonnormative or explicit public sexual cultures." And, further, "those conventions conjure a mirage: a home base of prepolitical humanity from which citizens are thought to come into political discourse and to which they are expected to return ... Intimate life is the endlessly cited *elsewhere* of political public discourse" (ibid., emphasis in original). In their discussion, Berlant and Warner illuminate how a variety of acts not seen as often related to sex – a long list that includes taxes or "family-size" groceries (555) – support this privatization of sex in heteronormative culture as a "utopia of social belonging," thereby describing a "constellation of practices that everywhere disperses heterosexual privilege as a tacit but central organizing index of social membership" (ibid.). In contrast, they urge us to focus on queer world making, which develops intimacies "that bear no necessary relation to domestic space, to kinship, to the couple form, to property, or to the nation. These intimacies *do* bear a necessary relation to a counterpublic – an indefinitely accessible world conscious of its subordinate relation" as well as of its fleetingness and fragility (558, emphasis in original). They imagine a queer project that supports "forms of affective, erotic, and personal living that are public in the sense of accessible, available to memory, and sustained through collective activity" (562). We do not contest that we create queer counterpublics in this book. However, what we do suggest is that to begin to conceptualize the politics of popfeminist performance and digital feminist activism, we must engage with "nonheteronormative bodily contexts" that are firmly embedded in publics (ibid.). Moreover, to do so, we ourselves must understand the intimacies with which we approach the material as a way of creating counterpublics. The academy is also organized by heteronormative culture's relegation of intimacy to the private sphere, where encounters with intimacy and ethics of care are usually displaced by an ethic of "work" and "busyness." The act of writing *Awkward Politics* engages in a very different public act of intimacy aimed at creating a counterpublic for a feminist academy. This counterpublic might not be queer in the libidinal sense, but instead awkward, embracing not only critique, discomfort, and negativity but also care, connection, and community as essential to the fabric of academic work.

Informing our line of questioning in establishing just such intimacy are our own historical trajectories. We both cut our feminist teeth in the mid-1990s when feminism was defined by self-induced threat – the threat of being passé, of being ineffective, of being unable to live up to the political legacy established by the second wave. At the same time, feminist politics was informed by theory as much as it was steeped in performative practice. In the twenty-first century, both of us have· entered the academy in what Meredith Haaf, Susanne Klingner, and Barbara Streidl, in their book *Wir Alphamädchen* (We Alphagirls), describe as the professionalization of feminism. According to them, in the 1990s, feminism retreated from the streets and into the university and the political establishment or mainstream (Haaf, Klingner, and Streidl 2008, 193). While in *Awkward Politics* we do reflect on our position as academics, our stories and our examples also call for a less linear and more interconnected understanding of what feminist politics were, are, and can be in the contemporary moment. Technologies of popfeminism that consider both gender and race tell a messier, more complicated story than what has been told to this point.

Scene 1: Maria in Southern Germany

Imagine two girls in a small room. My friend asked me to sing karaoke to Madonna's "Like a Virgin" (released in 1984); I did not actually know the lyrics very well (yet) and, due to my parent's decision to "allow" their children to grow up without television, I was not familiar with the music videos either. As a result of that, my karaoke was certainly an awkward affair. Nonetheless, with the clear feeling that I needed to catch up to be "cool," I did, however briefly, become a Madonna fan. A few years later, while affected by teenage angst over beauty norms, I began to listen to second wave feminists with great interest: some were my teachers, some were friends of my mother, others were people in my community of friends. During my high school years, I met regularly with a group of female friends, first for what we called "hen-parties," an idea that I now suspect a feminist English teacher put into our heads, and later for wine parties where we cooked and got tipsy together. These girls' nights were, for me, formative for a sense of female solidarity. As far as I remember, these evenings were just about us, not about boys, love interests, and intrigue. Some of my girlfriends of the time and I went on train and bicycle trips across Europe during summer vacation, during which we learned to assert ourselves against unwanted sexual advances, to speak other European languages, and to identify as, somewhat awkwardly and vaguely, part of a European subculture.

It was when I encountered alternative music and culture, when Nirvana's "Teen Spirit" arrived in southern Germany, and when I made friends in the (very small and small-town) Punk and Goth community, that I started to form what I considered a political identity. In the early 1990s, we protested new restrictions on asylum and demonstrated against neo-Nazi activism and organizing in our area. I read Pippi Longstocking as I grew up, but the German anarchist's version of the title song from the popular Pippi movie, adapted by Heiter bis Wolkig and entitled "Rote Zora" in support of the defence of a squatted building, became the anthem of some of my friends who identified with such anarchist squatter movements.[12] The first lines of this song roughly translate as "state, power, and money, vide-vide-vit, and the pigs / everyone big and small will take a hit / we create this world vide-vide-as we want it / fight against capitalism, illegal, legal, no matter how."[13] Our gestures were always far more radical than our actions. While most of the political groups I joined identified as anti-fascist and generally leftist or anarchist, the gender dynamics within my circle of friends were still rather heteronormative – even if we thought of ourselves as inclusive because a few of our group's members were openly gay. We made an attempt to form an all-woman's subcommittee of sorts within our anti-fascist youth group, but this group met only once, regardless of the fact that we all felt very empowered after our first and only meeting. Our activism was driven by a sense of political righteousness, and, while dedicated to anti-racism and being proud of the visible racial diversity of our group in a predominantly white and middle-class rural community, we did not actively and theoretically engage with racism or theories about race. The assumption on our part was certainly that our activisms and identifications alone put us on the non-racist, "good" side. After most of my friends and I graduated high school in the early 1990s, some of us went directly to Berlin to join an exciting alternative cultural and squatter scene there; others left for smaller university towns across the southern half of Germany. I do remember the feeling of wanting to get out of the rural south of Germany, but I was also very aware of the fact that I was privileged enough to be able to do so. When we left, friends less educated, which often also meant of lower-middle class or working-class families, were left behind.

I discovered the riot grrrl movement in the mid-1990s, as a student in the humanities and a radio activist in the mid-size city of Karlsruhe in southern Germany. I distinctly remember a conversation with a male friend who asked me what I thought about the fact that the band about to give a concert in a squat where we used to hang out was going to send all the men to the back of the room, mimicking their North American riot grrrl counterparts such as Bikini Kill. Two of my peers at the university and I formed a feminist reading and discussion group, which gave us a sense of empowerment in a male-dominated university environment. My roommate at the time was a fiercely independent young businesswoman who did not identify as "feminist" but was very openly and assertively sexual, smart without a college degree, founder of an alternative music store, and about ten years older than I; most of my closer friends in the political scene, however, were men. We produced awkwardly amateurish independent radio shows, we mingled with the (albeit small) squatter scene, and we organized large-scale parties. Under the pretence of sexual openness and gender experimentation, I often felt locked in and judged by very heteronormative expectations. I also started to have the vague feeling that something about our "activism" was off, that we were clinging to notions of activism from the 1970s and 1980s that failed to have political effects beyond allowing us to mark ourselves as "activists." I started to disengage from activist politics in Germany and started to immerse myself in gender studies as I continued my graduate education in the United States.

Scene 2: Carrie in Portland, Oregon

Imagine a lone teenage girl in thigh-highs and Doc Martens, standing on the edge of a tattooed and pierced throng on the sidewalk outside a graffiti-covered storefront, messenger bag slung over her shoulder and nowhere to put her nervous hands. I grew up in the "dream of the '90s" that was Portland, Oregon, dominated by a music scene that defined itself against Seattle and Olympia, Washington. I attended Reed College in partial fulfilment of my high school degree, and, on the afternoons that class was not in session, I would go downtown to West Burnside, a few blocks off the waterfront, most often by myself, to the now long-defunct X-Ray Café to hear afternoon shows. It was here that I saw the band Team Dresch, founded in 1993 by Jody Bleyle, female drummer for the relatively successful band Hazel, which had gained considerable notoriety and had released its two albums off of the Sub Pop record label, along with two other members. Around the same time, Bleyle launched the record label Candy Ass Records, which – while releasing many female punk, queercore, and riot grrrl bands – also put

out the 1995 CD *Free to Fight!*, a compilation that featured all-women
bands on topics related to self-defence, rape, and harassment, along
with a seventy-five-page booklet with self-defence tips and instructions
intermingled with contributions by thinkers such as bell hooks.[14]

I do not remember how I came to own the CD and booklet, whether
I bought it or it was given to me. I know I did buy the LP *Personal
Best*, which was Team Dresch's debut album, but of the origin of this
later, more political and collective album, I am unsure. What I do
remember is reading the booklet and listening to the rough and aggressive sound (a stark contrast to the ongoing loop of the in comparison harmless-sounding Ani DiFranco, which was then the anthem of
the liberal-arts-college feminist) in my dorm room at Bard College in
Annandale-on-Hudson, New York, where I had gone off to study. In
stores up and down the east coast, when buying an album in Boston or
a dress in Providence, shopkeepers would ask me whether I liked the
Spinanes or knew Built to Spill after seeing the address on my personal
cheque. My Portland-native status bought me street-cred in the music
and performance communities that were still distinctly offside of popular. But, by contrast, the community presented to me in *Free to Fight!*
was confusing for it brought up a sense of pride in and nostalgia for
place, but it also made me feel as though I could not quite call that place
my own. That is to say, I had no sense of participating in what, in hind-
sight, can be seen as the tail end of the riot grrrl movement, nor did I
believe that I had any personal experience with gender-motivated hate,
harassment, or violence. Nevertheless, the music, lyrics, and drawings
brought up a keen urge to belong.

But now, in retrospect, this moment of relative personal awkwardness
combined with the first-hand experience of feminist politicized performance was and is seminal for my understanding of politics, performance, and activism – and my intimate place among these. The musical
tracks on the album *Free to Fight!* are interspersed with spoken word
stories, beginning with a story of a woman reacting to a flasher while
riding the Greyhound bus, and including instructions on self-defence,
which is defined as: "Fighting with our fists, yelling, telling him to stop
looking at us, running away, listening to our gut instinct, getting support, knowing that we are worth defending, talking about what happened ... And playing rock."[15] Furthermore, included in the booklet
are not only cartoons, drawings, and poetry but also a blank page
entitled "My Story," inviting the listeners-readers to write their stories about harassment, sexual violence, or rape. Here, both in practice

and instruction, the performance and the political are intertwined in a DIY fashion.

The aesthetics of the performance scenes of our formative memories are, of course, indebted to riot grrrl consciousness. This consciousness is captured in the 1991 manifesto, which includes the following statements:

> BECAUSE viewing our work as being connected to our girl-friends-politics-real lives is essential if we are gonna figure out how [what] we are doing impacts, reflects, perpetuates, or DISRUPTS the status quo.
> BECAUSE we don't wanna assimilate to someone else's (boy) standards of what is or isn't.
> BECAUSE doing/reading/seeing/hearing cool things that validate and challenge us can help us gain the strength and sense of community that we need in order to figure out how bullshit like racism, able-bodieism, ageism, speciesism, classism, thinism, sexism, anti-semitism and heterosexism figures in our own lives.
> BECAUSE we see fostering and supporting girl scenes and girl artists of all kinds as integral to this process.[16]

Such statements express the way in which music and stage shows, including female-owned labels, performance venues, and topics, come together in the riot grrrl movement in the 1990s with a clear political position that is rooted in feminism. Artistic DIY production and alternative forms of consumption lead to a redefinition of a feminist alternative community.

The riot grrrl movement, as well as the feminist consciousness-raising of the 1990s, is often termed the third wave of feminism in North America, a consciousness that – erroneously, to which Maria's story in scene 1 attests – is often seen not to have taken place in the post-unification Germany of the 1990s. The third wave coincides with a broader academic and non-academic reception of poststructuralist feminism and Judith Butler's *Gender Trouble* and, based on these theories, attempts to do feminist activism in a new way. "Deconstruction" and "performativity" were key words for the theoretical discourse that was, ideally, intended to inform a new feminist practice, contrasted sharply from second wave feminist forbearers. Feminist theorists and historians have told the story of this evolution,[17] and we do not intend to focus on the historical connections and dissonances between second and third wave feminism here since, in telling a linear story, one might be tempted to either emphasize how deeply steeped new feminist theories and practices are in previous feminist theory or how third wave feminists deconstructed the very premise of second-wave feminist activism – namely, the categories of "women" and "men" in and of themselves. As many scholars have pointed out, both of these stories are true. When told together, they shed some light on the complexities of feminist histories and the complicated connections between feminist activism and theory.

Since our readings and theorizations aim to avoid any kind of evaluative stance regarding what kind of feminism works better for politics, we reject linear stories of political progress or feminist failures. This does not mean that we are outside of history; on the contrary, we argue for a decidedly historical perspective that understands socio-political realities in interaction with new forms of engagement that create different ways in which we read for and do politics. Political activists do not learn from the past's mistakes and progress from there; rather, they incorporate these pasts (wittingly or unwittingly) in their responses to new political realities, new forms of discriminations, exclusions, and injustices. Past engagement with feminist generations, particularly those that specifically discuss the third wave's departure from the second, has been mindful to highlight the similarities and differences between both movements, many discussions of which are couched in generational squabbles (see Whelehan 1995; Henry 2004). In an article written on the heels of 9/11, E. Ann Kaplan considers the possibility of feminist futures in the form of a fourth wave. In this she argues for 9/11 as a caesura of sorts for feminism, at least in the United States. Asking whether we have "arrived at the need for a 'fourth' feminism in a so-called era of 'terror'" (Kaplan 2003, 47), she pursues a set of challenges she sees as integral to future feminisms. These include three aspects that are related to the world prior to 9/11: first, the need for feminism after having ostensibly achieving what she calls "modest feminist goals" (47); second, the legacy of the feminist academy in the form of the institutionalization of Women's Studies; and, third, the impact of technologies and globalization (52). A fourth challenge emerges from the post-9/11 world, which she describes as the "traumatic effects" of the attacks and the challenge to conceptualize a "'fourth' feminism" (ibid.). This latter feminism, Kaplan claims, demands a resituating of the previous historically based challenges and, therefore, a re-keying of the legacies of feminism for future feminisms, or "feminist futures," as she calls them.

In particular, she points to the way in which issues related to violence and race, religion, and media have transformed in the post-9/11 era. Further, she believes that the issues with which the third wave concerns itself, particularly precarity and employment, are given new light in this era.

Kaplan sees what she calls a fourth feminism to be integrally intertwined with the feminisms of previous generations. She writes:

> While third wave feminists were inevitably to some degree situated in a semi-genealogical relationship to second wave feminists, the fourth wave will be distinguished by bringing second and third wave feminists together to confront a new and devastating reality that involves us all, if not equally, then at least at once. This new reality ideally cuts across racial, ethnic and national divides. (Kaplan 2003, 55)

She claims, further, that the global situation has forced feminisms into their national contexts, which, in turn, demands "a new sensitivity to our national locations and, therefore, very differing experiences and standpoints" (56). Kaplan reminds us: "That there is no monolithic feminism is a good, if at times uncomfortable, fact: positions, actions and knowledge – constantly being contested, questioned, and debated – mean that feminism is alive and well," if in constant flux in accordance with context (47).

While Kaplan argues for a fourth wave defined by this new global reality in the wake of terrorism, we argue instead that the position of contemporary feminisms is and must be *beyond* the waves, a position to which we return in chapter 2. This is not to suggest a radical break from generational lineage or an ahistorical perspective (for we are in agreement that particularly the second and third waves do come into important conversation in the present period) but, rather, a simultaneity of feminist concerns, methods, and approaches in the digital age. Here we are in agreement with Marie Carrière's (2014) thinking around "metafeminism," a term she uses to describe French feminist fiction, which she sees as multidirectional and self-reflexive, but which also brings to the fore the "internally critical, indeed the self- or meta-critical potential of contemporary feminism." This metafeminism brings together the global politics described by Kaplan with the intimate concerns of the personal in a manner that is in keeping with Joan Scott's understanding of feminist reverberations. As Carrière points out, the word "reverberations" allows for understanding feminism as a movement that radiates outward from multiple points. As Scott (2002, 11) herself writes, the word "carries with it a sense both of causes of infinite regression – reverberations are re-echoes, successions of echoes – and of effect – reverberations are also repercussions." Speaking from her position in 2002, Scott claims that reverberations are a good way to think about the circulation of global feminisms following 9/11 as the word suggests circuits of influence re-echoing around the globe. She emphasizes that this is so because a reverberation has not one but multiple starting points and is constantly shifting (13). From our position, now roughly fifteen years after 9/11, feminist theory and feminist political actions are closely – and circularly – tied to technologies and political discourse on local, national, and transnational levels. The search for the political is the main and possibly only constant that could serve to define any movement. An understanding of feminisms today as metafeminisms beyond the waves also implies that we depart from nationally centred perspectives that often focus on Western and white master-narratives. To think about political movements as reverberations and echoes describes a political landscape that does not construct its narrative of political progress as originating in the West and then reaching the rest.[18] This means that locations and spatial divisions do matter but that we need to think from multiple locations and look from multiple perspectives as we trace the political impact of activisms in the digital age.

Moreover, awkwardness speaks to our immediate cultural moment, but in a way that is aware of history. In a 2014 essay for the online edition of the *New Yorker*, Elif Batuman (2014) writes of the broad-spread use of the term "awkward" and all of its variants in US pop culture, citing in particular the more than six hundred entries in the online *Urban Dictionary*. Referencing Adam Kotsko (2010), who, in *Awkwardness: An Essay*, dates the surge of the term's usage to midway into the first decade of the twenty-first century but does not link it to the 2001 terrorist attacks on New York City and the Pentagon, Batuman looks to a shift from irony to awkwardness following 9/11. He identifies this timeline as important due to the manner in which the rhetoric around terrorism, particularly as utilized by the George W. Bush administration, attempted to streamline the issues with black and white discourse of the so-called "Axis of Evil," but notes that this "rhetoric didn't stick" because it made no sense; the threat of terrorism and the resulting fears were amorphous at best. He writes:

> Awkwardness is the consciousness of a false position ... "Awkward"
> implies both solidarity and implication. Nobody is exempt. Awk-
> wardness comes from the realization that, when you look around
> the world it's difficult to identify anyone who isn't either the vic-
> tim or the beneficiary of injustice. Awkward moments remind us
> that we are never isolated individuals ... Awkward moments are,
> by definition, relatable. (Batuman 2014)

Here, the tension between self-awareness of the awkward position
combined with solidarity and community built through awkwardness
is essential to our conception of awkwardness as a feminist politics.
Further, in contrast to anxiety's neurotic roots, "awkwardness is exis-
tential, universal." He goes on to claim that awkwardness is "familial"
for it highlights the hypocrisy of the simultaneous condemnation and
condoning of sexual urges found in family structures.

That awkwardness, or the awkward, as inherently both pop and
political can be seen in Batuman's discussion of the Taylor Swift video
for her song "Shake It Off." In it, the singer – herself the focus of numerous websites devoted to GIFs of her dancing awkwardly[19] – plays on her
own awkward dancing to show that she is not as skilled in movement
as are the professional black dancers and rappers alongside her, in Batuman's (2014) words, "as if to say, 'I know my ancestors once enslaved
your ancestors, and therefore I am physically and metaphysically less
graceful than you.' That's not a comfortable sentiment ... Awkward
moments have a way of pitting us against our own history." The Swift
discussion is interesting, not only for its production of awkwardness in
a way that exposes the historical tensions resonating in pop but also for
the manner in which it references the debate around twerking, particularly between Annie Lennox and Beyoncé, but also others such as Miley
Cyrus.[20] What makes these particular pop cultural debates about feminism awkwardly political is precisely the way in which they highlight
how a racist past and present continues to haunt feminist discourse.

The various moments cited by Batuman open up essential inroads
into the awkward in art and social practice, particularly related to the
historical and the popular in feminist actions. It is telling that Batuman
cites 9/11 as kicking off the "Awkward Age" in which US culture, in
particular, now finds itself, while Kaplan also claims 9/11 as the turning point for feminist futures. If we bring these two narratives together,
we see an interesting collision between the transformation of a cultural
tone and feminist political meaning. Irony, along with or followed by

the notion of camp, for example, defined cultural-political interventions in the 1990s as legible and decipherable.[21] Feminist performative activism in the 1970s and 1980s had a more satirically serious and, in some cases, darkly humorous tone, with clearly defined targets of critique.[22] The awkward, in contrast to both trends, creates diffuse and uncomfortable politics that always also reflect back on "readers" or "interpreters," implicating them in a sometimes-unwanted or unwitting solidarity. It is this transition to awkward politics from previous modes of feminist cultural presentation – be they satiric, ironic, or camp – that we trace briefly in the next section and that marks the examples in the rest of the chapters. This does not mean that satire, irony, or camp play no role in describing popfeminist awkwardness; however, these strategies are tangled up with awkwardness, which propels them to new levels of affective connection to the recipient, audience, or reader. Feminist activism in the twenty-first century, or, to stay with the above constructions, in the post-9/11 era, is multipronged and infused by pop culture, although, due to the essential role played by digital culture, that pop culture is no longer monolithic (or at least cannot be understood monolithically). Conversely, feminism has entered pop cultural moments and infused them with politics. These infusions, however, do not have a clearly determined political effect; rather, they are intersectional in that they often trigger discussions of race, class, sexuality, and gender that are inherently confusing and awkward. The confusing and awkward moments are mainly a result of unclear political positioning, of a political position that is not always clearly legible, that is on the move – and slippery.

"PITTING US AGAINST OUR OWN HISTORY" – PERFORMATIVE ROOTS

It is this lack of legibility and slipperiness that sharply distinguishes these contemporary performances and activisms from their forbearers, even if the historical legacy is obviously apparent. Contemporary examples of popfeminist protest performance art, digital as well as analogue, are steeped in the historical context of feminist performance art and closely linked to feminist happenings and performances of the late 1960s through the 1980s, though the political resonance is quite different, both in intention and reception. Since the late 1960s, performance art has worked with excess and parody, pushing the limits of form and audience reception. The international art movement *Fluxus* and the

Austrian artists known as the *Wiener Aktionisten* (Viennese Actionists)
provide two quite famous examples.[23] Due to the focus on the redefinition of art in the works of the artists associated with these movements, the politics of such performances are almost always integrally
linked to questions of form and aesthetics as well as to the audience's
collective experience. Indeed, the word "happening" goes hand-in-hand
with the description of these performances, but "happening" is also
often defined by what kind of audience effect it is intended to incite,
such as provocation or audience integration and participation (Dreher
2001, 15). Because of this interconnection between media, mode, and
audience reaction, such performances have often asked the audience to
question accepted norms and boundaries through transgression.

Nowhere is this transgression more apparent than in feminist performances, in which the body is the site for performative creative production and, as visibly gendered, is mobilized for feminist-specific
concerns.[24] Indeed, the use of the body to "impl[y] sexual liberation and
resistance to cultural constraints" is a key commonality to the political importance of these early performance artists' work (Striff 1997,
1). However, feminist engagements with art did not always focus solely
on corporeality. In *Radical Gestures: Feminism and Performance Art
in North America*, Jayne Wark (2006, 31) traces the manner in which
the political climate of the late 1960s, particularly the women's and
civil rights movements, was consciously inserted into art through feminist performance in a manner that focused on the "disruption of dominant narratives and the assertion of counter-paradigmatic narratives
through storytelling" as a further "powerfully politicized strategy of
engagement." In this, Wark continues, the aspect of agency was the central appeal of performance over other art forms for feminism enacted
by women as "agents of social and political change" (32). Thus both
body and "text" (whether as a narrative to be told or as a patriarchal
script to rewrite) come together in the origins and trajectory of feminist
performance art.[25]

Austrian artist Valie Export's performance "Aktionshose: Genitalpanik" (Action pants: Genital panic) provides a famous example. The
performance took place in a cinema in Munich in 1968 (the photo-documentation taking place during a Viennese exhibition in 1969), and it
displays a clear-cut engagement with – or rewriting of the text of – the
male culture of the gaze, violence, and the objectified female body.[26]
During this performance, Export, sporting a head of wild hair and a
steely expression, wore pants with the crotch removed and walked the

rows of the theatre brandishing a machine gun.[27] Her performance, therefore, confronted the male viewers with their sexual desire by presenting her exposed genitals to them in lieu of the women on the screen. However, by not embodying the ideal of femininity in her manner of appearance and, further, by equating sexual desire with violence, she clearly politicizes not only her own body but also the space in which it moves (here a cinema) and problematizes the unwitting audience taking part in the performance. The tones of the performance as well as the photo-documentation, moreover, are extremely earnest, though the markers of its politics are overdrawn with a hint of satire (the crotchless pants, representing the sexualization of women; the machine gun, representing violence to the female body through the gaze) as the intent of these markers is unequivocal.[28]

The combination of text, politics, and body in more traditionally defined feminist performance art is not only shared by those members of more established groups or movements pushing the boundaries of artistic acceptability, it is also seen in creative production by female visual artists, filmmakers, and literary authors with an agenda based in feminism or sexuality in the German-language context (including, for example, Export, Elfriede Jelinek, Pipilotti Rist, Marianne Wex, Charlotte Posenenske, Ulrike Ottinger, and Monika Treut). Transnational examples include Cindy Sherman, Marina Abramović, Susie Bright, Yoko Ono, and Annie Sprinkle.[29] The fact that Jelinek received the Nobel Prize in Literature in 2004 and that the Museum of Modern Art placed a Sherman exhibit on display in 2012 indicates their entrance into the realm of respected "high" culture, in spite of the fact that, at certain points in their careers, their works have been received as pornographic, shocking, and "gross."[30] The positioning of these transgressive women within established institutions that are hierarchical – even patriarchal – in structure and that bring with them cultural and financial capital, produces, furthermore, a tension between creative and political content and context for reception. While the provocation in the content of the works in question is not minimized, the intended impact may indeed shift directions, be heightened, or disappear all together. Moreover, the close-knit relationship between the reception of the work and that of the woman, as is regularly the case with regard to feminist creative production, receives another layer of complexity as the mode for disseminating the material and the discourse around that dissemination are simultaneously popularized. They are deemed acceptable for mass consumption and, as such, are problematized in that the validity of their placement as radical feminists speaking at and for the margins is put in jeopardy.

This is illustrated in Abramović's citation of Export's 1968 performance: she restaged "Aktionshose: Genitalpanik," along with six other late 1960s and early 1970s performance pieces, at the Guggenheim in New York as part of her 2005 exhibition *Seven Easy Pieces*. By so doing, Abramović, herself a long-time feminist performance artist emerging out of this same period, places the piece within acceptable museum space. Such a move muddies the clarity of intentional impact on the viewer, space, and body of the performer.[31] When placed within the acceptable context of the museum, and therefore elevated to the status of high art, the politics of the pieces lose their clarity; the performance is questioned in terms of feminist-political and artistic validity, even as that "validity" is confirmed by sheer inclusion in the Guggenheim. This is not to say that the piece suddenly becomes awkward in the same way that we identify as pertaining to the more recent pop-feminist actions, but its serious satire is transformed into serious art as museum-goers watch.

The shift that occurs in terms of feminist performance in the 1990s, then, is one of tone and context, although in many ways some of the same directed political intent can be found. Through the riot grrrl movement much of the feminist performance of the third wave was found in the music sector, including not only small-scale concerts discussed in our personal memories but also the beginning of large-scale feminist music events such as Lilith Fair or, later, Ladyfest, that reached the mainstream. In their political ciphers there are references to previous performance work by women, but there are also reverberations in today's actions. For example, Kathleen Hanna's scrawling of "slut" across her naked midriff at Bikini Kill concerts in the early 1990s immediately calls to mind the naked protests of Femen or the scantily clad SlutWalks. But it also references the way in which performance artists that came before utilized the body as a narrative and textual strategy, here by imbuing the word "slut," and, along with it, the music industry, with revolutionary power. It does so, however, with a clearly playful whiff of irony; instead of the use of satirical exaggeration the consumption of the female body on stage is ironized through the "girl power" used to appropriate the word "slut." A further example is the US-based group the Guerrilla Girls, established in 1985. These women take on the pseudonyms of dead female artists and appear in public wearing guerrilla masks to point towards sexism in the art world. They subvert and provoke through their playful use of irony (placing a guerrilla mask on a nude statue, for example).

This is not to suggest, however, that the more serious performance art of the earlier decades is smoothly replaced by the irony of the 1990s, making way for awkwardness in the current period. Such a periodization would be forced. Indeed, there are contemporary examples, too, that easily fall into similar categories of earlier performances. One such example would be the very real and personal protest performance of Emma Sulkowicz, a Columbia University student who, in 2014, decided to carry a mattress around with her on campus to represent the burden of being raped by a fellow student on a similar mattress. Stassa Edwards, writing in the *Hairpin* about the performance, draws parallels to previous feminist work, such as Yoko Ono's 1968 film *Rape*. But here there are also resonances of the awkward: the manner in which Sulkowicz's *Carry That Weight* criss-crossed digital social media also inserts an aspect of consumption and event culture into the performance, thereby unseating the personal-political nature of the work.

It is perhaps not surprising that the increased visibility of feminisms in the popular sphere comes at a time of the (nostalgic) return of many third wave and riot grrrl icons, a sign both of the ascent of a generation to middle age and acceptability, perhaps, but also, it might be argued, a sign of unwillingness to let go of a sense of feminist belonging that has not lost its relevance but, rather, has gained new relevance in a new context. Kathleen Hanna, lead singer for Bikini Kill and later Le Tigre, has come back on the music scene with the music project The Julie Ruin, and a documentary film on Hanna's career entitled *The Punk Singer* (by Sini Anderson) premiered at South by Southwest in 2013. In January 2015, Sleater-Kinney released their first album since 2005, drawing on band member Carrie Brownstein's success on the television show *Portlandia*, which debuted in 2011. The movement has also entered the academy – for example, with the establishment of the archive "The Riot Grrrl Collection" housed in the Fales Library and Special Collections at New York University, built of the personal collections of individual people, the names of which are listed on the library website. Further, the 2010s have also seen publications devoted to the riot grrrl movement, such as Sara Marcus's *Girls to the Front: The True Story of the Riot Grrrl Revolution*. Like the library archive, the book is framed by the personal, the author's own teenage-self: "I missed out on the first few years of Riot Grrrl" (Marcus 2010, 1). In each of these cases, much like our own case in this book, personal experience cannot be disentangled from the objects, performances, and politics embedded in the material. At the same time, like the recontextualization of feminist performance art in more acceptable spaces, narratives of riot grrrls' coming of age have left the stage – stopped the riot – and arrived, comfortably, on (feminist) bookshelves.

Hanna's work with The Julie Ruin continues to engage with performance and politics, as the 2013 song and video *Girls Like Us* (Harris and Gribbin 2013) attests, though in a manner that somehow differs from her earlier work. The song, which also features lead-vocals by trans-woman and queercore artist Vaginal Davis, includes lyrics such as:

girls like us might flock to scandals
but girls like us don't give a shit
girls like us pick up the hot handles
and burn our hands and we get over it
girls like us use highlighter pens
especially to write our poems
girls like us stand back to back
just because you know we want to know[32]

Here, unlike the song "Rebel Girl" from Bikini Kill's 1993 album *Pussy Whipped*, which includes such lyrics as "that girl thinks she's the queen of the neighborhood / I got news for you, she is!" and "when she talks, I hear the revolution,"[33] in this more recent song, the political and the notion of "girl" has become strangely familiar and is based in everyday actions. Further, the video posted on YouTube features Barbie dolls in a variety of staged scenarios – on a field with deer, in a bowl of popcorn, in a tiny wheelchair eating cherries – and wearing homemade DIY dresses. In the final two scenes of the video we see three Barbies, sitting around a bonfire lit by copies of popular US magazines such as *People*. As the music stops, we hear the sound of crackling fire, the dolls' backs to us around the campfire. When the image changes we see the same scenario – dolls around the campfire – but this time, the image is replicated on an iPad, around which the same Barbies are crowded, in various states of recline, on a bed. The band name and record label as well as its mode of distribution, iTunes, are overlaid on the final image.

The video alludes to the proximity, closeness, and utterly serious political messages of second-wave inspired feminism, but, at the same time, it uses the distancing and irony of the third wave, these strategies coming together on multiple levels: the lyrics, no longer suggestive of

1.1   "Girls Like Us," The Julie Ruin

the politics of rebel girl but instead of lifestyle-feminism, are overlaid
on an image of Barbie dolls, the ultimate in anti-feminist consumption. The collision between these modes produces awkwardness in its
political illegibility. The final shot of the technological medium for doc-
umenting the memory of Barbie's political act (burning popular magazines) suggests dissemination, made troubling by the embrace of Apple
products – the iPad and the advertisement for the song on iTunes – that
have become ultimate symbols of global consumerist corporatization.
Thus *Girls Like Us* shares with feminist performance art a playfulness
(Fox 2010, 110), its aesthetic and affects are sticky and awkward.

What characterizes the earlier examples of feminist performance art,
steeped in second wave politics, is their play with existing parameters of
acceptability, form, and available materiality, whether this means pushing the boundaries of language, the boundaries of aesthetics and beauty,
the boundaries between the body and representation, or the boundaries
of exhibitions space and the distance between performer and performed
body. While it is important to remember Griselda Pollock's claim that
periodization in art history follows a masculine model of curatorial
work that is, according to Oriana Fox, "anti-feminist" (Pollock 1996;
Fox 2010, 109), simplistically speaking, the female body as presented in
early performances art is legible and straightforward. In this way, these

performers lay the groundwork for the decades of feminist creative production to follow, including that of the third wave. What happens, however, in the later restagings of these performances, as well as in the reinterpretation of performance art in the context of the revival of riot grrrl DIY aesthetics, is that the politics of reception become less clearly defined, as is seen in the aspect of consumption and media highlighted in this final example. This illustrates a shift from political provocation to political disruption, from irony to awkwardness. By framing our circular reflections about popfeminist activism and technology with stories of how the personal and intimate are steeped in and tied to politics, to locality, and to circulations, we propose that, in order to describe and tease out the locations of political activism in the twenty-first century, we need to craft and read stories in a different way, and, heeding Cvetkovich's call quoted above, do the work of critique differently.

ENGAGING WITH TROUBLING TIMES

In a March 2014 talk at the University of Alberta, Donna Haraway (2014) called for listeners to "stay[] with the trouble" – "trouble," here, referring specifically to her discussion of our damaged and dying planet. Staying with the trouble, according to Haraway, offers a way to counter cynicism, despair, avoidance, and denial and to productively engage with the destruction we inherit by practising joy and embracing pleasure, collectively and individually. Of course, our individual, intimate experiences of the political possibilities of feminist performance collide with the appearance of essential feminist and gender theory from the 1990s. In her now-seminal *Gender Trouble*, Butler (1990, 146–7) suggests that gender normativity can be destabilized and de-essentialized – troubled – in a playful and performative way: "As the effects of a subtle and politically enforced performativity, gender is an 'act,' as it were, that is open to splittings, self-parody, self-criticism, and those hyperbolic exhibitions of 'the natural' that, in their very exaggeration, reveal its fundamentally phantasmatic status." In order to engage in troubling, we must uncover those aspects of performance that are part of each iteration of gender production. To do gender means to get into trouble. Butler concludes that, when it comes to gender activism, "the task is not whether to repeat, but how to repeat or, indeed, to repeat and, through radical proliferation of gender, to *displace* the very gender norms that enable the repetition itself" (148, emphasis in original). The call to activism, then, requires a circular and constant repetition of precisely that which is to be undermined: the category of normativity, whatever shape that might take.

All this does not mean that we intend to nostalgically remember 1990s gender activisms. The global ruptures of the early twenty-first century have posed new challenges to (feminist) activism. These challenges, in keeping with the above discussions of Carrière, Scott, and Kaplan, have also asked us to rethink the technologies of feminism, the discourse around it, the legacies and breakages of feminist histories, and the political viabilities of feminist futures diffusely engaged. Our intention is to find a language to describe aspects of these new feminist activisms, to capture their (however messy) political interventions, and to develop ways to think about contemporary political expression, global connectivity, and communities of care. *Awkward Politics* develops a political approach and it tells a story – a story of disruptions and continuities in the aesthetics and ethics of political intervention. The shifts and continuities are neither self-evident nor easily traced as a linear story; they need to be uncovered carefully – with a new kind of popfeminist methodology for awkward reading. Something shifted in the 1990s that led to a different location of political moments – technology and global circulations of such technologies played a crucial role in this shift. This does not mean that older or more traditional feminist and political causes disappeared, they were and are very much alive and relevant; nor does it mean that everything that happens under the label "feminism" is political. A new kind of political is located somewhere else; it is fleeting; it is connected to digital technologies; it is playfully pop but radically disruptive. This kind of politics does not make one happy, which may produce complacency and most definitely connotes progress, but it does erupt in joy, which is spontaneous and undirected, fleeting and playfully irreverent even in its seriousness. It might look light-hearted, but it is effective because it disturbs, questions, and disrupts not only gender norms but also conceptions of beauty and style, sexuality and pleasure, racialized perception, ageism, and classism.

In the 1990s, Butler's theory offered a way to depart from the identity politics and implicit essentialism of the arguments between radical and socialist feminists, and, more generally, between second wave feminists altogether. *Gender Trouble* opened up new ways of thinking about gender for a new generation of gender activists and riot grrrls. In the second decade of the twenty-first century, however, this trouble has become ever more urgent. Moreover, feminists also pointed to Butler's troubled relationship with race, anti-racist feminism, and intersectional feminist activism.[34] In this new trouble, every act bears the responsibility of locating the actor in a political playing field where gender is defined, and gender norms are either confirmed or new possibilities of doing and undoing gender evolve. The new trouble, however, was of a different quality than the trouble feminism was in before Butler – if we want to give Butler the credit for defining such a watershed. Understanding anything we "do" not only as political but also as performative creates a certain self-consciousness of action, which, we argue, is a facet of political awkwardness: the self-awareness of doing gender. This self-awareness also shifts from performer to audience, at times bordering on self-parody that is not always intentional or not always legible as such, and on subversion that can also look like co-option.

The challenge, then, is to find a position from which to engage with and theorize feminist activism in the contemporary moment that acknowledges multiple forms of intersecting oppressions and forms of exclusions. The trouble we find ourselves in today concerns being faced with the need to do feminists politics in spite of the fact that feminism only seems to address a fraction of what might be at stake, politically. Rather than remain with cynicism and despair in the face of our political (second and third wave) inheritance, we use popfeminist joy to push back against such cynicism. We must stay with the trouble by embracing the circularity of feminist politics as an awkwardness that communicates joy, collaboration, and community.

2

Feminist Activisms and Local Contexts: Forms and Trajectories

Rather than locating our theorizing of popfeminist awkwardness solely within academic and theoretical discussions, our first chapter emphasizes that our thinking grew out of collaboration around our own questions about feminist politics in the digital age. Where to locate the political, how to do activism, the function of solidarity today, and the effectiveness of certain political strategies that, more often than not, mix non-digital and often performative forms with digital dissemination are part of such questions. In this context, access and location as well as economic and social hierarchies become crucially important. To clearly connect our discussions of and theorizations around popfeminist digital activism to political contexts means to sketch out the political landscape and history within which it emerges. For this book, the majority of the examples come from the German context, starting roughly in 2007 and reaching until 2015. By looking at the German case, we tell a story of feminist engagement that is unique to Germany but that is propelled forward by global flows. To begin this story of feminist activism in Germany might falsely imply that feminist history could be written within one national or linguistic context, but we show that – especially when we trace digital feminist activisms – it is more complicated and confusing than that. From this discussion of Germany-specific activisms and their circulations into and out of different national contexts, a broader discussion of different forms of global and feminist activism is possible. The local and the national matter, but local and national politics shift in the context of digital circulations and new kinds of localities emerge (Tuzcu 2015). In turn, regardless of how "digital" and "global" circulations and activisms are, the local remains crucial for how any such activism plays out politically.

As quoted in chapter 1, E. Ann Kaplan claims that 9/11 is an essential moment for thinking about feminist futures and for rethinking feminist pasts. While 9/11 as a marker of national transformation does not bear the same weight for Germany as it does for the United States, it does denote a shift in the national relationship to the global, or, it could be said, a new understanding of the political urgency of transnational discourses. Discourses that were already emerging in the pre-9/11 era gained ever-increasing ground as part of what was seen as a transnational and national crisis. These discourses included the racial and ethnic dimensions to the European demography debate, the increasing growth of the precariat as a social class, and questions about unregulated and uncontrollable monetary speculation, leading to the 2008 Eurozone crisis following the global economic crisis. Already in 1999, Ulrich Beck describes the transformations that go into creating what he calls a society based on risk. In *World Risk Society*, Beck (1999, 2 and 5) explains that globalization and global risks that occur simultaneously and affect Western and non-Western societies alike, though the latter more heavily, increasingly determine the patterns of life – including employment, progress, and exploitation. He defines risk as the way in which societies attempt to control the "various unintended consequences of radicalized modernization" (3). In the substantially rewritten and expanded German-language version of the text, Beck (2007, 29) further explains that risk is not the same as a catastrophe but, rather, the possibility of a future catastrophe that does not yet exist. Therefore, the society's state of being is one of constant and threatening anticipation, whether of an environmental apocalypse or economic collapse. Or, as he says in *German Europe*, risk society is a society living in the subjunctive (Beck 2013, 8). What is notable is Beck's claim that such attention to risk by a society replaces any previous discourses that were political mobilizers, especially class-, race-, and gender-based inequities (Beck 1999, 4). However, one could also argue that the replacement of risk with a notion of crisis in the aftermath of the economic crisis of 2008 reintroduces in the form of the precariat the possibilities of global protests that are very often about class, race, and gender. Indeed, if, as Kaplan (2003, 5) claimed in 2003, employment is bound to be one of the areas of concern for feminist futures, the rise of the precariat underscores her thinking as a reality, but it also firmly reinserts feminism as a major discourse of power into the world risk society. Based on a 2011 study, in Germany specifically, 80 percent of the precarious positions (those which are only part time or are fixed contract) are held by women.[1]

Germany provides a useful case study for exploring these issues for several key reasons. As Myra Marx Ferree (2012) notes in *Varieties of Feminism: German Gender Politics in Global Perspective*, the history of German feminism, tied to but markedly distinct from Anglo-American feminism, provides a significant counterpoint for considering the transnational flow and the local contexts of feminist theories and actions. The resurgence of interest in and debate about feminism over the past decade, timed almost concurrently with the economic crisis and the height of the demography debate on Germany's declining birth rate,[2] brought with it a reconsideration of the nation within transnational discussions of migration and multiculturalism and the rise of Islamophobic discourse. Finally, because of its unique history and its crucial role within Europe today following the Eurozone crisis, a topic central to Beck's claims in *German Europe,* Germany represents a key site for considering the intersection of feminist activism with questions of sexuality, citizenship, race, ethnicity, religion, and economic disenfranchisement. The emergence of a German transnational feminist protest culture simultaneous to such national concerns and driven by digital media and other technologies is our point of departure for this chapter.

These reflections capture the complicated mechanisms at work in contemporary feminisms and provide reasons for the selection of our examples, which circle around a specific national context – that of Germany. After offering a sketch of the landscape of feminist discourses in Germany in roughly the last decade, that is – starting at the turning point for feminist activism described above – and laying the groundwork for answering the question of why Germany matters for our study as a whole, we turn to examples that illustrate the complex politics that develop from political and feminist protests and digital engagement. These examples include the emergence of Femen activism in Germany, the #aufschrei campaign against sexual harassment and violence, and blog-based discourses. Through these and other examples, we theorize more generally the space of art and political practices in the twenty-first century on a global scale, which leads to a discussion of pop-activism and popfeminist strategies. With these larger questions about political activism and its histories, and in combination with the previous chapter's examination of personal and performance histories, we set the stage for the ensuing chapters, in which we draw on specific examples to theorize reading for awkwardness as a popfeminist methodology that mines for the political.

THE PATH TO GERMANY'S NEOFEMINISM IN NEOLIBERALISM

Beginning with the advent of the new millennium, popular and academic publications across the Western world have grappled with *Reclaiming the F Word* (the title of a 2010 co-authored text by Catherine Redfern and Kristin Aune, subtitled *The New Feminist Movement*). Such texts suggest that political concerns of the second and third wave – including the liberation of women's bodies, equity in home and work, and violence – persist but that the question "why feminism?" (Redfern and Aune 2010, 205) – or better yet "which feminism?" – is nevertheless posed again and again. This generationally founded positioning was acutely felt in Germany, where feminist activists and scholars repeatedly insisted that the third wave had not reached the country in the 1990s, as it did other nations.[3] However, there are other factors at work as to why Germany provides a specifically interesting starting point for a discussion of contemporary feminisms – one that allows for a springboard to the larger theoretical and methodological feminist claims we are developing here. As Ferree (2012, 5) notes, German politics on the federal level draw not on individual rights or opportunities as would a liberal state but, rather, on "conservative views of patriarchal authority and social democratic ideals of justice to forge a social welfare state that prioritizes family support and the social reproduction of the nation." Further, German unification and the ultimate discrediting of East German socialist equality measures as part of the outgoing repressive regime complicate the historical legacies at work in contemporary feminisms in Germany. Ferree underscores how these and other stark differences in Germany collide with similarities to other nations, including the effect of transnational flows and the positions of religion, class, and ethnicity (6). She writes: "The shifting global balance of power, in which liberal institutions are growing but American-style feminism is no longer the trendsetter, is both cause and consequence of changes in what German and other national women's movements embrace" (7). Germany, therefore, offers a unique location in the reading for currents and crosscurrents in feminist political practice. The German context also offers a salient example of a Western nation whose national concerns increasingly clash with global issues. Within this clash, a model of "the West" as an entity is increasingly under scrutiny. Germany as one such Western nation, of course, continues to exist as an idea that drives and fuels – in some cases rather desperately so – political and economic agendas. But in the face of the social reality of a multi-ethnic society, the political reality of a Germany embedded in Europe, and globally connected financial markets, a much more complicated picture emerges.

Because of this complex set of global influences, the current state of feminism can only be described as beyond the waves. Previous waves of feminism, as Ferree shows, are also the product of global flows; however, we can often trace these flows back to a set of certain national, or even local, political triggers. The second wave feminist movement in West Germany, for example, came out of the radical student and other counter-cultural movements sweeping many nations in 1967 and 1968, also in response to the devastating conflict in Vietnam. Mobilizing West German women politically was the topic of abortion rights, a topic on the agenda of many other national feminist movements (Ferree 2012, 62). A very different, more local moment caused German feminism to first coalesce in the form of protest: when during the national assembly of the German Socialist Student Association (Sozialistischer Deutscher Studentenbund [SDS]) in September 1968 the chair of the meeting tabled a feminist critique of the SDS submitted by Helke Sander on behalf of the Action Group for the Liberation of Women in Berlin, Sander threw tomatoes at the chair, with others joining the fray (Ferree 2012, 53). In its spontaneous performance of protest, this action was effective because it replicated the SDS's own gesture of radical critique – the cobblestones the students threw at public targets – therefore suggesting that the SDS members were just as oppressive as were the structures against which they agitated. But this protest also had a directed political trigger: Sander's critique specifically outlined the problems of West Berlin mothers in mobilizing politically due to their role as caregivers of children (Ferree 2012, 57; Smith-Prei 2013).[4]

Third wave feminism, too, begins in reaction to a larger sense on the part of feminists that their story was not being told, this time by fellow feminists. The inception of the third wave in the United States came as a response to the perceived political unity of a movement that the second wave embodied. It countered this unity with multiple feminisms characterized by difference, set out in numerous articles that appeared in popular venues such as *Ms. Magazine* and the *Village Voice* in the early 1990s (Garrison 2005, 249–51). As outlined in chapter 1, the riot grrrl movement took to the stage, protesting against gender- and race-motivated violence through punk and rock performances. The story of what we term third wave feminism in Germany also begins with a localized moment that is theoretical, performative, and transnational: Judith Butler's 1997 lecture in Berlin. As Ferree (2012, 176) writes rather personally of this lecture: "Arriving at the city library where she would speak, I realized I had stumbled into an event more like a rock concert than an academic lecture ... Understanding gender as performance arrived in Germany with a bang." This event coincided with the transformation of language of gender at the level of the European Union, including a focus on gender mainstreaming – a transformation that caused some feminists concern. However, as Ferree notes: "Awareness of how gender intersected with sexuality, race, age, and other inequalities also opened space for gay men to ally with lesbian and feminist activists and highlighted the marginality of racial/ethnic and immigrant women in European feminisms" (177). These new spaces for alliances also meant that the voices of feminists of colour who had tried to infuse feminist discourse in Germany since the 1980s finally became part of the conversation.

At the same time, the individualizing strategies, as Ferree calls them, of gender performance and mainstreaming seemed to further insert a neoliberal model into feminist politics (see Baer 2012a; Gill and Scharff 2011; and Scharff, Smith-Prei, and Stehle 2015). Ferree (2012, 180–1) writes that, in the wake of Butler's talk, German debates over structuralism and poststructuralism were viewed as having a real impact on feminist practices but that poststructuralism seemed to be individualistic and neoliberal: "Neoliberalism, used as a derogatory term meaning placing capitalist values over social solidarity, was a common critique against the market-based restructuring of welfare states that began to accelerate worldwide after the collapse of the socialist regimes of Europe." The new attention to poststructuralism meant also a new attention to the neoliberal model of individual agency as part of feminist discourse (181). This is not to say that German feminists wholeheartedly embraced the neoliberal model; instead, the insertion of the neoliberal model into the discussion illuminates the increasingly transnational, while still firmly national, character of the discourse (see also Scharff in Gill and Scharff 2011). In particular, the manner in which the tensions over unification and the end of the Cold War exposed the problem of not having anything to replace the "dying dichotomies" also played out in gender discourse (Ferree 2012, 182). Thus, while the third wave was never labelled as such in Germany, it could be argued that this moment marked a shift in the language used to think nationally about feminist politics on a European and transnational stage.

When discussing the political context of activism and protest performance since roughly 2007 and the complex circularity in these actions, the German context provides a set of questions related to the interplay between historical trajectories, ground-swell feminist actions, and neoliberalism. Ferree (2012, 226) summarizes:

> By looking carefully at a political context that is not politically liberal, the German case illuminates the radical potential of so-called liberal feminist ideas of self-determination, individual freedom, social autonomy, and civic culture to challenge state-driven, protectionist varieties of feminism from the grassroots ... To equate the political aspirations of classical liberalism with the social depredations of neoliberal market fundamentalism overlooks a transformative power that feminism has always claimed.

In her analysis, Germany offers a unique place for engaging with feminism entrenched in liberalism in a way that illuminates but does not over-emphasize transnational neoliberal influence. Ferree goes on to discuss how, in the German context, activists bridged the gap between activism and liberalism in feminism's concerns by forming political groups to pursue a common project (227). It is this common project around the political aspect of feminism that we are concerned with in *Awkward Politics*; however, instead of suggesting commonness as being common goals or intentions, we suggest a different notion of community forged through disjuncture and disconnect, circularity and messiness, but also through joy and collaboration.

Ferree describes a period of German feminism that historically precedes the time period with which are concerned here. However, the legacies of Butler's talk and the discussions around new or neo-feminisms (starting around 2007 in Germany) continued to breathe life into discourses about feminisms. When we began our conversation about and collaboration on popfeminist politics in 2009, German media were abuzz with discussions about feminism – neo, post, and pop. These media debates continued in the following years, despite the financial crisis taking a central position in political concern and public conversation. Hester Baer describes this in her discussion of sensationalized media debate triggered by the publication of Charlotte Roche's novel *Schoßgebete* (Wrecked), following on the heels of her surprise success *Feuchtgebiete* (Wetlands, a text we discuss in chapter 5). Baer (2012b, 59) writes:

In summer 2011, as European stock markets plummeted and EU
leaders tried to stave off the impending Eurozone crisis, a debate
took shape in the German media about sex and feminism. The
protagonists in this debate were Charlotte Roche, the best-sell-
ing author of two immensely popular novels and a self proclaimed
young feminist, and Alice Schwarzer, publisher of the established
feminist magazine *Emma* and, for over thirty years, Germany's
best-known feminist.

Timed with the global financial crisis, artists, writers, and performers
as well as journalists, media personalities, and conservative pundits
addressed the question as to whether the "f-word" mattered anymore
and what feminist practice looked like. That these discussions were car-
ried out by representatives of second wave and neofeminism as well as
by neoconservatives suggests precisely this simultaneous appearance of
classical liberal feminism with activist and neoliberal cultures identified
by Ferree.

The renewed interest in feminism in Germany also came just as the
demography debate had reached its heights, also around 2007. Since
the turn of the millennium, social scientists, scholars, and politicians
were convinced that the German population was dying out as a people
because women (read: white German women) were no longer having
(enough) children. Popular non-fiction titles such as Eva Herman's *Das
Prinzip Arche Noah: Warum wir die Familie retten müssen* (The Noah's
ark principle: Why we must save the family, 2007), Iris Radisch's *Die
Schule der Frauen: Wie wir die Familie neu erfinden* (The school of
women: How we are reinventing the family, 2007), and Dieter Thomä's
Väter: Eine moderne Heldengeschichte (Fathers: A story of modern-day
heroes, 2008), or government-sponsored publications by then family
minister Ursula von der Leyen such as *Familie gewinnt* (Family wins,
2007) and *Füreinander da sein, miteinander handeln* (Being there for
one another, acting with one another, 2007) disseminate the specifics
of contemporary family politics into the public sphere. The reasons
given for the waning normative family were most often placed on the
shoulders of women, one specific reason identified as women's choice
of career over family. Shared by many of the reactionary or neoconservative texts, in particular, is a belief that the '68 movement, along
with second wave feminism, was the catalyst for the (negative) familial
transformations in the twenty-first century.[5]

At the same time, Germany saw increased interest in and public discussion of the state of feminism. Publications such as *Wir Alphamädchen:*

Warum Feminismus das Leben schöner Macht (We Alphagirls: Why feminism makes life better) (Haaf, Klingner, and Streidl 2008); *Neue deutsche Mädchen* (New German girls) (Hensel and Raether 2008), and *Das F-Wort: Feminismus ist Sexy* (The f-word: Feminism is sexy) (Stöcker 2007) all wished to reclaim feminism for a new generation of "girls": "We want to be feminists again" (Haaf, Klingner, and Streidl 2008, 20).[6] The antifeminist demography debates played a massive role in sparking renewed interest in the "taboo-word" "feminism" among young women (Stöcker 2007, 10).

A (false) perception that German feminism is dominated by second wave icon Alice Schwarzer drove such authors to define themselves repeatedly against their forbearers. Schwarzer (2007, 172) herself warns such women in her contribution to these discussions, the publication *Die Antwort* (The answer): "Ok, understood sisters, you have to have your own experiences, but: please don't start everything again from scratch."[7] By asking these "sisters" not to reinvent the wheel, Schwarzer suggests that issues facing German women today should be approached with strategies developed by feminisms of the past. Scholars such as Margaret McCarthy, Hester Baer, and Christina Scharff describe how these debates played out in German literature, media, and social discourse. Most often, they are framed as a generational conflict between second and third wave feminists who do not agree on what feminist politics should or might be all about.[8]

This impression is fostered by the obsession of many neofeminist publications with the legacy of Schwarzer and with defining their thinking against that of the previous feminist generation. *Wir Alphamädchen* includes a chapter devoted to the history of feminism in which, within fifteen pages, the authors attempt to sketch out feminist history starting in antiquity and covering US feminism and West and East Germany. They, too, end with Schwarzer as the long-standing "institution" for feminism (Haaf, Klingner, and Streidl 2008, 196). Stating that feminism in Germany needs them, the new generation, they conclude this history section with a call to women to finally claim "their half" (197). This history, however brief, emphasizes the importance of second wave feminism to contemporary iterations and explains the fact that feminist issues disappeared from the spotlight in the 1990s as other issues took its place: a focus on career, consumption, and pop culture (193). Without using the term, these authors are describing a neoliberal atmosphere that fostered the depoliticization of what was then perceived as private issues and that led to the belief that we had arrived in a postfeminist era (193). Jana Hensel and Elisabeth Raether (2008, 14), too, take as their starting point an engagement with feminist history in the form of their disagreement with the politics of Schwarzer, particularly her stance on Islam and prostitution: "Time has caught up with them, their rhetoric is worn-out, Alice Schwarzer and her women have become history."[9] Describing a press conference with Schwarzer as the impetus for beginning their collaborative book, these "new German girls" go on to write about friendship, relationships, love, sex, identities, and roles – a personal book about "what it is like being a woman today" (16).[10] Like for the Alphagirls, second wave history becomes the point of departure for neoliberal individuation, and, also in keeping with many of its fellow publications, references to intersectionality, race, and class are absent (Baer 2012a, 370).

What these discussions, including their counterparts in North America,[11] display is competing terminology around feminism, the use of rhetoric that emphasizes generations, and the importance of considering the influence that a neoliberal economy has on social activism and gender constructions. All of these aspects display tensions around assessing impact, meaning making, and the necessity of feminism that we describe as circularity. Such terms as "postfeminism" and "lifestyle feminism" (and the continual suggestion of replacing "feminism" with the word "humanism") work towards making feminism palatable, apolitical, and ahistorical. Postfeminism and lifestyle feminism are used to describe a middle- and upper-middle-class attitude of young women who take from feminism whatever helps them to further their personal goals, while disregarding its larger social and political goals.[12] In Germany, these terms show the influx of neoliberalism in contrast to the political tradition of social forms of feminism. Scharff summarizes this debate about postfeminism, theorized also by Rosalind Gill (2007) and Angela McRobbie (2009), as describing a time when feminist and antifeminist discourse exist simultaneously, when feminism "is taken into account and simultaneously repudiated" (Scharff 2014a, 837).

Postfeminism, then, in part describes a true trend in Western countries in the later 1990s and early twenty-first century, but it is also a tool to lump together various forms of feminisms that continued to have a rather activist agenda and, at least discursively, to depoliticize them. A poignant example here is the increasing visibility of feminists of colour in Germany during the 1990s, a fact for which such generalizations cannot and do not account.[13] Rather than creating the sense of a malicious and clearly politically intentional media conspiracy that leads to such generalization, neoliberal market forces might have driven these trends towards depoliticization and apolitical readings of emerging movements. We think here, for example, of appropriations of the rebellious and visually "other" as the new cool by music television channels like MTV and Viva in Germany. Baer (2012a, 370) writes of the failure on the part of many of the German texts discussed above to "engage with many insights of feminist theory" and, therefore, also their "failure to recognize white privilege or to achieve a consciousness of the intersectionality of oppression," this due to "popfeminism's assimilation of postfeminist discourses that have become commonplace under the sign of neoliberalization in Europe." Such neoliberal appropriations do not mean that new forms of visibility are void of political messages. They do, however, often serve as arguments in debates over gender inequality, race, and racism in Germany; namely, that, since so many women and non-white people are now on TV, Germany – or what is often called the new Berlin Republic of the 1990s due to the move of the country's capital from Bonn to Berlin following unification – has clearly overcome racism and sexism. Especially when it comes to race, such calculated visibility often over-compensates underlying historical hauntings and attempts to render invisible forms of racialized discrimination that are based, for example, on class, legal status, or religion. It further justifies a discourse about "normalization," whereby the mainstream public is increasingly comfortable with referring to racial (and often also gendered) stereotypes as funny and innocent since racism is considered to no longer be a (real) problem in a supposedly postracial society.[14] A similar argument can be made for gender – to over simplify, a Germany that has a female chancellor must, by definition, be a country where feminist issues are passé or where feminism has become a "lifestyle."[15] New forms of exclusions that revolve around concepts of religion and faith, mainly Islam, take the place of earlier discriminations that revolved around race or gender.[16] This is not to suggest that gender and racial discriminations disappear; rather, they are papered over with a new and equally problematic construction of a monolithic idea of religiosity that is considered "backward" and certainly "other." "Homonationalism" as defined by Jasbir Puar (2007, 2013), is also part of this general trend whereby Western nations utilize certain concepts of inclusion (here of homosexuals, but also of women or people of colour) to position themselves as superior against a backward (often Eastern or Southern) religious other. The creation of such new forms of racialized and gendered exclusions, of course, is precisely what calls for new forms of politics. And the appropriation of the language of liberation, emancipation, and equality in these exclusions is what makes the creation of new political forms so complicated. Thus, certainly in the twenty-first century, forms of discrimination and exclusions do not come in "waves" but, instead, intersect and clash in messy ways. It is within this mess that spaces for equally messy feminist political interventions open up.

POPFEMINISM

This production of unclear political meaning speaks to the situation of contemporary feminisms in popular discourse and, potentially, in the academy. An alternative term, specific in its use to Germany, that came out of these discussions is "popfeminism" (*Popfeminismus*; see Baer 2011, 2012a; Seidel 2015). Popfeminism evokes feminist traditions of creative work, particularly performance art since the late 1960s, as discussed in chapter 1, but it also points to their shortcomings in today's contexts. It is a reaction to, and even an incorporation of, second wave feminist-political tradition, third wave DIY creative aesthetics, and the contemporary depoliticization of feminism. In particular, it uses feminism to recode pop culture and pop to rewrite feminism. First theorized by Eismann (2007b, 10) in the edited volume *Hot Topic: Popfeminismus heute* (Hot topic: Popfeminism today), popfeminism provides a feminist approach to pop culture, but it also critiques and redefines both feminism and pop culture: "Pop culture [should] be perforated and rocked by feminist strategies."[17] Eismann's attempt to reclaim feminism for a new generation is, on the one hand, a reaction against the popular understanding of feminism in Germany as second wave feminism and, on the other hand, a correction of the missing radical voice and a reinsertion of politics drained from post- and lifestyle feminism. But while popfeminism is a playful politics of personal experience taken to a theoretical level, it is constantly – and consciously – in danger of becoming an object of consumption for it uses pop culture on a global scale to look for local spaces of change and resistance.[18] Eismann, like her other neofeminist counterparts, also assumes that Germany lags behind (particularly the United States) in both feminist and pop-cultural developments (10–11; cf. note 19), but, at the same time, she positions German popfeminism in a decidedly political sphere. Rather than providing a history of feminist activism in Germany or globally, the essays in *Hot Topic* focus on demands for the present and the future in order to create links to, specifically, third wave feminism in the United States. The different contributions by scholars, artists, and gender activists in *Hot Topic* cover such diverse areas as sexuality and sexual identity, body and body image, media and work, DIY activism, music, and comics.

While the volume as a whole follows a rather intersectional approach, questions of race and racism remain largely absent.

The circularity inherent in the critique of pop culture by popfeminism, and, in turn, the popularization of the feminist image in that critique is central to thinking through the politics of performative and popular forms of activism. Moreover, the term "pop" in the German context does not refer only to the popular. In her study of the crosscurrents between US and German pop, Agnes Mueller (2004, 4) writes that, in Germany, popular culture is a "response to the formation of subcultures, as it is an integral component of the hegemonic power's dominating culture. Pop culture, then, can also exemplify a further hybridization of subculture, by integrating the dominant culture into its struggle for a new identity." Since the 1960s, the "pop" prefix in the German context has been used to denote a specifically "German" subcultural phenomenon floating on the surface of global mass culture (see Arnold and Schäfer 2003; and McCarthy 2015). German pop recodes signs of popular culture through quotations, pastiche, and cut-up methods, resignifying and redefining the original subject in a manner that reflects, exposes, and even problematizes superficial aspects of everyday reality. In their foreword to *Pop seit 1964* (Pop since 1964), Kerstin Gleba and Eckhard Schumacher (2007, 12) explain that pop is a way to remake and remodel culture, utilizing artificial exaggeration in its approach to reproduction and copying: "Pop is ... a strategy, a posture, an attitude."[19] This focus on pop as an attitude underscores the fact that pop is a performative act of self-stylization. Pop's artificiality intentionally subverts "dominant notions of taste" (Jenkins, McPherson, and Shattuc 2002, 27). As a subversive element, pop thus produces intentional unrest and unease that, in its politicized form, can lead to aesthetic acts of resistance. Gleba and Schumacher (2007, 14) see this to be a German phenomenon: "Only [in Germany] is pop always also a problem."[20] It should be noted that pop in the German context is almost always associated with the reformulation of the term in the mid-1990s, following pop's first appearance in the late 1960s. In the 2011 essay "Das Ende der Popliteratur" (The end of pop literature), Schumacher writes, however, that pop should not be understood as synonymous with pop literature; instead, pop constitutes a gesture, one of many literary approaches, which is marked by a tendency "to continuously undermine definitions – where appropriate in seemingly opposite directions" (Schumacher 2011, 65).[21] Returning to popfeminism, this concept of a disturbance and resignification is central to grasping the impulse behind the manner in which pop and feminism come together as an activist concern: the understanding of pop as gestures that go in opposite directions corresponds to the movement described by awkwardness.

As these discussions imply, the timeframe in which such new forms of street and digital activisms emerged in Germany is not coincidentally the same timeframe that marks the emergence of new forms of activisms across the globe. As Todd Wolfson (2014, 2) argues in his 2014 study *Digital Rebellion*,[22] in the 2009 aftermath of the financial crisis, a "cycle of resistance" emerged as what he describes as a "diverse but singular moment of rebellion." In these diverse movements, Wolfson identifies common traits such as "the creative use of new media and social networks," "the desire for meaningful democratic participation, the physical and virtual occupation of space, and the leadership of young people" (2). These traits, in Wolfson's reading, helped "to form the silhouette of a new figure of resistance, a new sociopolitical formation" (ibid.). He understands these movements as developing through a dialogue with social movement actors – and forms, we would add – past and present and in close connection with a material world that is their main concern as well as their primary object of critique. This material world, which, in the current neoliberal moment, is defined by a "network society," includes digital forms and, as Wolfson calls them, "networked formations" (3) that are, simultaneously, the target of critique and the means for organizing political resistance.

While Wolfson emphasizes the way in which these new movements – and he starts with the Occupy movements and what he terms the "*Cyber Left*" (emphasis in original) in particular to investigate examples of new left organizing – utilize new forms to fight equally new forms of capitalist exploitation, he also insists on their connection and interplay with historical forms of resistance. These forms of organizing, so his main point would have it, "ha[ve] shifted spatial and temporal configurations" thus "creating new possibilities for organizational structure, democratic governance, and media strategy" (4). His conclusion, however, is rather pessimistic in that he argues that "the logic of resistance and therefore the strategies, practices, and organizations that have emerged in the last two to three decades might not have the facility to build power and create real-world change, at the scale of the Old Left" (193). We return to some of the specific forms of digital activisms in chapter 4 when we map the discourses around digital circulations and activisms; however, in the context of this chapter, Wolfson's emphasis on historical references and connections, on the one hand, and new forms of communication and organizing in digital activisms, on the other, is significant since a similar tension is at work in the digital feminist activisms outlined here. Our contention, though, as we state at various points throughout this book, is that, rather than looking for quantifiable change in an evaluation of the political effects of these movements, we need to focus on forms and aesthetics that produce, however fleetingly, moments of political challenges in order to gain a better understanding of political process and change in the digital age. To acknowledge the historical connections of contemporary activisms, in our analysis, offers a way to look beyond the idea of historical waves and to let history and the present circulate, merge, and clash in new ways. We need to forgo the evaluative, goal-driven stance in order to uncover political moments in contemporary activist movements. These moments, at times, emerge when we least expect them.

As we turn now to outlining a selection of protest actions that engage both pop and feminism in their activism within the context of the broader reach of contemporary feminism in Germany, these connections between historically anchored forms and new technologies of activism become apparent. We focus on the way in which the German context makes legible the collision between transnational flows and national legacies, even as these remain murky in their interaction. The selection of examples below merges the more traditional social-radical concerns of German feminism with neoliberal consumption tendencies, although, in this, the selection is by no means exhaustive and should not be seen as representative of all that has happened over the past few years and is still happening in feminist activism in Germany at the popular level. The very nature of contemporary digital activist work is its constant proliferation and manifestation. It does this by relying on traditional feminist platforms – for example, taking to the street (protest marches and rallies), written communication (in the form of publications, such as zines), and community building (women's centres, cafés, or bookstores) – but transforms these through digital tools and pop means. Feminist engagements in the digital realm specifically emphasize information sharing, connections, and solidarity with a view to empowerment through not only discursive but also visual means; the interplay between the discursive and the visual is what creates the specific aesthetic reach of such activisms.[23] Further, digital culture is an integral part of pop cultural circulation. If digital culture distinctly drives popular culture today, then, following popfeminism, feminist activisms not only use but also productively disturb the digital economy; however, this means that the digital economy disturbs and reconfigures feminisms.[24] While these examples offer diverse modes of engagement, they and the debates around them are also fraught with a type of altruism that suggests that, in feminist political work, there exists one clear agenda, one goal, and one possible outcome to label as success. By reading for and acting with awkwardness, as we theorize in more detail in chapter 3, we develop a methodology that insists on the necessity of political action and feminist protest in the face of its often messy and circular effects.

POPFEMINIST ACTIVISM

The Street

One such activist group that illustrates a mixture of pop and protest, historical forms and digital means, and transnational and national contexts, is the international group Femen.[25] Co-founded by Anna Hutsol (in the initial years together with Wiktor Swjatskyj), a Ukrainian economist, Femen started as a Ukrainian feminist protest group in Kiev in 2008. The group organized topless protests against sex tourism, religious institutions, and sexisms in general with its "sextremist" actions. Sextremism is "a non-violent but highly aggressive form of provocation; it is an all-powerful demoralizing weapon undermining the foundations of the old political ethics and rotten patriarchal culture" (Femen, official website). From the Ukrainian context, Femen grew to a self-proclaimed "global women's movement," defined on its website as follows:

> In the beginning, there was the body, feeling of the woman's body, feeling of joy because it is so light and free. Then there was injustice, so sharp that you feel it with your body, it immobilizes the body, hinders its movement, and then you find yourself your body's hostage. And so you turn your body against this injustice, mobilizing every body's cell to struggle against the patriarchy and humiliation. You tell the world: Our God is a Woman! Our mission is Protest! Our Weapon are bare breasts! And so FEMEN is born and sextremism is set off. FEMEN is an international women's movement of brave topless female activists painted with the slogans and crowned with flowers. FEMEN female activists are the women with special training, physically and psychologically ready to implement the humanitarian task of any degree of complexity and level of provocation. FEMEN activists are ready to withstand repressions against them and are propelled by the ideological cause alone. FEMEN is a special force of feminism, its spearhead militant unit, modern

incarnation of fearless and free Amazons. (spelling and grammar in the original)[26]

The reification of the female body in Femen's self-description here is joined by a revelatory call to arms, thus suggesting that any aggression to be harnessed arises out of a body that naturally senses injustice. This focus on the body can be described as what Miriam Stehling and Tanja Thomas (2015) call decontextualization, or the unlinking of the protests from clear contexts, in Femen's self-mediation, which further leads to the group's potential depoliticization. Discussions about Femen in the media and among academics are often rather critical of the group but are also in awe of its success. Both the critique of and the theory about the success of Femen circle around the topless protests of the rather normatively beautiful, often white, blond, and young protesters involved in Femen actions. Further, it is clear that, without such – carefully calculated – media attention and Femen's active participation in digital media and social networking platforms like Twitter and Facebook,[27] this success would not have been possible.

In her research on Femen, Jessica Zychowicz (2011, 217) asks a question similar to the one we are posing more broadly – namely: "What would it mean to stop arguing over whether Femen's members are 'good' feminists, and instead, to consider them critically as a performance group with a political constituency?" She reads Femen in the tradition of feminist protest art and concludes that she feels "the need to advocate for alternate approaches to them [Femen], approaches that go beyond conventional understandings of protest as a means to an end" (224). Zychovicz argues that Femen frame "the 'perfect' female body, held sacred by society, with laughter and shame," which, according to her, makes them controversial and "lends them a shred of political legitimacy beyond allegations that their actions merely comprise cheap showmanship or reactionary antics" (219). Not just the group itself but also its mode of protest became popular at the same time as the global financial crisis reached its peak. Since then, many Femen activists have left Ukraine. Nonetheless, members of the group continue to be active in Ukraine, for example, orchestrating a protest action on the same day the Crimean Parliament voiced its will to join the Russian Federation.[28]

The specific actions of Femen in Germany point to some issues of feminism in the contemporary moment that we discuss above: in solidarity with the topless protest of Tunisian activist Amina Tyler (Sboui), for example, a German Femen group publicly protested against women's oppression in Islam by standing in front of a Berlin mosque with bare breasts and with slogans such as "Fuck your Morals" and "Fuck Islamism" written on their bodies. This action triggered a counter-protest by Muslim women in Germany who claimed that Femen was trying to steal their voice. Muslimah Pride (also known under #MuslimahPride and organized via Facebook as "Muslim Women against Femen") protested in the same space as had been occupied by Femen, with signs reading "Ich bin schon frei" (I am free already), "Freedom of Choice," "There is more than one way to be free," and "Gegen Unterdrückung" (against oppression).[29] When photographs of the two protest events are juxtaposed, pertinent political questions emerge about body politics, race and voice, intersectionality, space, context and location, and, generally, the global politics of feminism. Tyler's documentation and digital dissemination of the initial protest and the following actions offer starting points for a range of political statements and discussions around such events as "Topless Jihad Day," which, in many ways, played out much like what is seen in the discussions of contemporary German feminism (see above) – that is, along generational lines, with Alice Schwarzer somewhat surprisingly taking the side of Femen (Weber 2015a). The examples of these Femen protests and the counter-protest also show, as Beverly Weber (2015b) contests, the Muslim body as a hypervisible site for the negotiation of political and religious issues, such as those surrounding the headscarf, yet invisible as an agent of activism. One reading would be that such feminist activism fails to address the complexity of the political questions that matter in the twenty-first century. Another reading might suggest that the messy issues that arise in this example point to exactly why feminist protests matter today: they draw attention to the questions that remain unanswered, politically pertinent, and explosive.

This is just one example in which Femen activities in Germany specifically underscore the tensions caused by transnational flows and national histories. In form and content, Femen activism offers moments of disruption and disturbance; however, its protest is enabled by and is a product of neoliberalism, which is easily appropriated for the cause of the Western nation-state, in this case German nationalism against a supposed "backward" Islamic other. The almost exclusively white and often bare-breasted protesters of the group, and their target of patriarchy as either Islam or Putin, is easily incorporated into the German press landscape as once again confirming the superiority of the West over backward Eastern and Middle Eastern cultures. The juxtaposition between the white skin of the Femen activists and the clothed bodies of the Muslim activists work within a binary that has a long tradition in German media.[30] The way in which – mainly because of protests by Muslimah Pride – voice, image, and agency clash and intersect highlights racism in Germany and opens up a, however messy, space for more complicated forms of feminist solidarity. Further, the digital sphere becomes a place where activists are able to "reveal the gendered and racialized politics of visuality at work in public digital spaces," thereby challenging racism and demanding visibility in a way that also allows for agency (Weber 2015b, 3).

Further, Femen's aesthetics have become part of the popfeminist repertoire; indeed, it is arguable whether its aesthetics are new, or whether its members, in their use of the naked female body, engage in a citation of second and third wave feminist concerns. For example, the German author Renate Rasp appeared topless in 1968 at the Frankfurt Book Fair to protest the role of women in the literary sphere, to much outrage.[31] As mentioned in chapter 1 in the context of performance art, Kathleen Hanna wrote slogans on her naked body during her riot grrrl performances with Bikini Kill in the early 1990s. In its form, Femen utilizes the female body as a performance tool, but even in its obviously problematic entanglement with race, beauty, and class, there is a sense of radial joy in its disturbances. In this manner, it replicates other performative actions that occur on the street and that move digitally, such as SlutWalks or the "feminist flashmobs" that, under the label "One Billion Rising," were organized around the globe in the aftermath of the brutal rape and murder of a woman on a bus in India.[32] As Carl Nasman (2014) writes in the *Deutsche Welle* describing the feminist flashmobs in Germany:

> The global campaign "One Billion Rising" staged more than 150 demonstrations in Germany and many more abroad to highlight a sobering United Nations statistic: More than one billion women – or about one third of the world's women – will be beaten or raped during their lifetime.

The flashmob references traditional protest forms, one might even think about the Situationists' idea of creating disturbances in space, but these forms are transported into the twenty-first century in that the performances are recorded and digitally disseminated. They are grounded locally but coordinated globally. They intentionally cause a disturbance, of course, creating a situation in which suddenly, in a space designed for another use (e.g., shopping), a mob of people breaks out into dance. The physical bodies of the dancers are the centre of the protest and they form the content for the digital dissemination. The global simultaneity suggests connection and solidarity across the world in response to a brutal rape and murder case. Traditional feminist causes remain at the centre of such protests; the form of the protest is playful, physical, and spatially specific. The physical action of dancing in local spaces and the global reach of the protest through global organizing and ensuing digital dissemination are not at odds; rather, they form the very core of the political project.

On a theoretical level, the question of what is considered "normal" becomes the new focus: a crowd breaking out into dance in a public space intentionally creates a disturbance to underline the disturbing fact of rape and violence in public spaces that often goes unpunished. And yet, the silly dancing clashes not only with the "normal" action of people walking through public spaces or shopping malls but also with the brutality and violence of the event against which the flashmobs protest. Like the bare breasts of the Femen activists, here the silliness might distract from a politically serious message or from a clear call for action. As the stories of this brutal rape circulate globally, videos of the flashmobs appear on YouTube and social media platforms. The relationship between the body of the victim and the bodies of the people dancing in protest and the form of mainly digital, global dissemination of the visual result of that relationship is simultaneously intimate and abstract.

A very different yet persistently global form of street activism is seen in the ever-proliferating SlutWalks. The SlutWalk began in Toronto, Canada, in 2011 and was, in the following years, organized in various cities across the world. Initially, the action was a response to a lecture by police officer Michael Sanguinette, who counselled students on safety issues on the York University campus. His advice that female students not "dress like sluts" triggered protests against victim blaming and rape culture on college campuses. Through digital dissemination, mainly via Facebook, SlutWalks organized across Canada and the United States and spread globally. Jessica Valenti (2011), co-founder of *feministing.com*, claims that, "in a feminist movement that is often fighting simply to hold ground, SlutWalks stand out as a reminder of feminism's more grass-roots past and point to what the future could look like." The aim is to create an anti-rape, pro-sex message and to use forms of organizing that come from the ground up; are street based, playful, and visible; and digitally and globally disseminated. Similar to Femen's protests and its members' use of the naked female body, the use of the term "slut" and some of the strategies of the SlutWalk protests have become the target of fierce feminist debate, which makes use of the evaluatory language of success and failure.[33] For example, in the German context, SlutWalk Berlin triggered heated discussions among the participants based on a slogan that was written on one of the banners – "do away with gender – do away with men first"[34] – which some participants found to be sexist. The group that held the banner claimed that the phrase conceptualized gender as a social construct.[35] Further critiques pointed out that, in the first Berlin SlutWalk in 2011, in which thirty-five hundred people took part, people of colour, sex workers, and people from economically disadvantaged groups were underrepresented in favour of middle-class, cisgendered women (Baer 2015b).[36] Further, in SlutWalk Berlin 2012, Femen activists showed up to again protest Muslim covering, this time wearing blackface (ibid.). The online reaction following these incidents led to a rebranding, and then the closing down, of SlutWalk Berlin.

In their introduction to *Transnationalism, Activism, Art*, Kit Dobson and Áine McGlynn (2013, 15) suggest that artistic production challenges the "economic determinism of our times" but also, in a sense, participates in such determinism, citing Richard Florida's discussion of the functionalizing of culture and creativity in urban centres towards the marketing of cities for tourists and investors. "Disruptive aesthetics" as Dobson and McGlynn call creative street practices, do offer an alternative narrative to the economic forces behind art in a way that uncovers the transnational reach of activism, art, and the movement of capital that both seek to address. Nevertheless, as they write, "cultural work takes place and agitates towards social change, but it is also, absolutely, part of the structures it contests" (17). This is certainly true for the examples discussed here, since the protest events themselves, SlutWalks and Femen protests in Germany, are embedded in a securely Western framework and remain closely linked to traditional feminist concerns. At the same time, as the discussions above show, they produce their own critique. By exploring the controversies around SlutWalks and the Femen protests in Berlin, we broaden the context in which pop-feminist activism needs to be understood: to read for awkwardness in such protest events is to infuse them with a political edge and uncover the moments at which cultural work takes place and where disruptions and agitations happen. When read through the lens of awkwardness, their aesthetic theatre becomes a self-reflexive act of disturbance. The awkward elements of these protest events and making use of exactly this awkwardness for political activism might not always be intended, it might even be a cultural by-product that only surfaces in the controversies about these protest events. Further, as these examples indicate, such activism is historically rooted and locally embedded but globally inspired: it circulates in and out of specific national contexts, it goes viral, and, in some cases, it disappears from view rather rapidly.

The Word

While the above-described actions are digitally distributed and inspired by transnational movements and causes, they strongly rely on feminist activist forms of the 1960s and 1970s in that they focus on the street level of protest as well as on public disturbance of (or even as) large-scale events. The fact that they are popularly consumed online broadens their reach beyond the local street context and national media outlets. Another form of feminist work that makes use of historical forms but relies on digital reach are feminist blogs and websites. They borrow the style and political thrust from recognizable feminist methods of communication that work with the written word, specifically the 1960s flier or leaflet (in the context of the second wave) and the 1990s zine (popularized by the third wave). These small-run printings of political communications disseminate a message, but they also suggest unified action. Blogs, today, continue disseminating a traditional feminist message in their interest in dialogue, communication, and community, particularly in producing and passing on information related to equity, body politics, and protest.[37] A key part of this "printed" discourse is its relationship to the open movement, which, among other things, shapes broader understandings of global feminist rights. The White House's fact sheet, "The Equal Futures Partnership to Expand Women's Political and Economic Participation," released on 24 September 2012, for example, specifically cites both Creative Commons and the OpenCourseWare Consortium, two open access companies, as being central to the economic and political empowerment of women and girls around the world. Other types of digital dissemination of feminist texts come in the form of websites, such as *agirlsguidetotakingovertheworld.co.uk* and *feministing.com*, which collect feminist imagery circulating on the web and redisperse it through digital community-building platforms, such as blogs or livejournals that encourage participation from a number of users, with the express intent of inciting revolutionary change.

Here, we examine two forms of written communication, the site *maedchenmannschaft.net* and *Missy Magazine*, the latter appearing in print and in digital form. Both venues strive for intersectionality and inclusivity in their analyses. *Mädchenmannschaft* regularly posts analyses of issues related to race or immigration, more recently highlighting a dossier on the topic of exile and protest on its main page. Reyhan Şahin (Lady Bitch Ray), for example, writes a column entitled "Ask Reyhan" for *Missy* that addresses questions of racism and prejudice. *Mädchenmannschaft* collects a variety of blogs on feminist topics while also presenting original writings authored by house-feminists. The site was started in 2007, and out of it grew Mädchenmannschaft e.V., a group that works on- and offline for education on "the situation of girls and womenlesbiantrans in Germany and worldwide."[38] Thus, the online presence sparked offline work, which highlights the importance of digital platforms for all forms of activism today. Mainstream media honoured Mädchenmannschaft e.V. for its digital political work: the blog-site won the Deutsche Welle Blog award in 2008 and was nominated for two other media prizes in 2009: the Grimme Online Award and the Alternativen Medienpreis (Alternative Media Prize).

Missy, on the other hand, is a self-expressed popfeminist magazine started in 2008 by Sonja Eismann, Stefanie Lohaus, and Chris Köver, among others, and fashioned after US-based magazines *Bust* and *Bitch*. In 2015, "Team Missy," headed by editor-in-chief Katrin Gottschalk, launched a successful crowd-funding campaign on Kickstarter, yet another digital tool that allows for broad-based participatory action for feminist and other causes, to expand and diversify the magazine's digital presence. Although *Mädchenmannschaft* and *Missy* do cover some of the same issues and topics, the former is clearly politically pedagogically positioned, and the latter is firmly rooted in popular culture: "*Missy* is a magazine for women, who are interested in pop culture, politics, and style – simply for women like us."[39] They write about music, fashion, crafting, and cooking but also about sex, pornography, and law "with an attitude that consistently questions the status quo with a grin. Because we don't (yet) live in an equal society ... Feminism is passé? We don't think so. Therefore: *Missy*."[40]

Because the content of these two different venues is so wide reaching, we focus here on a very small comparison of writings on the topic of motherhood. As seen in the above discussion, motherhood (and with it, childrearing) is a topic that is foundational to feminism in Germany. The issue of mothering and the manner in which it kept new-leftist women from joining their male compatriots on the street motivated politically oriented women to organize (Klimke 2011). In the contemporary period in Germany, mothers, mothering, and motherhood is inextricably linked to the demography debates, which saw and continue to see the low birthrate to be, in part, due to the (neoliberally coded) choice of women to pursue a career over birthing or raising children. These discussions are also racially motivated, as is seen in Thilo Sarrazin's (2010) *Deutschland schafft sich ab* (Germany does itself in), in which the politician controversially blames both women and immigrants, particularly Turkish immigrants, for Germany's falling birthrates.[41] Thus motherhood, as one of those pressing issues for feminism (historically, contemporarily, and intersectionally), provides an angle on the unwieldy question of the collision between pop and social action and how these are engaged with in the digital sphere.

One of the tools on the *maedchenmannschaft.net* site is a lexicon, which defines, among other standard terms, "Mütterfeminismus" (motherfeminism) and "Müttermanifest" (mothermanifesto). The definition ends with: "Some feminists see the birth of a child also as a chance for the 'birth of a feminist consciousness': the assumption to have already reached gender equality can be questioned by motherhood and the restrictions that come with motherhood."[42] This German-specific feminist historical reference preceding the lexicon's contemporary political considerations roots its discussion of motherhood in second wave feminist causes. The digital presence of *Missy Magazine*, too, runs a lexicon of sorts in the form of the "Parent ABC" ("Eltern ABC"), a semi-regular column that features writings about parenthood by recognizable figures, ranging from those in the German pop cultural scene to those in the academy, organized alphabetically: the lead singer for the band Wir sind Helden, Judith Holofernes, takes on V for *Verantwortung* (responsibility); US sociologist and masculinity studies expert Michael Kimmel addresses Q for quality time; and author Kathrin Röggla writes about O for *Ojemine* (Oh my!). Each entry is illustrated by Ana Albero. While feminism is not a specific focus in these vignettes, they do tackle topics that are rarely the purview of women's magazines, such as children experiencing their parents having sex or mothers' disappointment at having children.

Of course, the standard online activist engagement in the digital sphere when it comes to motherhood is the so-called "mommy blog." This online venue becomes an autobiographical format for telling the personal story of motherhood. It serves community building through advice-giving, but it also becomes a place to display the commodification of motherhood, including sponsorship, advertising, and product-placement. Finally, the blog can also become a place to engender activism, whether in terms of linking up or giving voice to subcultural communities (in the case of transmoms or queer motherhood) or large-scale mobilization for global causes.[43] The "Muttiblog" (mommy blog) contained within the site *maedchenmannschaft.net* and "Fuckermothers," appearing as a summer 2012 guest blog within *Missy Magazine*'s digital presence, each offer potential for illuminating popfeminist intervention in a standard format. The "Muttiblog" runs as a semi-regular series on the site and, by its title, differentiates itself from all other series – "Der F-Blick in die Politik" (The f-view into politics), "Sex am Morgen" (Sex in the morning), "Wilde Mädchen" (Wild girls), or "www Girls": "Muttiblog" merely replicates the format recognizable to most blog readers and thereby connotes neither girlish rebellion nor feminist activism. The questions or discussions related to motherhood posted therein are removed in tone and audience from the other series and, therefore, from the entire framework of *maedchenmannschaft.net*. Confirming this standard approach to motherhood, the posts logged in the "Muttiblog" range from stories about returning to the workforce after maternity leave, feminist analyses of children's songs, discussions of economic policy or fathers, with a smattering of posts on the colour pink or cultural politics of breast feeding. In other words, while all very relevant to the feminist-political discussion of family in Germany, the topics of the posts replicate standard questions of time-use equity, body politics, and shared housework.

"Fuckermothers," the guest blogger for summer 2012 at *Missy Magazine*, also turns to motherhood. The title is already in keeping with the riotous-rebellious nature of popfeminism, this also supported by the background imagery: we see the name of the riot grrrl band Bikini Kill nestled among images of mothers – including transmothers – in popular culture. The self-expressed intents of the blog are to expose the ideal of motherhood: "In order to disturb and destabilize this ideal, Fuckermothers wants to broaden the perspective of how wo/man can be mothers today and show the diversity of possible lifestyles, body images, and emotional states."[44] The blogger contests that, for mothers, the only theoretical approach available is "difference feminism" and second wave activism.

For this reason, Fuckermothers wants to investigate the different possibilities of feminist mothering(s), queer mothers, hip

mothers, non-mothers, anti-mothers … the trans-mothers, father-
mothers, sexy mothers, marginalized mothers, pro-sex mothers,
cripple moms, traditional mothers, the critical mothers who live
in traditional relationships nonetheless, the manly mothers, the
motherly men.[45]

By placing this long list (of which this is an excerpt), which speaks
of inclusivity and performativity essential to popular writings on popfeminism in the blog's vision, the ideal against which the blog wishes
to work is replaced by another, multifaceted ideal. The categories of
the posts, moreover, speak to this new ideal. While the blog does cover
topics similar to those approached by the Muttibloggers (a critique of
pink and blue clothing at H&M, for example), it also includes discussions of transfamilies and roller derby moms, a queer summer camp,
and a narrative about an "anti-mother" leaving husband and children
via divorce. Further, the final blog for the guest post of *Missy Magazine*
covers reproduction and parental rights in Germany and abroad.

This brief analysis shows that, when it comes to the "mommy blog,"
posts contained in the more politically framed *maedchenmannschaft*
.net are distinctly less radical, revolutionary, and perhaps even less
political than are those penned by "Fuckermothers" for *Missy Maga-*
zine. However, at the same time, the sense of queer idealism in the latter does not translate into the broader digital community; most posts
contain no more than two or three responses, whereas the posts in the
"Muttiblog" received upwards of thirty-six comments. Further, while
the actual site *fuckermothers.wordpress.com* clearly aligns itself with
the open movement by using a creative commons licence, the guest-blog
reframing within a magazine that uses a pay-model in its print format
clearly disturbs that impulse.

Interestingly, the blogs share only one similar post, and, through this
post, they come into conversation: the critique of Anja Maier's (2012)
Lassen Sie mich durch, ich bin Mutter (Let me through, I am a mother),
which venomously criticizes the mothers living in the Prenzlauer Berg
quarter of Berlin, known for its many young, hipster families. In the
"Muttiblog" post entitled "Mütter sollten ihre Möpse bedecken – jedenfalls wenn sie rechnen können" (Mothers should cover their boobs –
at least if they can do math), the author pursues the "Mütter-Hass"
(mother-hatred) she sees not only in the excerpt of the book published
in the Berlin-daily, the *Tageszeitung* (TAZ),[46] but also in the comments
made by readers in the online platform of the newspaper. The book

describes Prenzlauer Berg as populated by cows (mothers) who, supported by working fathers, do nothing all day but sip lattés and whip out their "Euter" (utters) to feed their children. While the blog entry counters this discussion by telling a personal narrative about living in Prenzlauer Berg as a working mother and by discussing the research on the effect of nursing on the public perception of mothers (breasts = stupidity), it is less the book that the blogger finds problematic than the online comments of the TAZ readers, who focus their critique not on the problematic equation of mothers with bovines but on the clear East-West debate (referencing the local East Berliners and the many West German Swabian transplants found in that quarter of Berlin).

The companion piece by "Fuckermothers" is entitled "Prrrnzlbrg-Mütter: Eine Ursachenuntersuchung" (Prrrnzlbrg-mothers: A diagnosis). While the focus on breastfeeding was already clear in the title of the first critique ("boobies"), here the reference to the riot grrrl movement in the triple "r" of "Prrrnzlbrg" sets up the critique for a specific tone and intent. However, the post itself is made up of one long quote from the "Muttiblog" piece, to which the blogger adds only two postscripts related to other examinations of the Prenzlauer Berg scene and mother hate through the lens of race and poverty. The popfeminist riotousness implied by the title, then, is not in the content of the piece but in the form: it re-mixes a variety of aspects related to the debate as pop culturally driven, thereby draining mother hate, which is ultimately a neighbourhood hate, of its interpretative meaning, particularly in light of socioeconomic considerations and racism of the comments.

In neither of these blogs does a true counter-image of motherhood emerge. In the final pairing, a moment for truly disturbing the national-cultural imaginary as it emerges in a very specific demographic and neoliberal space of former East Berlin is recognized but, unfortunately, not mobilized. The East-West tensions implicit in the changing demographics are acknowledged in the first blog, although the reasoning for anchoring these tensions on public breastfeeding – that is, on the mother's body – are not fully explored. Instead, the focus remains on the scientific reasoning behind the negative associations with breastfeeding. However, when this information comes into digital conversation with other critiques (and critiques of critiques) of the Prenzlauer Berg mother-scene in the second blog, the imagery on both sides (dominant and subcultural) is opened up to the question of poverty, race, and sexual orientation. But the imagery is reconfigured in a way that does not merely replace that imagery with a new ideal.

The construction of popfeminist motherhood, the mother's body in feminist digital culture, is neither wholly able to be encapsulated within popular culture nor entirely mobilized and politicized by contemporary feminist-queer impulses. Indeed, as the "Fuckermothers" blogger contests, the only theoretical framework available to an analysis of motherhood is a throwback to second wave feminist concerns and notions of difference.[47] While the Muttiblog in some ways embraces, or at least accepts, this without question, "Fuckermothers" struggles with this notion and wishes to present a varied and queer portrait of motherhood that would rewrite pop cultural and historical feminist discourse, an attempt that is ultimately perceived as a "queer failure" of sorts.[48] "Fuckermothers" tries but does not manage to depart from evaluative stances, judgmental notions, and other affective charges that surround these discussions of motherhood as a form of class-infused and racialized biopolitics and that operate as prescriptive forces on the female body. The elements denoted here as "failures" are exactly the elements that, in the next chapter, we argue can be made politically productive as awkward.

Feminist Activist Communities

In these examples of feminist street activisms and feminist writing, community building remains a prime target of politics, be it online or offline; here, a multitude of voices can participate, comment, and come together thereby producing a sense of community that is disembodied and open while at the same time, in topic and form, tied closely to concerns with the body and subjectivity, voice and narrative. In the twenty-first century, these forms of community building and protest organizing happen on and through social media sites where protesters plan their actions, call for participation, reflect on their protests in online communities, and, of course, use the digital realm to share images and trigger responses. Similarly, blog sites report and comment on street protests and local organizing. Some forms of community building appear to import traditional forms of political communication into the digital. *Maedchenmannschaft.net,* for example, goes beyond the written format of information dissemination with the category of "Selbermach Sonntag" (DIY Sunday), which works more like a town hall meeting. Each week, readers are called upon to share links, things they read, comments, and thoughts in the comment section following a short announcement: "This week, too, we are looking forward to your links:

what have you read or written yourself? Which announcements would you like to make? What questions remain? As always: go ahead and put it in the commentary and we wish a happy Sunday!"[49] Comments range from links to, for example, a pdf version of a bell hooks article to people's blog entries, to theatre performances and other "feminist-related" events, to self-promotion for art projects. In effect, "Selber-mach Sonntag" is a digital bulletin board on which anything can be posted. The digital form allows for a sense of wider-ranging connections in that the reader can be immediately transported to the site or object posted by clicking a link, but the idea behind the board remains closely tied to familiar forms of participatory information dissemination.[50] The reference to DIY techniques central to third wave feminist aesthetics, particularly the zines of the riot grrrl and queercore movements, injects a sense of irreverent pop into the space. That irreverence is, however, quickly tamed, for by linking the DIY impulse to Sundays, the implication seems to be more that of the amateur repairer, "tinkering" with feminism at home.

In a similar manner, hashtag activism engages the traditional feminist participatory model and builds communities of users who join with common interests and share stories, pictures, or outrage (see Baer 2015b; Drüecke and Zobl 2015; Stehling and Thomas 2015). In some cases, communities can be closed, while others remain open, which also means they are open to people who disagree, make nasty comments, and attack. To share and like on Facebook; to link social networks together by linking pages such as Facebook, Twitter, and Instagram; allows certain images and causes to go viral and circle through various social contexts, repressing others as they get lost in the web. Such hashtags can also circle well outside of the digital sphere and across national borders, as was seen in the popularity of #RegrettingMother-hood in April 2015 in Germany. This English-language hashtag was sparked not by an online comment or source but, rather, by a news story published in a German print newspaper (Göbel 2015) that itself was prompted by an academic article by Orna Donath (2015) in the journal *Signs*. #RegrettingMotherhood became a near-instant phenomenon, not only being used by women expressing their shame at being unhappy in the role of mother but also resulting in anti-feminist and misogynistic backlash (Heffernan 2015).

The #aufschrei campaign is the to-date most successful Twitter-based campaign in Germany, during which women posted and shared their experiences of sexual violence, assault, and rape utilizing the hashtag.

Suggested by Anne Wizorek as a way to mark and collect sexist moments in everyday experiences on Twitter, the hashtag was quickly taken up by standard media organs such as print newspaper and television.[51] Again, traditional feminist causes remain at the centre of this campaign, and the participatory model closely fashions itself after forms of feminist activisms from the 1980s onwards. The open form of the campaign, which includes its reach, its circulation, and its (potential) co-option, is the distinguishing factor, for #aufschrei quickly also became a way to negatively mark women who were speaking out about everyday sexism. The success of the hashtag and the resulting talk show interviews led to Wizorek's (2014) publication of the book *Weil ein Aufschrei nicht reicht: Für einen Feminismus von heute* (Because an outcry is not enough: A feminism for today), which Tina Groll referred to in the online edition of *Die Zeit* as a "manifesto," potentially on par with Schwarzer's 1975 classic *Der kleine Unterschied* (The little difference). The book covers topics from women's quota, beauty ideals, body politics, and generational debates, but it also turns to look extensively at the digital sphere in Germany. The latter aspect she places under the section header "Wir sind viele. Ein Rekrutierungsversuch" (We Are Many. A Recruitment Attempt), thus, in many ways, suggesting that the digital is a tool for collectivity and solidarity in feminist activism. She writes in the introduction: "I love the Internet and its possibilities! I watched it grow (and still do) and experienced, how more and more possibilities were added. And finally did I not lastly find out through the Internet that that, which I stand for, is feminist – no big 'BUT,' rather only a 'Fuck yeah!'" (7).[52] The digital sphere, of which #aufschrei is a part, becomes a place for feminist instruction, but in a manner that is pop, as is indicative of her use of the expletive in English.

While these activisms' new open forms rely heavily on and in some cases start with the digital, the reception of their causes remains tied to second and third wave feminisms. Their digital components are often what are recognized in mainstream media as important political interventions, but it is also this reliance on the digital that activists criticize as mere hashtag activism that lacks any kind of real political consequences or push towards social change. The way in which some of the causes here are easily co-opted by mainstream media and politics – as can be seen in the Femen protests and their anti-Muslim slogans, the Mutti-blogs in their negotiations of motherhood as *the* issue for women, or #aufschrei's tendency to create a generalized category of "women" – illustrates yet again the tension between, on the one hand, a rising awareness of violence against women that is far-reaching and, on the other hand, a sense that these kinds of activisms can easily and simply be funnelled back into a mainstream, neoliberal, and, in some cases, even nationalist discourse where they lose any kind of politically progressive edge. The insistence that feminism in and of itself is a political cause rather than a focus on form, dissemination, circulation, and connection beyond what the "waves" of previous feminisms define as "feminist" limits the political impact of these campaigns. By suggesting, however, that we can read such activisms as awkward, we attempt to get at the political within their circular, in some cases viral, motions in a different way. Feminism becomes pop in its relation to and tension with other political causes – questions of racism or economic inequality, for example – and pop becomes feminist by the awkward references to political causes that infiltrate the popular. It is by reading these forms of activism awkwardly, as we explore in greater detail in the following chapters, that we can insist on their political relevance in the face of political impossibilities. A popfeminist activist community, then, emerges based on an intersectional position that insists on awkwardness as a moment of political disruption. The charge for us then, in this book and beyond, is to infuse these circulations and disruptions with a – however awkwardly directed – sense of political agency and willfulness (Ahmed 2014b).

ART AND POLITICAL PRACTICE: AWKWARD POPFEMINIST FUTURES

At the time of the writing of this book, we find ourselves already nearly a full decade beyond the debates outlined at the beginning of this chapter. And, as the charge for awkward readings illustrates, while these debates and positionings are our starting points for examining the impulses behind popfeminist activism today, they are not where we remain. The debates on the forms of new German feminisms outlined above – whether considered lifestyle, post, or popfeminism – all germinated at a time just prior to the outbreak of the global financial crisis of 2008. For this reason, in their discourse, phrasing, and imagery, these neofeminisms speak to a specific type of positivism that, following the financial crisis and the increasing visibility of activism all around the world, was no longer viable (more on that positivism in chapter 3). Instead, as the world revealed itself to be interlocked like never before, neoliberalism came to be a bad word in everyone's mouths, and the inequality of the distribution of wealth became central to protests and mainstream representations alike. Thus, as we argue at the outset of this chapter, the global financial crisis and the ensuing Eurozone crisis can be seen as a watershed moment for the politics of feminist futures – much as Kaplan argued 9/11 was for the United States. This moment shapes and reshapes forms of feminist activism.

The circularity inherent in popfeminism, the way in which feminist causes circulate in and out of political contexts, are contested, debunked, reworked, and criticized (illustrated by our discussion in chapter 1), informs that political action. Such action, however, is often muddy, certainly messy, and can be nonspecific. This lack of specificity serves to highlight form and mode of dissemination as well as the reach of circulation, which, we argue, is often politically more important than content, message, or goal. In this sense, such opaque activism has indeed been politically productive, though in a very different way. What popfeminist activism does is undermine or interrupt, if only for a moment, what in *Cruel Optimism* Lauren Berlant calls "slow death" in the post-financial-crisis age. "The phrase *slow death* refers to the physical wearing out of a population in a way that points to its deterioration as a defining condition of its experience and historical existence" (Berlant 2011b, 95). Berlant uses the phrase to open up what she calls a space in which to "conceptualize contemporary historical experience ... where it is hard to distinguish modes of incoherence, distractedness, and habituation from deliberate and deliberative activity, as they are all involved in the reproduction of predictable life" (96). She suggests, further, that such experience "reframes the ways we think about normativity in relation to sovereignty" (ibid.). While Berlant addresses these terms as a way of considering the science of biopolitics and governmentality, such rereadings of the terms "normativity" and "sovereign agency" apply here as well. In a post-2008 Germany specifically, and more broadly in the Western world following the financial crisis, there is an ongoing sense of being worn out, a numbness, that is momentarily interrupted by these affective and psychological bursts of digitally circulated activist energies. These energies reinscribe social and state-driven feminist pursuits into popular, event-based, and consumer-oriented actions, creating popfeminist engagements. However, because they are found within these moments, they, too, are caught up in the murky distinction between incoherent and deliberate activity, quickly and easily seen as "embedded in normative notions of agency" (99). Berlant engages in an analysis of "agency and personhood" as an "activity exercised within spaces of ordinariness that does not always or even usually follow the literalizing logic of visible effectuality, bourgeois dramatics, and lifelong accumulation or self-fashioning" (ibid.). For feminist activism in the popular sphere, we suggest that, although the disturbance of normative expectations around political agency occurs elsewhere than the traditionally political realm for action, it also occurs in the arena of the ordinary.

The popfeminist actions in the digital sphere described above operate within the circularity inherent in pop and feminism. They incorporate pop and consumer tendencies in that they not only rewrite neoliberal capitalism but also repackage themselves as part of that cycle. The manner in which performative street protests, blog discussions, and new forms of feminist community building in general can be harnessed politically is not always clearly evident, which often leads to the dismissal of their political effectivity. At the same time, the speed at which messages and images spread in the digital age and the new spaces for connections that emerge in the digital realm create clear moments of political intervention and disturbance. New forms of agencies and new actors emerge that directly engage in art as social or political feminist practice. The political disturbances take place in a self-referential and self-conscious politicking within the circularity of the current political moment. The political is not (just) in the protest gesture itself but in the circulations that surround or transport these gestures, and in the search for (art forms as) political practices that self-consciously engage with these circulations. Important political interventions are happening at a new pace and in newly created spaces because of the possibilities of the digital. Rather than analyzing single events, it is often the context in which they circulate that reveals political tensions and potentially productive interventions.

For example, in 2012, South African artist Brett Bailey organized an exhibit in the context of the Berliner Festspiele that was called "Exhibit B." The website of the Barbican Centre in London, which intended to host the exhibit in 2014, describes it as follows:

> *Exhibit B* critiques the "human zoos" and ethnographic displays that showed Africans as objects of scientific curiosity through the 19th and early 20th centuries. Translated here into twelve tableaux, each features motionless performers placed in settings drawn from real life. Collectively they confront colonial atrocities committed in Africa, European notions of racial supremacy and the plight of immigrants today.[53]

In London, the show was cancelled as a response to the protests that described the exhibit as racist. In Berlin, activist organizations, most specifically *Buehnenwatch.com*, also critiqued the exhibit extensively but could not stop its display. The exhibit itself allows for a distinctly neoliberal mode of consumption in that it tries to sell provocation as political art. This kind of provocation has long been incorporated into a mechanism of consumption for the (white) spectator, whereby the feeling of discomfort suggests the art is experienced as "political" since it is uncomfortable. The digital dissemination of images from this exhibit, taken out of context and deprived of the (however still) live performance, appears to simply perpetuate colonial modes of violence and racism in the imagery's objectification of black bodies. The exhibit itself might be provocative, but it is not a political disruption. The consumption of the provocative and the affective response by the presumed "white" visitors, which is a confirmation of white guilt combined with the confirmation of their superior position and gaze, is disrupted only by, at least in the German case, mainly digital protests and, in the British, petitions and demonstrations against these displays.[54] Only these protests – and even the cancellation and ensuing discussions about censorship of the arts – infuse this exhibit with the politics it was pretending to have or it was trying to unveil. The Femen protests outside the Berlin mosque, for example, work similarly: in conjunction with the protests against these protests, an interesting set of political questions and disruptions emerges. While itself not an example of popfeminism, the Brett Bailey exhibit illuminates the politics behind popfeminist activisms in the twenty-first century: in its intention, popfeminist activism tries to anticipate and think through this entire process of reception, protest, appropriation, and circulation and find or define spaces for political disruption. The process of coming into politics is an awkward one.

3

Awkwardness as Popfeminist Craft: Staying with the Trouble

Can you tell us a little about your work (as an academic and activist/performance artist)?

Lady Bitch Ray: Yeah, 'course I can! So, for me rap was too boring to do forever, so I read a whole bunch and wrote my doctoral thesis. I wanted to call myself "Dr. Bitch Ray" … and now I do! Isn't that cool!? My lyrics are essentially about my sexual experiences; for example, I write about how bitches can best pleasure themselves and everything guys do wrong when they're fucking – do you know my song, *Enlightenment*? On the side I'm designing my pussy-deluxe costumes under my line *Vagina Style-Wear*. My record label's called *Vagina Style-Records*, and I've kicked-off the third wave vag-movement in Germany! I want Vagina Power – I want Pussy Deluxe!

Dr. Şahin: Well, I finished my university entrance exams and wanted to study something to do with languages. Then I came up with linguistics and German literature …

Lady Bitch Ray: No, *I* studied linguistics because I love rap and was good with my tongue – and I'm not just talking about languages!

Dr. Şahin: (Whispering) Ahem – that'll do. I'm speaking now, I told you! So I completed my studies and worked for two years as a radio journalist. During that time I came across the topic of the Muslim headscarf. Since there wasn't any proper study about this I wanted to conduct the first comprehensive study. That was successful and my dissertation was published December 2014 by *Lit-Verlag* (Münster). I wish to remain in academia.

Lady Bitch Ray: As cunni-linguist, hahaha!

(Riot Grrrls, Bitchsm, and Pussy Power:
Interview with Reyhan Şahin / Lady Bitch Ray 2015, 5).

In this interview published in the *Feminist Media Studies* special issue on digital feminisms in Germany, linguist Reyhan Şahin and her alter ego, rapper Lady Bitch Ray, take turns answering questions about feminism, body politics, and digital cultures. This two-voiced interview reveals an essential feature of popfeminist awkwardness: the necessary collision of theory with practice. Activists are often also feminist theorists and are engaged in academic or intellectual discourse, as is seen in the case of Şahin here as well as in the case of Chicks on Speed (one member, Alex Murray-Leslie, for example, is currently pursuing her PhD in Sydney), the *Missy Magazine* founders (Sonja Eismann is also a popfeminist theorist), and others to whom we refer. Just as the lines between the physical body and its digital representations blur together, so systems of theory and practice fold onto and into each other. These processes produce awkward politics in that they disturb binaries and create new spaces for action and interaction. The two examples discussed in the following chapter – the performance, fashion design, and art collective Chicks on Speed and the Turkish-German porn-rapper, sex-activist, actor, academic, and author Reyhan Şahin aka Lady Bitch Ray – exemplify the results of this collision in different ways, allowing us to sketch out the range of political awkwardness in popfeminist work: historical yet contemporary, theoretical yet pop, digital yet physical, playful yet urgent.

The works of Chicks on Speed and Lady Bitch Ray are quite obviously pop and feminist, although the manner in which popfeminism is employed by these artists is very distinctive: body politics play out differently in the two examples, their engagement with technology and the digital takes divergent forms, their play with materiality in digital forms sparks a variety responses, and their local-global locations are set into motion by very different kinds of circulations. Further, both examples are positioned at a moment of transition between activist forms of the early twenty-first century and new forms of activism that developed with movements such as Occupy, Free Pussy Riot, and Femen. Thus, when taken together, their works illustrate the breadth and complexity of the political in popfeminist awkwardness. Activist theory and performative practice intertwine in both examples in a way that highlights not only how they work together but also how a collision of theory and practice can create awkward questions and, further, opens up space for a new, popfeminist methodology.

To read for the awkward in the popfeminist work of Chicks on Speed and Lady Bitch Ray uncovers the messy conveyance of meaning that remains nevertheless urgent within popfeminist discourse. In this, the term "popfeminism" functions threefold: first, as a way to situate ourselves within a political discourse that is popularized; second, as a term that describes the events we are analyzing in that they have been consumed en masse, produced by popular response, or clearly integrate the popular into their works; and third, as a perspective that we as researchers take – that is, one that captures our own personal investment in approaching creative work that emerges out of or engages with popular culture. The result is a methodology that utilizes the notions of circularity and disturbance inherent to popfeminism (as described in chapter 2) – that is, the insertion into or rewriting of pop by feminism and vice versa – in a manner that is conscious of popfeminism's melding of theory with practice. In this sense, the theoretical material with which we engage is not placed onto the object of study (performance, performer, action, creative result) as a framework to aid in its interpretation; rather, theory fuses with and is infused by the object at hand – and the other way around. The research outcome, then, is not an explanatory clarification but a process-based and creative intervention that is also inherently political. We use the term "methodology," therefore, not to describe a set of criteria for analysis but, rather, to describe a reading strategy, one that emphasizes process, craft, and creation. Reading for awkwardness as a popfeminist methodology means uncovering disruptions of the cruel optimisms of neoliberalism, discovering new avenues for connection and relatability, and searching for new spaces for feminist community and joy.

The tension between disruption and connection is a defining feature of this kind of political awkwardness, and it also defines both our relationship with pop and with feminism. Our development of this strategy – or methodology – is grounded in a set of theoretical inspirations mainly emerging from affect studies, transnational feminism, and queer studies. Awkwardness, as we exemplify in the readings in this chapter, becomes a "search term" that allows us to mine for the political in feminist creative work. The awkward is a search term because it is always on the move in these events or in between these events, sometimes produced in or internal to the content, sometimes occurring in the collision of media or material, sometimes occurring in the reception or theorization, sometimes inherent to the performer or audience body, and always retreating from view. It draws attention to normative representations of sexuality, gender, race, and the power of prescriptive regimes of representation while also putting on display the collapse of standard discursive or theoretical frameworks that might easily describe these representations.

The particular challenge posed by the works and performances of Chicks on Speed and Lady Bitch Ray is the manner in which the bringing together of theory with practice, bodies with technologies, and political agency with precarious subjecthood takes place within the highly mediatized current neoliberal moment. That which defines the possibility of the political in these activisms is also that which undoes it due to a reliance on neoliberal mechanisms of individual pursuit of success, upward mobility, and happiness, among others. They engage with this circularity in their work through an aesthetic and performative display of joy founded upon patriarchal structures of the industry. Further, their political posturing, particularly that of Lady Bitch Ray, indicates a belief in or a "desire for the political" (Berlant 2011b) that brings with it a positive, optimistic charge. In her 2011 germinal study *Cruel Optimism*, which itself has spawned an entire response issue of the journal *Social Text*, with engagement by prominent queer and affect scholars such as Sianne Ngai and José Esteban Muñoz,[1] Berlant writes of the optimism produced by the neoliberal promise of what she terms "the good life" as follows:

> Optimism is cruel when the object/scene that ignites a sense of possibility actually makes it impossible to attain the expansive transformation for which a person or a people risks striving; and, doubly, it is cruel insofar as the very pleasures of being inside a relation have become sustaining regardless of the content of the relation, such that a person or a world finds itself bound to a situation of profound threat that is, at the same time, profoundly confirming. (2)

Cruel optimism is the continued belief that success is on the horizon if only this or that object is attained or scene experienced, the object or scene being precisely that which stands in the way of attaining the promised success. The object or scene of cruel optimism can be love, the desire for the good life, or the wish for the political, including, of course, the feminist-political. The interview quoted above displays well the manner in which cruel optimism appears in these activisms, how it drives political attachment, but also how that optimism is destabilized. Both voices, whether in the semi-raunchy vocabulary of the rapper or the more restrained language of the academic, start from the assumption that empowerment, a "third wave vag-movement," is necessary, possible, and inherently positive: an optimistic stance. Such positioning is shared by most of the activists, performers, and artists we discuss.

Instead of refuting the circularity produced by cruel optimistic attachments, Lady Bitch Ray's works, as well as those of Chicks on Speed – exemplary for the other performance activisms discussed in this book – harness a joyful awkwardness that is entirely stripped of the distancing techniques of irony and that might not always look like joy. The interview displays this sense of joy in its playful use of two voices vying for space with the interviewer. However, the use of the pejorative "bitch" as the figure for the political development of the movement Şahin/Ray describes suggests a slightly off-putting nature to its subjecthood and sisterhood. In *The Promise of Happiness*, Ahmed (2010, 17) discusses figures that look for happiness in places that are conventionally unhappy, the "feminist killjoy, unhappy queer, and melancholic migrant." Ahmed calls for a dissociation of our conception of happiness from what is unquestionably "good," examining the "unhappy archives" each figure embodies as a way of illuminating alternative modes of living (ibid.). In her conclusion, she develops a concept of silliness as a form of unexpected happiness and of "the freedom to be happy in inappropriate ways" (222). Silliness is a counterpart to joy, just as "inappropriateness" is a facet of awkwardness. Killjoys, queers, and migrants, similar but also different to the ones Ahmed describes, are important characters of the technologies – the mechanisms – of popfeminist activism.

Joyful silliness and awkward inappropriateness are key descriptors for these activisms. What further connects the works is their insistence on political relevance in spite of their entanglement in a neoliberal culture industry that relies on cruelly optimistic relations. To return to Haraway's words, they insist on "staying with the trouble" and on troubling relationships, specifically between pop and feminism (Haraway 2014). We believe that scholar-activists, including ourselves, must do the same: stay with the trouble, continue to think through these troubling relations, and support but rewrite both pop culture and feminist politics. Bringing the characters Ahmed describes along with the concept of "cruel optimism" to Chicks on Speed and Lady Bitch Ray illustrates the way in which awkwardness emerges in popfeminist activism: as a disturbance to the workings of cruel optimisms, as a manner of creating feminist activist communities for the twenty-first-century, and as a new approach to feminist methodologies and reading strategies.

CHICKS AND BITCHES

The band and artist collective Chicks on Speed is a popfeminist performance group whose members explicitly understand their work in the
context of feminist performance art and as part of a global, political,
feminist culture from their beginnings in the late 1990s until today.
Their music, performances, visual art, and DIY fashion are infused with
the political project of feminism; in their works, they fight for feminist body politics. Both their geographic location and their political
position, however, are complicated and have certainly shifted since the
1990s. Fittingly, a critic's statement, printed on the back cover of the
2010 book and exhibition catalogue ~~Don't~~ Art Fashion Music, tries to
pre-empt any attempt to clearly define their politics by claiming the
book "highlights the pitfalls of defining their practice or attempting
to freeze the meaning of their extraordinary work." Chicks on Speed
are self-consciously and intentionally awkward, their approach is postmodern and deconstructive, and they explicitly attempt to make political popfeminist art. Their art, however, is mainly received as part of
an urban, middle-class, hipster subcultural movement rather than as a
broad political intervention. What further muddies their politics is the
fact that, over the course of a career that has lasted more than a decade,
the reception of their performances and the political moments that surface in these reception processes have undergone various shifts. Further,
in the later 2010s, their work entered the museum spaces, suggesting an
achievement of a measure of tameness and acceptability.

The multi-media art project Chicks on Speed started performing in
the late 1990s, often live on stage. The band members Melissa Logan
(United States) and Alex Murray-Leslie (Australia) met at the Academy of Fine Arts in Munich where they studied fine arts and jewellery
making, respectively. They started to host illegal parties together (at the
moving party event "Seppi Bar") and organized art exhibits. During
this time, they met the third founding member, Kiki Moorse (Germany),
who left the group in 2006 to continue her solo career with Toffeetones
Records. Since 1999, Chicks on Speed have released eight albums –
The Un-Releases (1999), *Chicks on Speed Will Save Us All* (2000),
The Re-Releases of the Un-Releases (2001), *99 Cents* (2003), *Press
the Spacebar (with the No Heads)* (2004), *Cutting the Edge* (2010),
UTOPIA (2014), and *Artstravaganza* (2015) – as well as various sin-
gles, EPs, and compilations such as the CD release *Girl Monster* (2010).
They have also published in the form of books and zines, including
~~Don't~~ Art Fashion Music (Chicks on Speed et al. 2010), *It's a Project*

(Chicks on Speed and Schönauer 2004), and *Cultural Hacking: Kunst des strategischen Handelns* (The art of acting strategically) (Chicks on Speed and Düllo 2005). Their performances and publications blur the boundaries between high and low culture (Clark 2010, 39), and street and studio art, as they continue to perform in galleries, clubs, and theatres as well as on streets and plazas across Europe, the United States, Australia, and Asia. Journalists describe their art as a mixture of a cut-and-paste DIY approach and multi-media performance. More creative terms for their art describe it as a political post-punk guerrilla gesture, as a "postmodern glamour of fake" (Eismann 2011),[2] approach to music and performance, suggesting the melding of political gestures with glam and camp, a melding described as equal parts naïve and consciously masterminded. Further, Chicks on Speed's stage performances and fashion choices mirror the mixing of contemporary trends with retro elements from punk and 1980s pop. In their performances they use knitting needles, sewing machines, and power tools together with polished and, in some cases, abstract, often neon-coloured video projections. Their stage outfits are regularly collages made of tape, plastic, and fabric pieces that look like they are stitched together hastily; these seemingly accidental forms, colours, and shapes are, of course, a carefully crafted part of the stage performance.

In their most recent work, they explicitly try to address what they describe on their website as "the current impressive collision between analog and digital worlds." The website describes their art, particularly their most recent project, *Artstravaganza*, as interlacing DIY aesthetic, activism, and "data spaces": "Their songs lie at the cutting edges of activism and media-pop-art, where the digital world embraces the hand made, rough and spontaneous, interlacing the programmed, the multi-layered and delicious data scapes."[3] Here we see an explicit focus on DIY pop aesthetics in the digital realm as displaying activist tendencies. The popularity of the performance-band Chicks on Speed supersedes the emergence of riot grrrl bands in the 1990s but precedes the making of the global superstar Lady Gaga as well as the political activism of punk groups like Pussy Riot. In conjunction with the rise of grunge, bands like Bikini Kill, Sleater-Kinney, L7, Babes in Toyland, and Hole appeared in the United States in the early 1990s, while only a few (riot) girl-bands emerged in Germany: Die Braut, Mobylettes, die Lassie Singers, die Lemonbabies, and the mainstream-oriented Tic Tac Toe and Lucilectric. In the early twenty-first century, bands like Le Tigre, Chicks on Speed, and Peaches continue this tradition of popfeminist music, fashion, and performance by combining feminism, pop, glamour, and (queer) sex, politics and private life, and form and content (La Hengst). The (queer) body, the visual, and the performative play a key role in the works of these artist-musicians.

The gendered body and normative expectations of female sexuality are essential themes in Chicks on Speed's works, and they generate a very specific kind of awkwardness. The bodies used and represented in their art and on their stages are pseudo-fashion models and improvising performers, they are sexy and angry, "real" and projection. The body is thus where authenticity and mediated event collide awkwardly, and it is the site at which these artists attempt to criticize mainstream representations of sexuality, gender, and body politics. In many ways, this exposes their 1990s roots in riot grrrl aesthetics and theoretical practice. When Chicks on Speed, for example, pose like rock stars while wearing so-called "skin-coloured" support underwear for women and "playing" cardboard cut-out guitars, they reference a normative body politics for women and the sexualization of female musicians while at the same writing awkwardness onto their very own bodies.[4] Rather than addressing questions of sexual and physical abuse or exploitation of women, as did their riot grrrl sisters, Chicks on Speed's bodies are almost post-bodies in that they linger awkwardly in a space between the performative body and its screen projection. This means that, in Chicks on Speed's art, the body is always also mediated and defined via its representations. The image and the physical body of the performers do not exist separately but, rather, are bound together in a kind of feedback loop. Their songs and the accompanying video clips are about the (female) body as projection. "Glamour Girl," one of the most famous songs from their first album, uses minimalist electronic beats to accompany the text, which reads like a compilation of snippets from different advertising campaigns combined with warnings against the dangers of femme fatales, "burlesque attitude / night-time thrill / she's a glamour girl / and her looks just kill / beware of her kiss / she'll suck you in / five times a day. love her breasts / forget the rest" (Chicks on Speed, "Glamour Girl"). These lyrics play with clichéd depictions of dangerous, beautiful, and glamorous women and playfully mix voices and perspectives. They appropriate standard anti-feminist rhetoric and leave open the possibility of empowerment through a voice that instructs the listener to pay attention only to the woman's breasts and to "forget the rest." In the context of Chicks on Speed's performances and musical acts, this playful objectification of parts of the female body is (made) awkward rather than deemed offensive.

Stylistically, Chicks on Speed's performances blend a DIY approach to fashion and music with polished fashion objects and multi-media performances that play with potentially endless reproducibility; however, their chaotic and spontaneous live performances turn electronic music and media into a happening, a one-time event that cannot be conserved (Torloxten 2011; Mansfield 2010).⁵ In this way, they create spectacles that are sometimes short lived and exist only in and for the moment but, at the same time, are highly mediated, and, at least theoretically, reproducible on the internet and in other media platforms. This simultaneity of the digital, analogue, and physical on stage is a hallmark of Chicks on Speed's performances. In addition to the performers on stage, the bodies of the audience members become a part of the act. Their approach to performance plays with but expands on earlier understandings of audience reception, as is indicated by the simulated-handwritten text scrawled across the first pages of ~~Don't~~ Art Fashion Music: "You Have Now entered the Performance Area, Anything you say, do, touch, Don't do is part of the Performance Art Rules Apply Here Be part of the Performance Scål." This means that not only the artists but also the spectators find themselves, at least potentially, implicated in this messy display of bodies and body parts in a physical sense and as projection. The disturbed look on spectators' faces as the noises of power tools and the shrieking voices of the performers enter their ear canals are, at least in theory, part of the artistic performance.

This incorporation of the audience is also seen in a 2013 performance at the Zentrum für Kunst und Medientechnologie (Centre for Art and Media) in Karlsruhe, recorded and posted on YouTube, in which the performers move through the audience and the sound installation is decentralized.⁶ The camera that films the event cannot help but record members of the audience as they stand awkwardly still, watching and listening. This performative strategy takes on a playful dimension in that Chicks on Speed are knowingly winking at the audience in their experience of disturbance. The performative here is intensely physical while at the same time the physical and corporal merges with the space and tools of the performance. They use what they call a "sonic carpet," a piece of art that looks DIY, with various fabric applications including the iconic Andy Warhol banana, but that is infused with electronic sensors that turn it into an erratic instrument. In the same year, during an opening performance to an exhibit in New Zealand entitled "Touch Me Baby I'm Body-centric, a Multimodalplosian" by Chicks on Speed and Lisa Walker,⁷ they also employ the sonic carpet. Additionally, the performers get trapped in what looks like a gigantic spider web, and, interestingly enough, in defiance of the title, the performers are not as close to the audience as they were in Karlsruhe and nobody seems near enough to "touch." Both performances rely on the collision between technology and the physical body, between proximity and touch. Rather than the body, the sonic carpet is "asking" to be touched. The bodies of the performers stay elusive; however, they play a crucial role in activating the carpet and in illustrating the ways in which physical bodies can get caught in (spider) webs. As a structure that bodies climb around in, and within which they are tangled up, this web might evoke the World Wide Web, the messy web of social pressures, or a mental map. In an e-mail snippet from Louise Gray (with reference to the work of artist Beryl Korot) to Murray-Leslie, reprinted in *Don't Art Fashion Music* with the header "Women's Work: The Center of Production," Gray describes Korot's work as "containing digital code, rather like tartans contain cultural patterns. It's the way of taking something that's traditionally thought of as female craft and grafting it onto – technology – perhaps feminising technology" (Chicks on Speed et al. 2010, 37). Chicks on Speed locates this discussion of female craft among images of looms that weave fabric with sound. Their work, too, contains digital code in their use of repeating patterns of fabrics and bodies as well as in their electronic sound and can, therefore, also be seen in terms of digital craft feministing – not feminizing – technology.

At first glance, and in contrast to Chicks on Speed, Lady Bitch Ray's awkwardness appears much less intentional and is often described, mainly by mainstream media, as unwanted effect. Lady Bitch Ray is the stage name of Reyhan Şahin, who holds a PhD in linguistics from the University of Bremen, where she completed her dissertation on the semiotics of clothing. She held a research position in media and communication at the University of Hamburg and is now a postdoctoral fellow with the Gerda Henkel Foundation. She first appeared in the public eye as Lady Bitch Ray after launching a lawsuit against her former employer, Radio Bremen, for firing her based on her online appearances in May 2006. She approached the German tabloid paper *Die Bildzeitung* with her story, and, due to the scandal-appeal of a highly educated Turkish-German porn-rapper, the paper gladly published her story. In the following months, Lady Bitch Ray became a media phenomenon, albeit at the time short lived. While her record label and line of clothing are entitled Vagina Records and Vagina Style, respectively, thus connoting female sexual empowerment merged with entrepreneurial prowess, her lyrics are riddled with what could be seen as anti-female pejoratives that retain much of their violent impact. Lady Bitch Ray's approach to female agency, which often causes unease in the audience or the imagined audience, is central to her performances, including also interviews and talk shows, where she physically embodies typical aspects of heteronormative erotic fantasy and visually cites pop-pornographic expectations of objectified desire, all the while expounding her own brand of feminist ideology. Until the release of her book *Bitchsm* in 2012, her work, moreover, was primarily digital and therefore mobile (in the form of downloads), fleeting (in that it can be censored, removed, or buried in cyberspace), and manipulable (through the participatory function of comment sections).

The public discussions around Lady Bitch Ray's work divide neatly along the lines of success within the contemporary feminist context or failure as mere titillating provocation and vice versa. But her performance work represents the variety of ways in which awkwardness circulates, and the need for a new set of methodological tools beyond those devoted to assessing intention and meaning through close readings of content based in a framework of gender or feminist media theories – for such tools consistently break down. This is potentially due to the intermixing of academic voice with joyful and humorous pop-porn gestures as well as a defiant and pedagogically inclined feminist activism found in her works, all of which hinge upon the body and person of Lady Bitch Ray and all of which walk a fine line between riotous success and utter failure, a line that is also seemingly self-consciously exploited.

Her own mediatization on her website displays this as well, as does her use of social media platforms. The website is primarily focused on the promotion of her book, *Bitchsm* (Lady Bitch Ray 2012b), although it also contains descriptors of her fashion line, her record label, and the Vagina Style Institute, an umbrella organization, so to speak, under which all activities undertaken by "Boss Bitch" are united – "feminist-oriented studies and concepts, bitch-rap-music, pussy art, bitchy cliterature, and fashion."[8] The description of the institute is accompanied by a photo of Lady Bitch Ray, squatting with legs spread in front of a Mercedes and wearing a body suit sporting an image of Salt-n-Pepa. The images and videos posted to the site are all high-resolution, glossy depictions of her work, the artist always the focal point of the imagery. Further, feminist causes feature centrally in the blog, but always in a manner that continues to place Lady Bitch Ray or the language of her institute in the forefront. The blog includes, for example, a pink poster displaying the words "Freedom for Pussy Riot" accompanied by a sketched image of Lady Bitch Ray, posed like the iconic Che Guevara, her beret decorated by the two-fingered symbol that is the logo of her brand. The text that goes along with this poster reads: "Tomorrow the BitchWalk from Lady Bitch Ray at the Frankfurt Book Fair. Eat this, Bitch!"[9] A later post includes a further poster that reads as a call to arms for the BitchWalk, in which complex concerns around race and sexuality that plagued the SlutWalks in Germany and that also mark Femen protests come together in her signature sexualized language: "Take off your clothes, put on a headscarf or take to the streets in a negligée."[10] In this manner, she herself and her work become the pop object that is inserted into feminist activism, both being rewritten in the process. The inappropriateness and joy outlined at the beginning of this chapter come together here to self-reflexively engage with feminist activism in a manner that recognizes and plays with its cruel optimistic mechanisms. The international reach of both feminism and rap culture also play a role, the references here transnational in origin (the Russian Pussy Riot or Canadian SlutWalk, but also the visual reference to US rap culture through the Salt-n-Pepa body suit and the Mercedes). Interestingly, at the time of this writing, the blog has not been updated since October 2012, while the associated Facebook page is regularly updated with images that precariously walk the line between self-promotion and self-objectification.

In her song and video "Aufklärung" (a term that, in German, means both enlightenment and sexual education),[11] Lady Bitch Ray (2012a) further exemplifies these strategies. In the video, Lady Bitch Ray, in her self-designed outfits, lounges on large beds with a group of mainly women – of different ethnicities – dancing and moving around in various sexual poses as she raps with texts that explain different techniques for making sex pleasurable for women. Except for the exposé, in which two black women announce the need for more rap from Lady Bitch Ray, and the ending, when Lady Bitch Ray appears to be on a beach, the video is filmed on two sets: one brightly lit bedroom and one dimly lit bedroom. She wears different, brightly coloured and self-designed outfits, the same Salt-n-Pepa bodysuit from her website, and some of her own merchandise. The video is flashy and poppy in its aesthetics; it uses special effects and close-ups of Lady Bitch Ray's face, cleavage, and crotch with a fabric strap-on. The imagery and the lyrics seem to suggest that the title refers to sexual education. The larger claim – that Germany needs to be "enlightened" by Lady Bitch Ray – lingers as a subtext. And what looks like the setting for an amateur porn film does not deliver images for sexual arousal but, instead, images of confident women mutually enjoying playful sexual gestures. The video and the song create awkwardness by consciously developing and then crushing expectations on different and seemingly clashing levels of discourse – of porn, of teaching sexual education or how to please women, of political progress, and of philosophical enlightenment, all embedded in rap visuals.

The awkward position of the body in Lady Bitch Ray's performances in and in-between media and discourses as exemplified on her website and in the video example is probably best illustrated in her most recent and, at least on first glance, least intermedial publication, *Bitchsm*,[12] a puffy pink book that replicates in style a soft porn scrapbook. It is in equal parts manifesto (based heavily on local references to German feminist history, Turkish-German relations, and German rap culture), fashion spread, and erotic style guide. In word and image, she engages in a simultaneously provocative and embarrassing play that works as sex-positivity and sexploitation, performative politics and erotic pleasure. While itself analogue, the book depends upon (and inspires) Lady Bitch Ray's digital works, including her media circulation (and that of others – for example, Pussy Riot or SlutWalk, as seen in the discussion above).

After struggling to finish the manuscript and searching for a publisher, Lady Bitch Ray saw *Bitchsm* appear in 2012 with a small publisher, Panini Verlags GmbH, in collaboration with her own publishing company, Vagina Style-VS-Verlag. *Bitchsm* is a playful mixture of a how-to-book, a political manifesto, and a soft porn magazine. Not only is it sex-positive in its approach to the female body, but it also suggests that successful female emancipation starts (and ends) with sexual liberation. The subtitle, "*Emanzipation. Integration. Masturbation,*"[13] further implies that the text addresses the relationship between sexual liberation and racial discrimination in Germany, confirmed by sections of the text that respond directly to media debates in Germany about headscarves in public schools, honour killings, and the failed integration of "foreigners" in general.[14] Because of the context in which *Bitchsm* was published, its multimedia reception, its formal use of intertextual and intermedial elements in an experimental collage, and its very clear development of a narrative-performative voice in the character of Lady Bitch Ray, the book functions like a piece of performance art and clearly illustrates the complex politics surrounding the sexualized body in Lady Bitch Ray's work. The book relies and draws on Lady Bitch Ray's previous work as a self-produced (porn)rapper, fashion designer, and media-savvy star. Her previous appearances were mainly fleeting and digital; the book seems to capture this fleeting appearance between a cushioned binding and on glossy printed pages.

The text's narrative-performative perspective unifies these potentially disparate elements of Lady Bitch Ray's previous performances as this perspective is consistently hedonistic and centred on female pleasure and lust. *Bitchsm* is a response to and builds upon the media frenzy that developed in 2008, following her lawsuit against Radio Bremen. At the time, Lady Bitch Ray appeared on talk shows and in interviews, published rap videos online, started her own label, and triggered furious as well as enthusiastic responses in chat forums and in the comments to her videos or other media appearances. But *Bitchsm* also builds on Lady Bitch Ray's claim to be a new feminist voice. The text begins with a "philosophical definition" and ethics (primarily concerning female solidarity), then it offers "Ficktipps" (fuck tips) and beauty advice. The second half of the book directly addresses questions around cultural politics, racism, sexism in hip hop, family politics, and Turkish identity in Germany. Each chapter is illustrated with a range of photos that are in a soft porn style, as is much of the writing. The photos show the author wearing self-designed lingerie as she demonstrates various sexual practices and exercises to improve self-esteem and sexual pleasure that she explores in the text. In large parts, *Bitchsm* is a sex-positive manual for female body-styling, and, although at times it slips from sex-positivity to sexploitation, body-styling does not originate in negation or negativity vis-à-vis the female body. And the gross, sick, or painful body does not appear in the text. Instead, Lady Bitch Ray describes the sexual, sexualized, and sexy female body as a site for and source of power, as is clear from the cover notes: "For emancipated bitches whose pussies can't get enough and always itch – stand up if you are a cunt! Bitchsm 2012, yeah!!"[15] At the same time, it turns this emancipation back on itself: the front and back cover show a black and white Rorschach-like smear, the caption reading "Original impression of Lady Bitch Ray's cunt."[16] Suddenly, the sexual body of the author-narrator is a little too close for comfort, a little too inappropriate – joyfully so.

This closeness is mimicked in the book's approach to its audience. The introduction of *Bitchsm*, for example, veritably screams the following directly at its readership: "Dear dogs and bitches, enjoy this motherfucking work! Bitchsm for bitches, bitchsm for live [*sic*], biaaaaaach!!! You can't ignore it any more. Finally I can publish bitchsm and no dick can interrupt me. Written by Mushido – Lady Bitch Ray's bushy pussy" (Lady Bitch Ray 2012b, 17).[17] Lady Bitch Ray's use of anti-female aggressive language recoded as empowerment is turned playful and self-referential by her amalgamation of the name of controversial

German rapper Bushido with "Muschi," or pussy. To this, she adds the "Fußnutte" (her playful neologism made of the German word for footnote and *Nutte*, or whore): "I asked Ms. ALICE SCHWARZER if she wanted to write the foreword to this Bitchsm work, unfortunately she did not answer, then my twat wrote it. It became much twatier" (17).[18] *Bitchsm* deploys negative semantics around female sexuality that often have a citational quality, thus becoming culturally intertextual in nature. Moreover, the text's performative position with regard to its audience and its assertiveness vis-à-vis racism clash awkwardly with historically driven German feminism, as is seen in the reference to Schwarzer. This intersectionality and intertextuality create a messy politics that consistently slips from interpretation. In an attempt to counter racialized stereotypes of victimized Turkish women in Germany, stereotypes that German mainstream feminism (from Alice-Schwarzer feminism to lifestyle feminism) endorses and fosters, *Bitchsm* employs the violent language of pornography and the sexist imagery of pop culture to create its pleasure-obsessed, hedonistic, and aggressive voice. The text highlights the awkward tensions that intersectional approaches to racial and sexual discrimination can present. The way in which *Bitchsm* attempts to escape the traps of either racist or sexist essentialism is by playfully circling the line between both. Thus, Lady Bitch Ray poses the question of political agency and of who is in control of awkwardness. The character of Lady Bitch Ray is purposefully out of control, which is simultaneously how she attracted attention and what made her a disturbance to public media forums and discourse. Şahin enacts the "free, possessive individual" of the neoliberal society (Hall 2011, 706) as a disturbance to this very society.

THE WILLFULNESS OF THE MATERIAL: READING FOR THE AWKWARD

The awkwardness displayed in our examples above corresponds to those activisms we discuss in the previous chapters, but here, the works consciously use the awkward moments that such feminisms generate to make these very moments politically productive. They deliberately produce awkwardness, anticipate its effects, and frame that awkwardness theoretically. This does not mean that their performances are clearly legible politically, but they take political illegibility as their starting point. Neoliberal pop-consumption is a precondition for this awkward activism to "work," as is the element of aesthetic creativity. Chicks on

3.1 "Mösen Medi," Lady Bitch Ray

Speed work politically if one presupposes a precarious subject position that exists in a mediated, digital, neoliberal world, a position that their acts then analyze and make productive. Similarly, Lady Bitch Ray assumes a certain political disturbance of the smooth surface of pop consumption as a starting point for her interventions. Her acts then deliberately reveal false binaries, stereotypes, and the cruel optimisms that are the foundations of neoliberal concepts of self-realization, liberation, and Western feminism. This assumption of a particular subject position that is precarious and engaged in acts of disturbance works much in the manner described by Ahmed (2014b) in *Willful Subjects*. She discusses the terms "willful" and "willfulness" as referring to something that goes against the general expectations of a certain structure. Using

3.2 "Cupcake," Lady Bitch Ray

3.3 "Shoe Guitar," Chicks on Speed, on Exhibit at Kunsthaus Bethanien (Berlin), 2011

the image of the willful child who stubbornly misbehaves and does not conform to parental and societal expectations, she discusses how to be willful is to be a problem, to be disobedient (3). In the works of Chicks on Speed and Lady Bitch Ray, we see precisely this misbehaviour as a mode of upsetting structures at work in neoliberalism and in feminism, in political performance and in pop.

"Misbehaviour" in the above examples is enacted through the manner in which materiality, which includes bodies and objects, is mobilized in the digital realm. Ahmed (2014b, 43) writes: "A body can become a willful thing, when it gets in the way of an action being completed." Further, an object that seems not to do as it is told by not serving its intended function becomes subjectivized, becomes viewed as willful. The willful body or object sticks out and is noticed, makes an impression as it misbehaves. The material willfully misbehaves in our examples above, for example, in the overt self-sexualization and self-commodification, and the obvious feminist agency rewriting any sexual drive on the part of the viewer. Lady Bitch Ray very specifically utilizes such willful misbehaviour with her own body, the implied bodies of her audience, and her material objects. For example, in an interview for the German-language version of MTV early in her career, she opens the conversation by offering the interviewer a panty-liner embossed with a dark pink (at first glance reminiscent of washed-out blood) outline of a female figure. Because she had been hyped in the press as a scandalous porn-rapper, the excitement on the part of the interviewer and audience around an expected sexually charged misbehaviour is palpable as she enters the studio. By beginning with the feminine product, she simultaneously defuses the excitement and ups the ante in a rewriting of her vagina style to highlight the (and, as the interview continues, her own) menstruating vagina. This willful misbehaviour also comes through in her fashion design, which often features cut-aways that sexualize the performer's body (mesh backsides or holes in the crotch reminiscent of Valie Export's "action pants") or additions – misplacements even – of oversized female or male genitals made of velvety fabric and sewn on in bright, poppy colours, all of which highlight and harness the female performer's sexualization in the industry.

In the case of Chicks on Speed, that willfulness is also geared towards the fashion and music industry. Their "shoe guitar" offers an example of their mixed-media approach to fashion, art, and music. A lady-gaga-esque shoe that appears in some of their performances and exhibits is musical instrument, fashion and fetish object, and art sculpture in one. Like Lady Bitch Ray's costumes, the shoe-guitar willfuly combines (high) fashion and design with a different function, here to become an instrument that is closely associated with a history of rebellious self-expression. Chicks on Speed also repeatedly reference guitars in their songs and visuals as a symbol for the male-dominated rock music scene that they at once reject and appropriate.[19] But, as in the case of Lady Bitch Ray's willful objects, the shoe guitar also takes on an impudent, inappropriate undertone when the "theorizing" of the object by Chicks on Speed is taken into account. In ~~Don't~~ Art Fashion Music they write of the guitar: "Taking the Prick out of Guitar, yes, now it is livable, wearable + requires better positions to play it. Lets wank around" (Chicks on Speed et al. 2010, 84, grammar and spelling in original). Wanking around imbues the shoe with genital-sexual undertones, as does the suggestion of better positions demanded of the guitar. These undertones reference the male body and the masculine dominance of the music industry, but these are transferred to their own, female bodies. In their performances, fashion design, and theorizations, willfulness is a collective and joyfully (and also sexually) charged collaborative act.

But the description of the willful body is also one that depends on the social and that continually breaks with the cruel optimism described at the outset of this chapter. Ahmed (2014b, 50) writes: "Clumsiness can be how a subject experiences itself: as being 'in the way' of what is 'on the way,' as being in the way of itself as well as others. A body can be what trips you up, catches you out." It is this clumsiness and bumpiness, or what she calls being not-attuned and out of time with others, that Ahmed suggests might produce a queer ethics, which "registers those who are not attuned as keeping open the possibility of going another way," as a "way of staying attuned to otherness" (51). The clumsiness and bumpiness of the body that is willful – that does not find itself in step with others – is not, therefore, something to be overcome: "Rather than equality being about smoothing a relation perhaps equality is a bumpy ride" (ibid.). There is a sense, therefore, that willfulness can be understood as a disturbance, a bumpiness, that arises when something or somebody is not passing, does not fit, is out of step or out of turn, and sticks out: is awkward. Similarly, we claim that awkwardness produced in these popfeminist performances is not to be explained away through failure or success but, instead, left to be acknowledged, followed, and potentially harnessed. Getting tripped up, therefore, is part of the material and becomes part of the clumsiness of the research that demands a different methodology, one that is aware of the interdependency of theory and practice as well as the circularity of meaning making and, thus, reads for the awkward. This is not only the method we develop and utilize in this book but also the one we suggest is necessary for research on the status of the political in many contemporary popular forms of activism.

Throughout her book, Ahmed (2014b, 7, emphasis in original) makes it clear that willfulness is a category of feminism (the willful child is almost always the girl-child), of queerness (the eradication of willfulness a "*straightening device*"), and of race: "Feminist, queer, and antiracist histories can be thought of as histories of those who are willing to be willful, who are willing to turn a diagnosis into an act of self-description" (134). Thus willfulness is also a call to arms in a clearly political sense. It can also be seen as a way of thinking about awkwardness as being on the path to political determinacy. In her final chapter, Ahmed turns to willfulness not as a way of prescribing a certain type of politics but, rather, as a style or mode of politics in and of itself: "Willfulness could be thought of as political art, a practical craft that is acquired through involvement in political struggle, whether that struggle is a struggle to exist or to transform an existence" (133). Further, she describes willfulness as "audacity," "standing against," and "creativity" (134). When thought in this manner as crafty and stubbornly creative, willfulness is both what the subject must do and how that subject as a body is transformed through that doing. This has implications for the taking up of arms, for political (self-)mobilization, or – our suggestion here – for feminist academic research.

The concept of willfulness applies to the artists, the theorist-artist or -activist, and the theorist-critic, and it marks another point of collision between these spheres and between the object of analysis and (us as) the analysts. Indeed, returning to the figure of the feminist killjoy developed in her earlier work, Ahmed (2014b, 152) claims that she shares the same affective horizon as the willful subject, as "the ones who 'ruin the atmosphere.'" Willfulness, she writes, is attached to the problem of the female character – a statement that can be applied to our object of study as well as to our search for a popfeminist methodology, a methodology that foregrounds the willful voice or the willful subject. In Ahmed's words, "we can hear what is at stake in how women who speak out are heard" (153), women charged with being disagreeable, too loud, too harsh, too forceful – too willful, or as not willing.[20] But this, Ahmed suggests, can become a project for feminism. The political charge is "to transform this judgment into a project," which "requires we make another willful translation. We are *willing not* to be willing: *not willing* translated into *willing not*" (154, emphasis in original). This willing not asks us to be loud and to not let the silence overtake us.

Ahmed's book offers a charge of willfulness, of taking on the project of willfulness, asking readers to accept this charge. What is specifically important for developing a popfeminist methodology and reading for awkwardness is not only the manner in which she discusses willfulness and the willful subject but also, and in particular, the language she uses around the urgency of the political. Awkwardness might describe what the willful subject creates in her wake. It might also describe her creative output. If the willful subject can become political, or at least a political project, through acceptance of her willfulness – or, to use the terms above, by willing not (that is, willing not to conform, to fit in, to be silenced) – then awkwardness is something that accompanies her whether or not that charge of willfulness is accepted. The awkwardness resonating, being produced by, or following the willful subject is itself political no matter the subject's decision to take up arms. Awkwardness as opposed to willfulness appears more coincidental, less powerful, and less militant. So, while awkwardness might accompany willfulness, awkwardness also implies a less directed will, a will that does not – or not yet – really know what it wants, that might even create "awkward silences," but that can also certainly be too loud, too close, and too forceful and, at the same time, not willing.

A less directed, but maybe also more joyful, connotation of awkward activism echoes with J. Halberstam's playful notion of "Gaga Feminism," which is an explicitly gender activist approach to a number of questions similar to those that we pose. In his short book, *Gaga Feminism,* Halberstam (2012, 28–9) advocates a new kind of feminism that sounds "pop" and that seems to touch upon a notion of awkwardness:

> Gaga feminism is outrageous. This is not a feminism for the faint of heart nor for the weak of knees … this is a feminism that has no truck with shame or embarrassment, it is for the freaks and geeks, the losers and failures, the kids who were left out at school, the adults who still don't fit in … [T]his feminism is not about sisterhood, motherhood, sorority, or even women. It is about shifting, changing, morphing, extemporizing political positions quickly and affectively to keep up with the multimedia environments in which we all live and to stay apace of what some have called "the coming insurrection."

Halberstam combines pop and feminism by asking why pop figures like Lady Gaga could not, in fact, "be new figures of feminism" (7). He defines "Gaga Feminism" as "a form of political expression that

masquerades as naive nonsense but that actually participates in big and
meaningful forms of critique" (xxv). While *Gaga Feminism* is a sort of
manifesto that calls for a new kind of "feminism" that "is outrageous"
(28) and not ashamed or embarrassed, our project asserts that this kind
of new feminism already exists (and that those perceived as outsiders –
"freaks and geeks, the losers and failures" (29) – are already firmly
mainstreamed) but that we need to develop tools to tell the story of its
political impact. Lady Bitch Ray and Chicks on Speed are "Gaga Feminists" in this sense. Their "losing" and "failing" – their clumsiness – is
part of their political act. These performers act out the freedom to be
joyful in unconventional or inappropriate ways.

By reading for awkwardness in popfeminist activism we bring
together the concept of willfulness and of "Gaga" to define the space
for political activism in the neoliberal, optimistic context. Popfeminism
is subject to the manner in which both feminist politics and pop culture are reliant upon neoliberal mechanisms even as these are radically
rewritten, manipulated, leveraged, and/or clash in popfeminist performance. A methodology that harnesses this is equally subject to and reliant upon such mechanisms. Feminism is a form of cruel optimism; it
creates a relation, or, in Berlant's (2011b, 1) words, "an attachment"
that contains promises such as liberation from oppressions, freedom (of
expression), choice of sexuality, and/or economic equality. The object
is the wish for the political that promises clarity of meaning (goals,
intent) and productivity (success, failure). The attachment lasts only
due to the fact that the promises are not (yet) fulfilled. Conversely, pop
culture (including media), creates an attachment based in consumerism that promises global belonging through participation. Popfeminist
actions are found (or consciously place themselves) in the middle of
relations that uphold cruel optimism; however, they also engage with
and exploit the assumptions that underlie these relations. To begin
with, feminist causes remain at the centre of their narratives, but emotional attachments are mainly formed via critical negativity towards
those causes. Furthermore, objects of popular consumption are also
at the centre of the story of protest, but negative emotions and critical
negativity with respect to these objects emerge as the primary point of
the performances. Popfeminism makes visible cruel optimism because
it openly uses feminist and neoliberal attachments and positions itself
negatively against them. As such, the examples we are discussing display the manner in which popfeminism refuses to accept conventional
understandings of success or failure as key to the feminist project while,
at the same time, not being evaluative in its consumption or coding

of neoliberal pop. Awkwardness emerges in the circularity, and it is in theorizing this awkwardness that we define a strategy that reads for the complicated and precarious positions of the political, positions that appear forceful and "willful" without a clear direction or goal.

ATTACHING AND DETACHING: NEOLIBERAL CIRCULARITY

In the final sentences of *Cruel Optimism*, Berlant (2011b, 263) writes of the problem of political action as demanding a necessary detachment from the world in order to confront or make a "claim on the present," while also necessitating the belief that the "world is worth our attachment to it." She writes of this as "cruel optimism's double bind: even with an image of a better good life available to sustain your optimism, it is awkward and it is threatening to detach from what is already not working" (ibid.). The current political moment is therefore "awkward" and one of transition – threatening to detach from what is already not working – a concept that also describes post-9/11 as a particular moment in neoliberal economic and political developments. Our search for awkwardness allows us to stay with this threat and to linger in the moment of transition, watching the politics that emerge. A related spatial metaphor we have been using throughout our discussions here is the notion of circularity, of moving in circles, whereby one constantly moves away from something only to return to the point of origin. In such circularity, detachment is also not happening even though it is a constantly present threat that is articulated over and over again, circularly. The threat of detachment is lingering, but whatever might be "on the move" stays awkwardly attached. There is no clear sense that this detachment will ever happen, so rather than focusing our political attention on the goal of what might or might not happen, we are interested in the current moment, in the formulation of a "threat." Similarly, though in different words and with a more negative trajectory, Stuart Hall (2011, 728) asserts:

> Neo-liberalism is in crisis. But it keeps driving on. However, in ambition, depth, degree of break with the past, variety of sites being colonized, impact on common sense and everyday behaviour, restructuring of the social architecture, neo-liberalism does constitute a *hegemonic project*. Today, popular thinking and the systems of calculation in daily life offer very little friction to the passage of its ideas. Delivery may be more difficult: new and old contradictions

still haunt the edifice, in the very process of its re-construction. Still, in terms of staging the future on favourable terrain, the neo-liberal project is several stages further on. (emphasis in original)

It is then the formulation of a "threat" and the insertion of "friction" against this hegemonic project that are the objectives of political activism in the current historical moment. Awkwardness, as we theorize it, is a constant – in some cases desperate and in other cases joyful – attempt to do just that: insert friction and formulate a sense of political will.

The examples of Lady Bitch Ray and Chicks on Speed offer two different kinds of framing and reframing awkwardness in the neoliberal age and in the digital realm that contain such moments of friction and, in some cases, formulations of a threat, and thus move towards political will. They make the legacy of sex-positive feminism and feminist performance art awkward by engaging with feminist body explorations and performance practices as they meet with either rap and pop-porn mainstream (Lady Bitch Ray) or pop-hyper-mediality (Chicks on Speed), among other mainstream discourses. Both use concepts of performativity that are reminiscent of feminist politics of the 1970s and the 1990s, but the concept of provocative or ironic performativity dissolves and evolves into disruptive awkwardness as it clashes with a neoliberal cultural sphere. A way in which both examples illustrate this is by becoming "too much" or "too outrageous/outraged": the bodies are too close, too sexual, and too intimate as well as too mediated, too intermedial, and too glossy. These seemingly hard-to-combine elements of "too much," which are nonetheless rather easily consumed and marketed in a neoliberal economy, are then countered with acts of disappearance. Before she published *Bitchsm*, Lady Bitch Ray left the public media stage as a performer only to reappear on the glossy pages of her own hedonistic book in over-exposed poses. Chicks on Speed's performances are improvised and fleeting and their stage is constantly on the move to different centres of hip-art and subculture venues and from street protests to museum spaces. Their danceable pop-performances merge into hard-to-consume, loud and long multi-media spectacles.

These examples of popfeminist performance are securely attached to the logics of neoliberal capitalist circulations of art, narratives, and images, but they also constantly threaten to detach from that very logic. This detachment is not necessarily or only immanent to popfeminist art; sometimes detachment happens in the circulations of popfeminist performance art and activism, a concept we explore in more detail in the next chapter. In the context of our discussion, however, a focus on circulations through different contexts means that Chicks on Speed, for example, are slipping away from appropriations according to the way in which political interpretations of their art shift in light of the actions of other performance groups, such as Pussy Riot. Similarly, Lady Bitch Ray's politics grow and get crushed as discourses around race, sexuality, and Turkish-German women in Germany shift.

In the German context, Lady Bitch Ray is racially other and often received as speaking mainly about and for (sexually) oppressed Muslim women. This places her in the middle of a messy political discourse that Reyhan Şahin both uses for and deconstructs in her performance and academic work. Mainstream media tried to cast her as the Westernized liberator of oppressed Muslim women, a role she played outrageously well, which, in turn, deconstructed it. While she used this mainstream approach to her work to get publicity, she positioned herself against the white, male German gaze and aligned herself with Muslim and Turkish women in Germany. In the headscarf debates, for example, which is also a topic of Şahin's academic publications, she clearly positions herself as a voice for and of women who do not choose to wear the headscarf and of women who do. Her disturbances as Lady Bitch Ray, then, are always meant for mainstream discourse that targets minority women as either oppressed or sexualized or both. This circularity is a further example of detachment and re-attachment. The constant references to discourses – in this case mainstream porn, racialized eroticism, (German) racisms and sexisms – offer moments of political critique that remain firmly attached to their object of critique at the same time as they disrupt these very discourses. Most recently, following the publication of her book *Die Bedeutung des muslimischen Kopftuchs: Eine kleidungssemiotische Untersuchung Kopftuch tragender Musliminnen in der Bundesrepublik Deutschland* (The significance of the Muslim headscarf: A fashion-semiotic analysis of Muslim headscarf-wearing women in Germany), Şahin (2014) began to offer highly successful "Bitchsm-Seminars" as Lady Bitch Ray, a combination of lecture, reading, performance, and conversation, to which we return in chapter 6.

In a circular motion similar to that of Lady Bitch Ray, Chicks on Speed's art and music constructs and self-deconstructs. The politics of their circulations are more self-referential and, at least on the surface, much more controlled than are those of Lady Bitch Ray. Chicks on Speed are globally accessible, albeit to a rather small artsy subculture. In their art, Chicks on Speed play with different notions of attachments. Our analyses reveal the fleeting and often (seemingly) accidental and

spontaneous moments when their work rather awkwardly "detaches" –
or threatens to detach – from what is not working. Awkwardness
functions intentionally and unintentionally in Chicks on Speed's staged
and polished DIY performances. Their self-referencing simultaneously
highlights and crushes the political effects of their performances. When,
in one of their "Utopia" performance videos,[21] for example, Chicks on
Speed performers tumble down staircases in skin-tight, neon-coloured,
and mixed-pattern exercise outfits combined with high-heeled shoes
only to end up in a huge pile on a stage, silliness and awkwardness,
painfulness and playfulness collide. The video uses slow, fast, and backward motion to emphasize the manipulated digital form of a recording
of this performance at the ArtSpace gallery in Sydney.

Both Lady Bitch Ray and Chicks on Speed are experienced performance artists who make music and design fashion, and who work with
multi-media platforms; however, Lady Bitch Ray's awkwardness relies
more heavily on a public political discourse. In contrast to Chicks on
Speed's rather abstract references to political issues, Lady Bitch Ray's
work is political in an immediate and interventionist way, mimicking
the fast-paced comment sections of digital social media and news sites.
Her political impact is bound to media events and discourses. This
might be the main reason why Lady Bitch Ray's work does not travel
(yet) beyond the German context, at least not with the political messages and implications she carries within the German media landscape.
In spite of her extensive references to mainly US female rap and hip-hop
artists and to transnational feminist protest movements, to this date,
her political interventions are located in a national context. Regardless,
since the digital realm is never confined by national boundaries, there
always remains the potential for the creation of new kinds of localities.

Productions of political awkwardness are intimately – and awkwardly closely – linked with the ways in which such images proliferate in digital spaces that are not contained by the nation but that,
instead, create just such new localities. The performances of Chicks on
Speed and Lady Bitch Ray rely on the proliferating effect of the sexualized body in digital space, but through these images of the sexualized body they reveal that the staging of sex as pleasure is a cruel
optimism. As performers they continue to promise fulfilment and intimacy that can be consumed but that they cannot and do not ever want
to offer. This mechanism generates a kind of playful and joyful awkwardness that escapes the logic of cruelly optimistic consumption. In
her performances, Lady Bitch Ray instrumentalizes "race and fashion

... to enable and enact an oppositional political economy of the body," which "animates the material realities of race, gender, generation, sex, and class that frame the (digital and real) production and consumption of fashion objects, images, and knowledge" (Pham 2011, 9). The kind of "animating" of material realities of race, gender, and sex is not accurately described as simply "performative," but it becomes political by highlighting the relationships between bodies, sex, race, and consumption. Chicks on Speed's performances illustrate this playing field of the sexualized body and the political differently; while race is a blind spot in their art, they manage to draw close attention to normative bodies by animating them as awkward or awkwardly. By staying with them, by staying too close to them and dancing around them, they joyfully deconstruct gender and beauty norms. In moving their work, mainly, into art spaces, Chicks on Speed protect their work from a certain kind of appropriation by the neoliberal pop culture market; however, at the same time, they subject their art to another kind of high culture appropriation that strips their work of politics by making it exclusive and deeming it "too artsy" for the mainstream public. By detaching from a pop-cultural counter-public and attaching themselves to gallery art spaces, Chicks on Speed escape a certain kind of pop-appropriation in exchange for the danger of becoming an exclusive and artsy museum piece.

The images of such performances that circulate digitally and globally never exist just in and of themselves and are, intentionally, referential. As our discussions show, this is rather obvious in the case of Lady Bitch Ray's porn poses, rap gestures, and talk show appearances as well as in the plethora of complex citations and references that define the work of Chicks on Speed. Less intentionally, maybe, images can also be infused with new political meaning by the continued circulation of new forms of activist gestures. The fact that Pussy Riot performances and the following protest actions in support of Pussy Riot are reminiscent of Chicks on Speed's earlier gigs reinfuses the work of the latter with activist politics. The colourful stockings, costumes, and performative and musical awkwardness of Chicks on Speed as it appears to be referenced in Pussy Riot's performance in the Cathedral of Christ the Saviour in Moscow not only aligns the two groups but also visually infiltrates the stages of Chicks on Speed with a new air of politics. Conversely, Chicks on Speed's effortless approach to art as politics and politics as art seemingly answers a question posed to Masha Alyokhina and Nadia Tolokonnikova at the First Supper Symposium – namely, how does the art world parallel their more political activist world? At this podium discussion in 2014, where Judith Butler and Rosi Braidotti asked Alyokhina and Tolokonnikova a set of pre-circulated questions mainly about the state of feminism in Russia, this question was met with awkward silence, in the middle of which Butler gestured the answer with her hand, which resulted in awkward laughter on and off stage. The moderator then concludes, "the answer was provided ... I liked Judith's sign language: they are not separate."[22] Here, theory and practice, as well as feminist generations, are embodied on stage. Butler's physical answer in the face of the activist-performers' clumsy loss of words suggests, however, a straightforward obviousness to art and politics that really does not and cannot exist in the contemporary transnational context. The tension between the hand (acting here as an index, a replacement for the missing answer) and the silence (acting as a question mark), then, opens up a new locality – an in between, an elsewhere – for the political to appear. This, again, illustrates how different spheres of influence are intertwined and how this intertwinement can create new localities for political activism.

APPROPRIATIONS AND WILLFUL ELUSIVENESS

Both examples, Chicks on Speed and Lady Bitch Ray, illustrate a shift from the politics of performativity of the 1990s towards a different kind of feminist politics that is less clear in intention, reliant on technology, and defiant of categorization. This new strategy is both neoliberal and contains the threat of slipping away from neoliberal consumption. Form and, more specifically, the interplay of different digital and non-digital forms, materiality, physicality, and digital projection play a crucial role in this process. While in constant danger of being appropriated for certain discourses around the body, sexuality, and gender, these artists strive for a position in which they remain "inappropriate" for consumption and, so we show, inappropriately awkward.[23] In the context of neoliberal pop consumption, they are and have to be always simultaneously appropriated and inappropriate, remaining on the move – circling or circulating – between these two poles. This kind of oscillation links back to joy and the figure of the feminist killjoy. At the very moment that either of these artists produce a promise of happiness or fulfilment, they disappoint – or try to disappoint. They then take joy in "killing" such promises. Their "seductive" behaviour, for example, becomes silly, clumsy, aggressive, or defiant. Their politics and the subject positions they take up do appear willful, for they are too loud, they are too close. But their willfulness might be most clearly highlighted when they are "not willing" and when they disappoint, when they disengage or disappear.

This points to another way in which one might be able to approach popfeminist circularity as politically productive beyond the metaphor of threatening detachment that Berlant suggests. Lady Bitch Ray and Chicks on Speed playfully engage with notions of appearance and disappearance, distance and intimacy, closeness and rejection. Above, we assert that, in their art, and in popfeminist art in general, the body is often "too close" and "too much," which directly relates to Ahmed's discussion of the willful subject. The willful subject can also, of course, be willfully elusive and invisible. Lady Bitch Ray disappears and re-enters the media stages in different roles; Chicks on Speed are elusive in their art in that they create spaces for improvised performances that will never and can never be recreated. Similarly, the presence of their art is globally on the move and exclusive. Both artists utilize costumes, stage personas, and forms of presentation that are as prolific as they are fleeting and play with the proximity and the elusiveness of the body in the digital age. Further, the audience members can never be certain that they read the images they see "correctly." It is the image on the move that makes the reception of images awkward, the threat that they might disappear, become blurry, or, in fact, become all too easily appropriated. Appropriation, however, is always already calculated into the production of popfeminist performances, which, as we argue, makes for their awkward – and, at certain moments, out of control – political messages.

Feminist media artist and theorist Hito Steyerl describes a similar process in her essay "In Defense of the Poor Image" (2009) and relates this process directly to "reality," which we understand in our context to be concerned with what is politically at stake. The poor image, so she concludes, is not about "the real thing" or about "the originary original": "Instead, it is about its own real conditions of existence: about swarm circulation, digital dispersion, fractured and flexible temporalities. It is about defiance and appropriation just as it is about conformism and exploitation. In short: it is about reality" (Steyerl 2009). While, certainly, our examples are about being seen, they play with the tension between hyper- and in-/poor visibility. It is not so much not being seen as it is the interplay between being seen and being loud – and willful – and disappearing from sight that adds a further level to the political awkwardness we trace and define in this chapter. The slippery meaning and the slipping in and out of "politics" of the image and the body in the image define these performances. In one sense, these slippages are precisely what place them in the neoliberal markets, with their flexible modes of consumption; in another sense, being on the move in often unexpected ways, they continuously escape an appropriation as suitable objects for cruelly optimistic desire. In order to talk more specifically about interventions and social change, we need to trace these movements and analyze their shifting forms and contents, something we do in the next chapter. We do not intend to remain with a vague claim for some kind of political moment merely to be read; rather, we mine for models of – joyful and willful – political engagement in the twenty-first century that we ourselves wish to appropriate in our theory and practice.

4

Movements, Circulations, Technologies: Awkwardness on the Move

On 4 October 2014, the Pussy Riot Facebook community page posted the following on their site: "Russia has not only Vladimir Putin and troops, but also great views, which we love. That's why we hate questions like 'Why don't you leave your scary country?'" And Pussy Riot – at least its two most famous members who maintain this Facebook community, Masha Alyokhina and Nadia Tolokonnikova – could leave after their release from prison and after they had advanced to become global icons of political and feminist activism.[1] Their insistence on being Russian and on returning to Russia is a very political statement within a Russian discourse that branded them as Westernized, as too Western, and as hostile to the Russian mentality. Their infamous performance in the Cathedral of Christ the Saviour threatened Putin's Russian identity, which is closely tied to Orthodox Christianity. The case against the three members of Pussy Riot (Alyokhina, Tolokonnikova, along with Yekaterina Samutsevich, who was released earlier than the other two) was based on "religious hatred," and their self-identification as feminists further positioned them as other, Western, and alien. Often, Alyokhina and Tolokonnikova do leave Russia: they appear on stages for podium discussions and roundtables around the world to discuss their human rights campaigns; they perform (or protest) at events and festivals; they meet celebrities such as Madonna, Bill Maher, and Quentin Tarantino; and they even show up in US popular culture, such as the series *House of Cards*. But to this day, they have also always returned to Russia and have publicized this return. Their insistence on retaining ties to Russia again points to the rather complex intertwining of the local, the national, and the global in contemporary feminist activisms. In spite of its seemingly seamless fit within a Western and neoliberal media circus, Pussy Riot's circulation between these contexts creates politically disruptive moments.

What the Facebook status of Pussy Riot highlights is that, aside from digital circulations, actual bodies and people travel. Post-1989, many Eastern Europeans and Russians tried to leave for political and economic reasons and attempted to find work in Central Europe; some were seasonal workers, some were students; some tried to settle, others returned, travelled back and forth, or stayed illegally. The questions of who or what can leave, who can travel, who must leave, who will be left behind, and who can return are possibly among the most contentious questions in the post-9/11 world and the current economic and political landscape. Neoliberalism is associated with such global movements of people, with the idea of flexibility and with the idea of a more interconnected world. In turn, however, the neoliberal economy also produces immobile subjects. In her collection of essays and a play, *besser wäre keine* (better would be nothing/nobody), German author and essayist Kathrin Röggla describes this process as a presumed increase of speed,[2] since the phenomenon of mobilization and flexibility seems to coincide with a new kind of immobility for parts of society. In the European context, such movements – especially from East to West – have become the centre of political discussions after the fall of the Berlin Wall and following the end of the Cold War in the 1990s; however, after 9/11 and the Euro crisis, these discussions have changed to include inner-EU migrations and an increasing discussion about the fortification of EU borders or even the idea of shrinking or abandoning the idea of the EU as an economic and political union altogether. Specifically, when confronting questions of migration, the interconnectedness – or assemblage (Puar 2007) – of gender, race, and national belonging come to the forefront, an interconnectedness that in earlier chapters we describe as a main feature of this contemporary moment of feminist activism.[3]

Building on this discussion, the concepts with which we wrestle in this chapter are movement, circulation, and speed in the context of popfeminist activisms in a neoliberal economy. The emphasis of our analysis is not economic, nor does it solely focus on the technical aspect of digital circulations; rather, we are interested in technologies as connecting social, technical, and cultural spheres and in how they create political disturbances within and across these spheres. The speed with which images, stories, and opinions circulate through different political and geographical contexts creates new challenges as well as new avenues for political interventions. In this chapter, the circulations of Pussy Riot activism in particular (activism of members of the group itself or in solidarity with them),[4] as well as a return to activisms previously discussed, such as SlutWalk and #aufschrei, serve as examples that allow us to more generally describe the circulation of protest activism and movements in the digital age and to explore political moments triggered in and by awkwardness on the move.

MIGRATION, CIRCULATION, AND NEOLIBERALISM

Discussions about female migrants in the global economy often revolve around questions of precarity and economic opportunity, paired with notions of gender-specific exploitation and violence to which migrant women, in particular, are subjected. Movements of people take vastly different forms: migrants can be political or economic refugees, highly skilled workers or seasonal workers, families, children, young people, or ethnic groups. Movements – or circulations – in a neoliberal economy are not simply or only motivated by economic reasons; more implicit effects of neoliberalism like ethnic or racial conflicts, wars, insurgency, or fundamentalist fervour cause millions of people around the globe to move or to join movements. While this is not the space to go into depth regarding this complex set of issues, it is crucial to keep in mind that, when we write about (digital, media, cultural) circulations, we emphasize the political urgency of these questions by thinking a connection, however tenuous and complex, between digital movements and humans who move, who get stuck, who are held back or even fenced or walled in, who are on the run, who return, or who decide to stay. Media representations are, as Myria Georgiou (2012, 792) argues in her introduction to the special issue on "Gender, Migration and the Media" in *Ethnic and Racial Studies*, not just reflections of reality: they also aid in the construction of reality since "our growing dependence on knowing about the world and about each other through media representations reaffirms and reproduces media's symbolic power." Thus, (digital) representation, political voice, and position in a political and social landscape, are, of course, intimately related. Some causes, however loudly they might enter the digital space, disappear from sight rather quickly, while others never circulate outside a local or national context. Agency is a murky concept in these circulations.

On the web, content "migrates"; digital circulations and digital activisms mirror the flows of the neoliberal economy and its subjects. In some cases, elements are swept up by neoliberal consumption; they become awkwardly part of neoliberal networks and they change the way in which marketing or branding might work, as the example of the reception of Pussy Riot outside of Russia's borders in Western neoliberal economies shows. In Russia, the reception of Pussy Riot has focused not on feminist concerns but, instead, primarily on their engagement with their archenemy Vladimir Putin and his entanglement with the patriarchal authority of religion in Russia.[5] The potential in such migration of feminism, then, is its ability to restructure neoliberal networks in the same manner as popfeminism rewrites pop; but, just as in the case of popfeminism, this restructuring also has a fundamental effect on the political impulses of feminism in that feminist politics are also restructured and/or rewritten by neoliberalism. That, in some cases, such change can only occur beyond the borders of origin is indicative of Western feminism's current dependence on the neoliberal model. Feminist activisms rely on mobility just as much as does neoliberalism. In their mobility, however, they do not just or simply emulate the structures of neoliberalism but challenge their very flow. In tracing examples of circulations of popfeminist activisms, characteristics of both digital and neoliberal economies, mainly the precarity and the crises of these economies, surface. But spaces for disruptions of these flows also appear to open up at sometimes unexpected, sometimes clearly calculated, moments. Neoliberalism, in its broadest sense, is a crucial concept in our tracings since, per definition, neoliberalism itself is not a static but, rather, a dynamic and unfolding process that creates "hybridized and mutated forms as it travels around our world" (Springer 2010, 1026).

We use the term "neoliberalism" frequently, particularly in connection with Berlant's definition of cruelty and capitalist relations but also when we discuss feminist politics in the neoliberal age. In *A Brief History of Neoliberalism*, David Harvey (2005, 42) defines neoliberalism as the "liberty of consumer choice, not only with respect to particular products but also with respect to lifestyles, modes of expression, and a wide range of cultural practices." As this short quote implicitly suggests, neoliberalism is not just an economic practice; rather, it functions in close connection with cultural practices and discourses (for example, the discourse around lifestyle feminism discussed in chapter 2). Such connection surfaced clearly in the face of the banking crisis and the following Euro crisis in 2008, when the notion of "crisis" seemed all-encompassing. Hall (2011, 705), relying on Gramsci and Althusser, summarizes as follows: "Conjunctural crises are never solely economic or economically determined" but, instead, "arise when a number of forces and contradictions, which are at work in different key practices and sites in a social formation, come together ... in the same moment and political space," thereby – and here he references Althusser – coming together in a unity that is itself ruptured.[6] Thus, what Hall suggests here is that the contradictory nature of crisis remains apparent nearly simultaneously to the crisis's emergence. Such contradictions are emphasized by the fact that, in spite of the ideology of free markets and choice that defines the neoliberal rhetoric, neoliberalism often works towards monopolization and consolidation and "has very little to do with a 'free market' ideology" (Wise, Covarrubias, and Puentes 2013, 432). Rather, they argue, "it entails the growing monopolisation of global production, services, and commerce along with increasing labour exploitation and environmental degradation. Overall, it embodies a plundering, parasitic, rentier, and predatory phase of global capitalism" (ibid.). The global flows of capital have changed, in a sense, the manner in which disparate bodies are fused together, bodies that go beyond national bodies to include the market-driven industries and economic structures forming their networks across the globe as well as the negative result of these networks. This relationship is also seen in the manner in which Beck addresses the simultaneity of globalization and global risks in *World Risk Society* (see discussion in chapter 2 above).

Wise, Covarrubias, and Puentes further describe a global system that, as a result of this capitalist restructuring, is rather interconnected and certainly violent in its response to such (built-in notions of) crisis. The crisis that came to a head at the beginning of the twenty-first century, they remind us, is "multidimensional (financial, overproduction, environmental, and social)," responses to which "have been short sighted and exclusivist" for they have not been directed at finding solutions for primary causes but, instead, attended to the rescue of large corporations (Wise, Covarrubias, and Puentes 2013, 432). The superficial measures taken globally to address the immediate results of the crisis have not reached deeper, nor have they touched individual people.[7]

What these examples of theories of neoliberal globalization illustrate is that, while the system seems to keep running, it is not running smoothly; it depends on crisis and ruptures to keep running while producing forms of violent exclusion and exploitation, often in the guise of "free choice." In the context of economic neoliberalization, alternative cultures and subcultures could easily and quickly be appropriated into commercial subcultures and even enter certain niches of an increasingly diverse commercialized mainstream. Large corporations incorporate subcultural movements in order to sell their products as "cool" and "hip," forging what Florida (2002) terms "the creative class" in their wake: crisis-chic is marketable. In turn, subcultural movements appropriated logos of corporations (as can be seen, for example, in the *Adbusters* campaigns), sometimes by playfully undermining them. Digital protest performance art can be described neither as capitalist nor as anti-capitalist, as neoliberal nor as anti-neoliberal. Our examples show once again that there is no "outside" of capitalism in a global neoliberal economy since neoliberal economies not only produce but, in fact, need crises; they often rely on their contestation to move forward. Protest movements, then, function similarly in that they – sometimes consciously or self-consciously so – use neoliberal tools to critique these very tools. This circularity that describes activism under neoliberalism does not mean that nothing can happen politically. But moments of change that could possibly challenge violence and exclusion inherent in such neoliberal structures are difficult to locate since they can pop up in multiple locations, appear uncoordinated and multi-directional, and are often messy in their effects and possible interpretations. The position of the "activist" in neoliberalism is similarly messy.

In *Ambiguities of Activism: Alter-Globalism and the Imperatives of Speed*, Ingrid M. Hoofd describes the tension in contemporary neoliberalism created by a certain expectation. towards productive citizens that ensures the system works well, economically, politically, and socially. She relates this discussion to questions of speed and notions of progress in the neoliberal economy as they intersect with political activism and political agency in general. Hoofd (2012, 7) traces the origins of the term "activism" in its reference to production and agitation to look more specifically to contemporary neoliberalism, for these terms "employ a valorization of productivity and progress." She continues: "As such, individuals and groups are increasingly called upon to 'subjectivise' themselves and to 'take action' under neo-liberalism, showing its intricate ties to liberal and humanist ideas of 'freedom.' Under an activist regime, then … the citizen-subject is *compelled* to be active, creative, and free" (ibid., emphasis in original). The relationship between neoliberalism, humanism, and creatively driven activism is fraught at best, and highly interconnected. Further, a "romaticisation of activism in turn uncritically accepts and repeats this essentially economistic theory of the subject and its technologies" (8). The participation in activism in an unreflective manner, therefore, circuitously drives the individualization and subjectivization of neoliberal societies forward. Hoofd applies this idea of taking action and progress to the speed and reach of technology in a digital age, where technologies may exacerbate this tension or inherent problematic of the neoliberal impulse at the base of activism. Activism thus feeds into the "techno-logical production of a new global elite that runs across markers of gender, race, and geographical location: the speed-elite" (11). As a sub-culture co-opted by this elite, feminist activist cultures also offer access to the speed and reach of the actions of such elite. Speaking specifically of the alter-globalism movement, Hoofd writes: "The conundrum of our responsibility resides hence exactly in the fact that alter-globalist activism on the one hand propagates new technologies and discourses of speed, while on the other must condemn the oppressive powers that these technologies and discourses are part of" (109). Here, she in effect describes the circularity of the activist moments outlined in the preced-ing chapters in that these, too, are part of those power structures they wish to undermine. At the same time, her assessment offers us a way to describe and theorize their circulations, such as those of SlutWalk or Pussy Riot activism, which counts on a certain neoliberal "speed" of dissemination of images and messages, on Western ideals of out-spoken and active citizens, and on the spectacle as part of consumable art. Nonetheless, there are moments in these activisms – for example, in the case of Pussy Riot, their original performances, their trials, their afterlife, as well as any creative references to their political struggles such as the Peaches video (with which *Awkward Politics* begins) – that clearly speak truth to power and condemn oppression and technologies of control and surveillance.

The organization of SlutWalks also illustrates these tensions. While they clearly borrow forms from previous feminist and political orga-nizing – the street protest – they also make use of new and globally disseminated technological forms that facilitate the speed with which such messages can be distributed – for example, by utilizing Facebook as a means of organizing locally and continuing discussions beyond the street, as evidenced by Emily Nussbaum's (2011) discussion of the 2011 New York SlutWalk in *New York Magazine*: "Even as we march, it is being tweeted and filmed and Tumblr'd, a way of alerting the press and a way of bypassing the press. I am surrounded by the same blog-gers I've been reading for weeks" (also quoted in Sadowski, 2015, 5). Further, SlutWalk's activism relies on concepts of political autonomy and individual freedom while, at the same time, voicing a critique of capitalist appropriations of the female body and sexuality as com-modity. The attempts to appropriate the term "slut" and to, in some cases, stage a protest that would certainly attract media attention and guarantee media circulation (albeit often circulations out of context and control of the protesters) are at the heart of this protest. Their first main goal (enabling women to freely and safely express their sexuality) is also quite compatible with neoliberal ideology, while their second main goal (to fight – and end – sexual violence) has defined feminist movements since the second wave. Controversies triggered by the Slut-Walks, mainly in the German context, emphasized that the protesters were mainly white, middle-class, cisgendered women (and some men) and that minorities and other marginalized groups who are often the targets of this kind of sexual violence were under- or not represented (Baer 2015b). Such claims illustrate not only that at least parts of the protest miss the main political issue that they are trying to address but also that the discourses around and the images from the protests force the spotlight onto these complex intersectional politics. The sustaining fantasy here is that free expression of sexuality is a goal for everyone, while in reality such free expression is often the luxury of only some – the people who have access to safe spaces, who conform to certain social norms, and who do not ask for too much. While not in itself politically awkward, such questions around the SlutWalks, and even aspects of the ensuing controversies, introduce awkwardness into the discourse, an awkwardness that disrupts and disturbs the sustaining fantasy that underlies this activism.

The fleeting digital platforms and forms; the street protests, news media, and TV reporting that they trigger; and the way in which such action and reporting, in turn, circles back to the digital platforms, describes the complexity of cultural and political circulations in a neoliberal economy. While neoliberal capitalism often appears to be a driving force behind the circulations, it is difficult to describe who, if anybody, profits from these movements directly. Profit is meant here both politically and economically; but, in either case, activists, media franchises, corporations, and/or governments are subjected to critique that then, again, becomes part of the digital circulation. The result is an at times confusing collision of digital imagery. A Google search for Slut-Walks, for example, generates x-rated image results together with websites describing the political organization of SlutWalks; images range from the pornographic to those showing political protest, high-resolution commercial images to DIY porn, and snap shots from SlutWalk demonstrations around the globe.

Steyerl (2009) describes the process of – in her example "poor" or low-resolution – image circulations in the digital age as

> both a platform for a fragile new common interest and a battle-ground for commercial and national agendas. They contain exper-imental and artistic material, but also incredible amounts of porn and paranoia. While the territory of poor images allows access to excluded imagery, it is also permeated by the most advanced com-modification techniques. While it enables the users' active participa-tion in the creation and distribution of content, it also drafts them into production. Users become the editors, critics, translators, and (co-)authors of poor images.

What Steyerl describes is a different way of reading the transitional and transient content in digital circulations. The poor image, as it circulates, stands for the potential of an awkward affective move in a different direction and away from (cruel) attachments of the neoliberal econ-omy to, possibly, new forms of political life. This process of moving in different or multiple directions, so we argue, does not exist outside of market capitalism, but it might nonetheless, and possibly always only for a brief moment, "save us from the greed of free-market economies" (Halberstam 2012, 137) by playfully and sneakily evading this greed. Steyerl describes these moments as possibly disruptive: "The circula-tion of poor images feeds into both capitalist media assembly lines and alternative audiovisual economies. In addition to a lot of confusion and stupefaction, it also possibly creates disruptive movements of thought and affect." It is not clear where such moments might lead, or if, in fact, they will – or should – lead anywhere. By mining for and attempting to describe these flows of images, bodies, and affects, we might, however, help to intensify such disruptive movements. As the case of SlutWalks shows, popfeminist activism awkwardly attaches itself to neolib-eral flows by highlighting some of the most confusing and precarious moments of these neoliberal attachments. Other circulations in and out of local, national, and global contexts, such as those of Pussy Riot, also produce awkward moments of disruption, moments where the images do not seem to fit or where they suddenly seem to fit all too well. Activ-ists may seem out of place or they effortlessly pass in their new envi-ronment, even though they sought to disrupt. In any case, their political messages continuously push – or are pushed – into new realms.

POPFEMINISM, CO-OPTION,
AND TECHNOCULTURAL DEBATES

Tracing patterns of dissemination and circulation of activist forms and contents, therefore, is not simply an intellectual exercise or a project of documentation but, in the context of our discussions, something that seeks to uncover complex structures of political agency and change in the twenty-first century. Since the economic crisis, the increasing speed and reach of activist cultures reveals some of the tensions that underlie these neoliberal economic structures. Political activism always, and in some cases consciously so, takes place within this complex set of tensions that defines the current global and neoliberal moment. As we have explored in the examples so far, in the digital realm, long outdated notions of normative behaviours, racialized oppressions, and gendered expectations persist. In some cases they become overly exposed and in others they become blurry, but they rear their heads in uncomfortable ways. In this context, Halberstam (2012, 16) wonders:

> As we go from analog to digital, from local to global, from proximity to virtuality, from community to social network, how is it that we can shift and alter our perceptions of so many of the building blocks of social life but we still cling to practically nineteenth-century notions of the intimate, the domestic, and the private?

Here, Halberstam tries to describe the complex relationship between perception, technology, and social reality. Despite technological advances, traditional social forms and ideas seem to persist, especially when it comes to intimate relationships. This is particularly true for feminism, considering the long-standing emphasis on the "private is political" in the various iterations of past feminisms. Halberstam seems to imply that one might falsely assume that technological progress, virtuality, and the digital dissolve old notions of community and local identifications and lead to something that is inherently more politically progressive. Local proximities and analogue communities, however, seem to happily (or less so) coexist with the digital or even, in some cases, appear to be enabled and solidified by digital networks. All the while, these alterations created communities in their wake. Halberstam's quote clearly voices the desire for a political shift in how we live and think intimate relationships, which is enabled by digital global networking and connection. That such a shift can be enacted, even becoming central to the activist performance, is well illustrated, for example, in the creation and dissemination of the Peaches video referenced at the outset of our book. Itself spurred on by an event that went from the analogue (Pussy Riot's protest event in the cathedral) to the digital (the video of said protest), Peaches's video began in the digital (disseminated call), turned to the analogue (performances in the street and private spaces of participants), and back to the digital (video, posted on You-Tube). Further, when the content of the video itself is examined more closely, the private performances in particular contain moments of intimacy through close physical proximity that are akin to those described by Halberstam. In these moments, the circular references to Pussy Riot contained in the colourful pop bodies of the performers are broken through in an awkward motion towards the viewer of the video, pushing that same viewer back and pulling her/him in at once, causing the viewer to experience a keen sense of belonging, not only her/his own (joining the outcry "Free Pussy Riot") but also those of the unnamed people who sent in their footage.

Berlant devotes the final chapter of *Cruel Optimisms* to "the desire for the political." Her assessment of the relationship between the digital and the intimate or personal starts with a seemingly more positive assertion – namely, that digital communities offer a sense of support whereby "any person can contribute to an intimate public a personal story about not being defeated by what is overwhelming" (Berlant 2011b, 226–7). Maybe even more importantly, participants in online communities, and in other mediated forms, can imagine themselves as part of a group, as belonging, even when they are only "lurking" rather than actively sharing their personal stories. Online communities can also – and some of our examples (most clearly Lady Bitch Ray) show this – be a space to define oneself negatively and aggressively against a certain movement. So-called "uncivil," highly emotionally charged, and offensive comments, including trolling, are rampant in responses to some of the performances we are discussing here. This, in Berlant's reading, new form of belonging (or, we might add, new form of communal disassociation) does not mean that these modes of political community building exist outside of what she calls "the system;" rather, they "confirm our attachment to the system and thereby confirm the system and the legitimacy of the affects that make one feel bound to it, even if the manifest content of the binding has the negative force of cynicism or the dark attenuation of political depression" (227). The system, in Berlant's understanding, refers to economic neoliberalism and the cruelly optimistic attachments that such neoliberalism fosters and thrives on, but it also references classic civic democracy, which upholds these structures due to the creation of a fantasy of political agency (reading a newspaper, listening to televised debates, voting), thereby confirming a deeply held belief that politics "work."

Towards the end of her book, Berlant (2011b, 261) imagines a political sphere that might move beyond or outside the cruel optimism of the "neoliberal present" by describing this current political moment as one of transition "between different animating, sustaining fantasies." She envisions a process in which sovereignty is reinvented "between crisis and response" in a digital space where people click, post, and send e-mails in some cases rather than – but in other cases in addition to and in yet others in order to – attend political demonstrations. She describes "the model of anarchist/DIY performances" – the model that is the subject of this book – as aiming to revitalize political action "not first by mapping out the better good life but by valuing political action as the action of not being worn out by politics" (261–2). These politically driven performances see "messes as ordinary, vitalizing, interesting, absorbing, personal, playful, and curious" (262). Such "new politics" are part of a moment of transition where new political forms of action have not yet been, but are *being*, invented. These new political forms are "in the middle of detaching from the fantasy of the good life" – cruel optimism – and aim to "produce some better ways of mediating the sense of [this] historical moment … so that it would be possible to imagine a potentialized present that does not reproduce all of the conventional collateral damage" (263). In our reading of Berlant, such potential could be understood as a sense of political agency that does not get caught in mechanisms that produce images of a promised better life that can never be attained but that, instead, fully embraces the messiness of the present instability. It would be false to assume that digital technologies *are* the enablers of this potential, but they do play a crucial role in formulating the process.

This process is awkward and circular, it is digital and includes a disavowal of the digital; the image is blurry and overly precise, everpresent and hidden. The voices of the performers, their bodies, and their agency are present and absent at the same time in digital circulations. They appear and disappear. This process produces a feminist awkwardness that is politically productive not because it decidedly incites political discourse or challenges social conventions in general but because it unsettles and disrupts any such fantasies of the good life.

Berlant's perspective on digital activism mixed with DIY strategies appears more positive, even optimistic, than what Halberstam describes when he assesses the possibility for "intimate" change in a socially networked and technologically interconnected world. In this context, it is important to consider that online communities not only create attachments and spaces for stories to be shared: they also create negative affective attachments by being often excessively verbally and visually aggressive and divisive. The spaces where we locate moments of transition are then not found only on the level of the content of one or the other "kind" of digital community but also in awkward movements within them and between or among them. Digital spaces are not static; they change, appear and disappear (or appear hidden), and discourses can be shut down or moved to a different platform. In these circulations, power is at play in sometimes ubiquitous yet veiled ways. The process of detaching from the fantasy of the good life and the search for new forms of political action that mirror a political present takes place within this messy push and pull between old forms and fantasies, and new images and processes. The struggle to communicate a political presence is essential.

Our discussions of this process in digital circulations are part of what scholars have termed "technocultural debates." Pham describes three different camps in these debates: first, the "techno-enthusiasts," who "view the widespread access to these new technologies as democratic"; second, those who stress the danger of technology as possibly eroding the "quality of public discourse"; and third, those who hold a "more nuanced" perspective, arguing that, "while ostensibly anyone (with a computer and a high-speed broadband connection) has access to these technologies, the very structure of networking systems, including the logics within which data is produced and by which it is distributed and made available in Web searches, is fundamentally antidemocratic" (Pham 2011, 2). The fact that the structure of technology is fundamentally anti-democratic and that technologies "operate within admittedly restrictive and inequitable conditions" (2) does not mean, however, that there is no room for political critique. As Pham points out, "cultural and social practices, especially those that enlist and produce racial, gender, class, and sexual subjects, have always been enacted under restrictive and oppressive conditions" (ibid.). Again, the question is not whether these forms are free of restrictions or are restrictive but, rather, how and where they are and to whom (much like the borders determining geopolitical restrictions). Sometimes, the restrictiveness of digital spaces becomes the very centre of digital projects and their main point of political critique. Digital surveillance and digital subversion, targeted advertisement and hacking, all arguably take place in the "same" digital spaces. Further, in the process of technocultural dissemination and proliferation, new and sometimes unexpected forms and associations emerge, even if only for a brief moment.

Steyerl (2009) describes the complexity of this process that enables appropriations – and, we might add, levels of "inappropriateness":

> Privatization of media production gradually grew more impor-
> tant than state controlled/sponsored media production. But, on the
> other hand, the rampant privatization of intellectual content, along
> with online marketing and commodification, also enable piracy and
> appropriation; it gives rise to the circulation of poor images.

This process also enables inappropriateness and impropriety, and a frantic competition over the control of digital spaces and consumer-based distribution of images. The poor image always stands in relation to the high-resolution, glossy image ready for consumption and ready to trigger targeted sales. These complexities again illustrate that, in order to locate political moments in digital technologies, we have to closely analyze these new forms of communication in context since they do not exist in a fixed form or clear location. They are on the move, in evolution, in transition, and always only exist in interaction with other forms. The reason "the digital" – or "the technocultural" – is so hard to define is that it is always part of a relation or part of a process. This is especially clear when digital events presume direct political and feminist involvement in body politics or in political or sexual violence.

The 2013 #aufschrei campaign in Germany (see chapter 2), for example, which aimed to protest sexual violence committed against women, shows this direct – and certainly awkward – connection between protests against physically experienced violence, digital activism, street activism, the political establishment, and global proliferation.[8] The digital enables a new kind of engagement with violence and body politics through not *dis*embodied but, instead, digitally embodied performances that allow for potentially endless repetition. The campaign made visible (digitally visible at least) the prominence of sexual abuse and sexist violence in women's lives. The many tweets of women as victims of such violence attempted to create a sense of solidarity and empowerment in order to enable them to fight back. At the same time, such an open platform allows for discursive interventions and comments that, yet again, turn a campaign like this on its head: images and stories of abused and victimized women, clichés of exaggerations, accusations of prudishness and of stifling political correctness, and perpetuations of racialized and classist stereotypes can run rampant in such public and open displays (see Tuczu 2015; Weber 2015b).[9]

When, in *Gender Trouble*, Butler describes the process of critical performative repetition as political intervention, she does not have the digital in mind. In the digital realm, gender is certainly revealed as "an 'act,' as it were, that is open to splittings, self-parody, self-criticism, and those hyperbolic exhibitions of 'the natural' that, in their very exaggerations, reveal its fundamentally phantasmatic status" (Butler 1990, 146–7). Such digital proliferations and exaggerations add a new level to the performative that has the potential to boost Butler's critical discussion of exaggeration, parody, and deconstruction, but they complicate the question of political agency, political and economic voice, and power.[10] Many examples of digital activism, whether strategic or nonstrategic, are not self-consciously performative and insist on non-ironic positions of agency and approaches to authentic voice. Digital activism and its circulations add intensity to Butler's claim that the task was "not whether to repeat but how to repeat or, indeed, to repeat and, through radical proliferation of gender, to *displace* the very gender norms that enable the repetition itself" (148, emphasis in original). While displacements certainly happen at a previously unimaginable speed, images and arguments are also replaced, manipulated, and put back into their places – and maybe "co-opted" – at a new speed. Digital campaigns often produce counter-campaigns that work with the same images, or even hashtags, to subvert the original message. This, yet again, illustrates that performativity as a politics in the digital age is not a matter of ironic provocation via a distancing from the body but, instead, one of emphasizing – and thus making awkward – the close affective relationship between the digital projection and the physical body.

An example from the German context that intended such political subversion is the German anti-quota campaign, mentioned briefly in chapter 1, that mirrored such social-network-based campaigns as "I am a feminist because" or "this is what a feminist looks like," in which people took photographs of themselves holding signs telling of their personal relationship to feminism. The anti-feminist campaign, which was launched by the German neoconservative party Junge Alternative für Deutschland (Young alternative for Germany) to voice its opposition to the institution of quotas for large businesses, replicated the visuals of the original campaigns; however, instead of displaying people holding signs in support of feminist politics, its signs read "I am not a feminist because every woman can decide for herself if she wants to be a housewife," "I am not a feminist because I want to read my goals through my own achievements and not through a quota," and "I am not a feminist because equality for women has been realized – it is now up to women themselves to make something of themselves."[11] These words clearly display the neoliberal logic of individual choice. The close relationship between the two campaigns is awkward in that one relies on the other to get its message across, thereby destabilizing the effectivity of both, leaving the visuals to act, instead, as the cipher. While performative in its initial form, the body and its signage in both the first campaign and its derivative are highly affectively charged and do not suggest ironic distancing. The co-option of the "I am a feminist" aesthetics by the counter-protest, instead, enhances the visibility of both campaigns without voiding the political meaning of either: the controversy adds affect and urgency to both.

Halberstam (2012, 135) uses the term "co-option" in his "Gaga Manifesto" to critique Slavoj Žižek's reading of the London Riots. He accuses Žižek of being one of the co-opters "in that he always anticipates co-option and even helps it along" (ibid.). In Halberstam's assessment, the London riots are "anticolonial and anticapitalist movements" with an unclear outcome: "All we know for sure," he writes, "is that the protests signal and announce a collective awareness of the end of 'normal life'" (ibid.). "Co-option" – or appropriation – is always part of the calculation when "pop" is combined with any kind of political activist position and, in a further step, when pop-activism goes or is digital. Halberstam is certainly correct in his assessment of Žižek: as a digital pop-philosopher, Žižek uses these very same strategies – including awkwardness – albeit with different impulses and resonances than do popfeminist activisms. As our examples of Chicks on Speed and Lady Bitch Ray illustrate, appropriation of the inappropriate is always anticipated. In order to infuse this project with the political, however, a lingering threat of "the end of 'the normal life,'" as Halberstam describes it, which can infiltrate these co-options, must be part of the project. In the case of popfeminist activisms, we describe these "threats" as disruptive moments.

Performative or performance-based popfeminist activism, such as Chicks on Speed or Lady Bitch Ray, works differently than do digital feminist campaigns like #aufschrei in that they do not just use digital proliferation but, rather, "co-opt" it by participating in, anticipating, and then tracing the process of digital proliferation. Similar in strategy to our popfeminist readings, whereby we read for disruption and connection in pop and feminism, activisms themselves mess with and reveal the mechanisms with which content is produced, disseminated, and reproduced in new contexts. To co-opt certain images, as, for example, certain porn-parody-images of Lady Bitch Ray, is part of a game with hyper-visibility and disguise. Co-option can proliferate and hybridize images to the extent that they lose their (intended) meaning. At the same time, they can remain dangerously close to the images they attempt to critique. This has become clear in our discussion of Lady Bitch Ray's pop-porn imagery. One might think here, for example, of the way in which her poses and costumes reference displays of the female body in soft-porn magazines and, added to that, seem to confirm the often rather sexual comments that frequently appear under her postings. The fact that Lady Bitch Ray designs her costumes herself and includes constant references to herself or to the vagina and female pleasure, however, subverts the core message of a magazine like *Playboy*, which exists for the pleasure of heterosexual men. The question of whether her work then truly promotes or undermines male-driven pornographic imagery cannot and does not need to be answered. Lady Bitch Ray does not critique, she appropriates; Lady Bitch Ray does not provoke, she disturbs. Her prolific images create a sense of hyper-visibility and the "real" Lady Bitch Ray appears as the agent behind these images even as she disappears as subject of them. Her own objectification makes her subjectivity hyper- and in-visible, overly vulnerable, and invincible. Similar to what Michael Connor (2013), in his editorial on Steyerl, asserts, Lady Bitch Ray's activism shows that, "although the aspiration to be invisible and the aspiration to hybridize through image proliferation seem to be incompatible, they are closely linked."

As protest events move geographically and as images circulate into hyper-visibility and in and out of context and meaning, the "feminist" and the "pop" in our objects of study are also on the move, in and out of the digital realm and into different realms of political realities, social realities, and intimacies. "Movement" in popfeminist digital protest events refers to directed action in moments of transition – that is, to political activist movements, geographic movements, and movements between cultural forms. As Berlant suggests, by describing these digital movements, we are describing a space not only of, but also in transition, not just on the level of technology, but also in form, content, and intent. Similarly, feminism in the twenty-first century, and specifically popfeminism, is defined as an intersectional relation between feminism and (popular) culture as well as, for example, among pop, racial, and body politics. This means that there is interplay between digital and non-digital forms and between different spheres of political protest and intervention. By relying on affect and images of bodies, digital protests are closely linked to (affective) physicality, and physicality is closely linked to image, representation, and to gender *as* representation. The fear that something might slip "out of order" triggers at least as "loud" – or willful – a digital response in the number of clicks and shares as it goes viral, as does the attempt to disrupt social norms and conventions that are deemed oppressive or exclusive. Rather than being puzzled, as Halberstam describes, by the fact that nineteenth-century notions have not dissolved in the shift to the digital, we might be puzzled by the awkward relationship between social convention, social change, and technological innovation. Popfeminist activisms operate within and with the clear knowledge of these puzzling relations. Through circulations and proliferations in tension with acts of disappearance, popfeminist activism makes relationships between gendered and racialized bodies, and history and social norms, awkward. Rather than pursuing a political goal, it is precisely this "making awkward" that allows these forms of political intervention to escape from being easily appropriated into the logics – and crises – of neoliberal capitalism. Their awkwardness makes them inappropriate.

PUSSY RIOT CIRCULATIONS

The example of Pussy Riot with which we start this book and this chapter is particularly productive due to its complicated circulations, media responses, and viral disseminations. What began as a local performance protest group in Moscow, Russia, triggered global cries for solidarity and for a new attitude associated with feminist protest. Through the imprisonment of particularly two of the group's members and their subsequent release, their performance in New York City at a concert in support of Amnesty International, and their protest at the Russian Olympics in Sochi in 2014, the political impact of the group and of what the public associates with "Pussy Riot" shifted as well. What in its intention and effect started as a highly political and provocative protest movement against Putin and his policies in Russia turned into an icon of global feminist protest and outrage and then merged into the campaign of (mainly) two global human rights activists on international stages.[12] From the "stage" in front of the altar at the Cathedral of Christ in Moscow (February 2012) to the stage with Madonna in New

4.1   Alyokhina, Tolokonnikova, and activists at a press conference at the
Winter Olympics in Sochi (Russia), 2014

York (2014) or with Judith Butler and Rosi Braidotti at the First Supper
Symposium in Oslo (2014), to the screen with Kevin Spacey in *House
of Cards* (2015) and the stage at Glastonbury (2015), Pussy Riot, or
their image, have certainly circulated in and out of new spaces.

The reception of Pussy Riot in Russia differs greatly from their
reception in the Western context.[13] In a position paper of sorts, Marina
Yusupova (2014, 604) states: "The Pussy Riot story was a story the
West wanted to hear. Western journalists, politicians, and celebrities
seemed to be unanimously inspired by the youthfulness and rebellion
of these courageous Russian feminists." A reason for the fact that a
broad majority of Russians, not just right-wing conservative and religious people, did not respond positively to Pussy Riot's act of political
protest is, according to Yusupova, that Pussy Riot is steeped in Western feminist theory not well known in Russia and that "has been lost
in translation" (607). This loss of political meaning starts with the English name of the group but extends to the fact that, according to Yusupova, the concept of "feminism" itself does not mean much to many
people in Russia – a claim for which she does not provide further support. She concludes by making an appeal for a Russian feminism that
takes local context into account and encourages Russians to speak in

their own language (609).[14] Interestingly, at the podium discussion with Braidotti and Butler, the very question of Russian feminism as having a long, albeit rather specific, history comes up as well. After the introduction of the panellists, the conversation focuses on the history of Russian feminism and, mainly, the legacies of state-mandated gender "equality" in the Soviet Union. Alyokhina then brings the conversation back to the contemporary by claiming that every generation has to develop its own feminism based on its particular situation, for which she garners applause from the audience and Butler. The discussion, however, continues to present Russia as a country that has "catching up" to do when it comes to feminism, which stands in awkward tension with the fact that the cutting-edge work of Pussy Riot themselves comes out of precisely this Russian context.[15] The attempts to place Pussy Riot within this Russian tradition illustrate the tension between national histories and contemporary, transnational circulations, which makes for an awkward fit. Negotiating this awkward fit, Yulia Gradskova (2013), in "Pussy Riot: Reflections and Perceptions," presents a complicated history of Russian feminism, the historic relationship between the state and the Orthodox Church, and conceptions of motherhood in contemporary Russia. Gradskova, however, concludes by praising Pussy Riot for making issues visible and for the continuing challenge they pose to the institutions of, for example, media, law, and the church.[16]

In response to this perspective, which focuses on the Russian context, one might argue that the very aim of Pussy Riot was to attract global attention to a national issue rather than to form a broad movement within Russia. Using digital platforms, like the dissemination of their video "A Punk Prayer" on YouTube, allowed for such global circulations and for a – mainly enthusiastic – Western response. The point of tension is the fact that their protest gesture, often understood at first as a gesture directed against Putin's patriarchy, was so easily incorporated into a Western master narrative of progress against a backwards "East," which then, in turn, fuelled a public reaction in Russia and on the part of Russian authorities that framed this activism as Western imperialism. Further, as Kendzior (2012) contends, one could argue that Western media completely misunderstood the actions of Pussy Riot "by focusing excessively on physical appearance and nostalgic notions of youthful 'punk' individualism." Such an anti-feminist and nostalgic reading of Pussy Riot in Western media resonates with the actions and media appearances of Pussy Riot as they both embrace and deconstruct such prolific imagery of the beautiful, defiant, and punkishly rebellious Russian "girls."

When, as a response to the "Punk Prayer" performance, Putin first jailed and then – in a publicity campaign that portrays Russia as respecting human rights prior to the 2014 Winter Olympics – pardoned the members of the group, it might be suspected that, in spite of all the political protest they triggered, Pussy Riot were and became (at least for a moment) a Russian instrument for manipulating the power of representations. After their release, however, Pussy Riot's art and music performances shifted towards activism against prison conditions and prisoner abuse, and against more general human rights violations. This visually much differently coded activism against prison conditions and abuse was only briefly interrupted by the protest at the Olympic games in Sochi. At this protest, security officers whipped members of the group as they were trying to perform.[17] The aim of this protest was less clearly defined than were those of previous performances, and it was the first protest event after their prison release that produced a new version of all too familiar images. Somehow, these images are awkward not just because of the flogging but also because they are so much like the images created in the punk prayer performance and so different from the new image of Pussy Riot as activists against prison conditions. Again, a video of this whipping was available immediately on YouTube. Simultaneously, in an open letter, other anonymous members of the group stated that the two now famous members of the group, Alyokhina and Tolokonnikova, were no longer part of Pussy Riot since they did not act according to the initial goals of the Pussy Riot movement, which include collective action and anonymity.[18] In 2015, the group of activists who claim to continue their work in the "true" spirit of Pussy Riot produced a video, published on YouTube in May (with forty-six hundred views by August 2015), that comments on the split between the actions of Pussy Riot and the media commercialization of Alyokhina and Tolokonnikova, which goes against the anti-capitalist and anti-commercial politics of Pussy Riot.[19] On YouTube, the video is described as a "series of unsanctioned performances"[20] of their new song "Aktsiia! Aktsiia! Pussy Riot Liquidation! Pussy Riot is dead." The performances were held between December 2014 and May 2015 in supermarkets and restaurants around Moscow. The Russian word "Aktsiia" means "sales," "promotion," or "special offer" while, at the same time, evoking the English "action" as well as possibly "shares" or "stocks." The lyrics emphasize the commercialization of art as well as the sexualization and exploitation of the female body in media imagery, the latter offering the most explicit critique of Alyokhina and Tolokonnikova *not* as individuals but, rather, as being swept up by the system. The chorus's taglines change after each verse, but the first one reads:

> Aktsiia! Aktsiia! Success and adaptation!
> Aktsiia! Aktsiia! Commercialization!
> Aktsiia! Aktsiia! Art-capitulation!
> Aktsiia! Aktsiia! Exploitation of you!

In the following verses, they explicitly turn to a critique of the nation/ "the fatherland" as corrupt and militaristic. They emphasize that their attempts to seek confrontation will continue, reference the infamous German left-wing terrorists of the Baader-Meinhof group (which was active in the 1970s), and, in the final line, call for Putin's "castration." The imagery, again, is recognizable as Pussy Riot – claimed by the "real" Pussy Riot – as three activists first perform in a shopping centre, where they dance on the conveyer belts at the check-out and then on the bar at a branch of Kentucky Fried Chicken in what looks like a mall food court. As they perform in front of signs for Western-style consumerism, most noticeably represented by the lit sign of the US fast food chain, they rip apart glossy cover images of pop and music magazines featuring Pussy Riot that they had pinned to their masks (such as the cover of *Rolling Stone* magazine). Rather than revealing naked faces, the ripping of the glossy images reveals covered and anonymous faces. The performers throw the pieces of paper and later what looks like (possibly dollar) bills into the watching crowd. During the action, their gestures and their dance moves are aggressive and their music mimics the improv-punk style of earlier Pussy Riot actions. While a crowd is filmed watching rather suspiciously during the performance, towards the end, the video also shows mall security talking on cell phones. A clear statement against media co-option and the commercialization of Pussy Riot's own image, this action did not get much attention in the Western media. The claim that Pussy Riot is represented by an anonymous collective of activists rather than the two famous former members of said collective is an attempt to regain control of viral and commercialized imagery while using the very recognisability of said imagery. These performances try to make the circulation of Pussy Riot imagery politically productive for continued radical protests against a patriarchal, corrupt, and sexist public. By remaining invisible as individuals, though, a key aspect of the political charge of this protest against the current circulations of Pussy Riot is a form of disguise. In this protest, further, we see a twist to pop-feminist circularity: much like Lady Bitch Ray's feminist reformulation of her own image as pop, the "real" Pussy Riot here engages in a feminist rewriting of the pop image of Pussy Riot in the West.

Regardless, media and the general public understood the protests at Sochi and all other media appearances, performances, and press conferences by Alyokhina and Tolokonnikova as actions of Pussy Riot, and their videos of the Sochi whipping certainly circulated globally as precisely that. Their brightly coloured balaclavas are now a "brand," meaning that simply alluding to them is seen as a statement of solidarity and certainly wearing them during a protest would signify that one is somehow "part" of Pussy Riot, a form of belonging forged by wide circulation and consumption. The most obvious tensions that emerge here are forged between nationally specific political protests and global appropriations, between an anti-capitalist gesture and global marketing or branding, and between the attempt to conceal the female body and a discourse that is all about female bodies in spaces where they do not belong, as victims behind bars, and as activists on a global stage. Most importantly, in all contexts, Pussy Riot's actions are depicted in digitally disseminated and manipulated images. What Steyerl (2009) describes with regard to the "poor image" applies to the images of Pussy Riot: their images are "heavily compressed and travel quickly" and "they lose matter and gain speed." Some images only lose some matter while gaining other, and their increased tempo might stutter with faltering and halting movements.

In these travels and circulations both digital and physical, aspects of the group's initial protests get lost or left behind (in Russia) and other aspects are added, mixed, and re-mixed. German and Western discourses use the example of Putin's oppressive rule to place (and displace) patriarchy onto the Russian and Eastern other, which is a well established and, in the German context, national(ist), cliché.[21] Eastern Europe and Russia become the racist and sexist other, where misogyny, discrimination against homosexuals, and neo-Nazism run rampant. The way in which this image surfaces in mainstream German press is not disruptive in any political way: the disruptions of Pussy Riot are tamed by framing them within a political context in which Putin and Russia once again, especially after the annexation of Crimea, appear as the political other to and for the Western world. Hanna Heinrich and Jacqueline Segschneider (2013), in *Pop-Zeitschrift*, conclude:

Made harmless by the media – they are often described as "girls," and not as "women" or "punk girls" – they offer themselves as foils for projections and figures of identification for people of very different political and social backgrounds. The bourgeoisie looks at them as an example of civil disobedience and the more radical left sees them as resistance fighters. Their media consumption serves a broad spectrum of Western recipients to offer them a moment of identification that does not threaten their own picture of themselves and the world. Their critical position vis-à-vis the Kremlin is also predestined for the Western press to scandalize the story about the "girls" who critique Putin and the Russian state loudly and were imprisoned for that action.[22]

This potential, which was certainly used to its fullest for political appropriation, does not mean that Pussy Riot have become void of politically disruptive power. It is precisely because of the speed in which images and ideas circulate, disseminate, and shift that new forms of and spaces for interventions open up. Heinrich and Segschneider caution that, "as long as [Pussy Riot's] political potential is not seriously analyzed in the context of performance art, they will be used in the mediated struggles over diverse political interests and can enter the mainstream discourse without posing a threat."[23] Our reading suggests that, on the contrary, it is this mediated struggle among different political interests that "events" like Pussy Riot and their circulations trigger and within which moments of friction, and maybe even "threat," appear. The circulations and shifts in their activisms question the contexts in which they emerge and the contexts – such as performance art, patriarchy, prison conditions, and human rights – that they use in their protests. For example, Putin's prison camps become a point of comparison for the US prison industrial complex as Pussy Riot tour prisons in the United States, an act that complicates any simple displacement of abuse onto the Eastern or Russian other.

Another example is the way in which their personas have shifted and keep shifting depending on the context of the protest: Pussy Riot's covered faces in their protest performances stand in an awkward tension with the recognizability of their faces following their arrest and during their then highly mediated campaigns. This tension poses questions about women's bodies and activisms, refers back to Femen's naked bodies in opposition to the Muslimah Pride protests, and poses questions about identity, physical integrity, and visibility and agency in protest in general, including the question of what protects Pussy Riot at which moment: their hidden individual identity as part of a globally recognizable protest movement or the global recognizability of their individual faces? Finally, the tension between Pussy Riot's global fame and their nationally specific messages, their global stage and their insistence on being Russian and returning to Russia, illustrate the complex relationship between national identification and belonging and a globalized media presence. These disruptive moments in Pussy Riot circulations are political disturbances that surface in these circulations. But they also illustrate how such activism, as it circulates, produces and contains its own critique.

In 2015, Pussy Riot appeared on an episode of the Netflix series *House of Cards*. This episode features a visit of the Russian president (very obviously modelled after Putin) to the White House. Pussy Riot (in this case, the "real" Pussy Riot – though represented by the two ostracized members – even though everything else in the show is "fake") are invited to the table at the White House dinner with the Russian president and they stage a protest action, which then prompts US president Underwood (played by Kevin Spacey) to also stand up to the Russian president. The Russian president, throughout, is depicted as a sexist misogynist who plays ugly power games, starting with Underwood by lusting after the first lady, Claire Underwood, herself a powerful political player. The entire episode is framed with protest. It starts with a fake protest for gay rights in Russia, and, at the end, the credits roll over images of a Pussy Riot–inspired protest that, due to the inclusion of a punk-style song, resembles a music video. In this final video, everyone pictured is dressed up in Pussy Riot gear except for the "real" Pussy Riot: they are wearing *House of Cards* T-shirts and show their faces. The appearance of Pussy Riot on the show is very styled, stylized, and sexy; the images of the protest at the end of the episode, however, seem modelled after the Peaches video. The difference is, of course, that this is a made-up protest in a Netflix series. Viewers encounter the "real" Pussy Riot in a fictional series that features a fake protest, which, ultimately, is not all that fake since the issues at hand are real political issues (i.e., gay rights in Russia). These awkward relationships make it clear that the appearance of Pussy Riot in *House of Cards* is more than appropriation; when taken together with the other "stages" on which the group – or its two more recognizable representatives – appeared, we can see this as the moment pop and feminism fuse, though awkwardly so, for even here in the commoditized world of pay television, there is a distinct lack of ironic distance. Instead, the utter seriousness of their politics remains, but the political has slipped off screen.

The example of Pussy Riot's circulations shows that, beyond the use of digital media to publicize political content, as the digital "moves," different kinds of political movements intersect with it. These events move in and out of the digital realm and through different realms of culture, such as alternative culture, museum spaces, national mainstream presses, and social networking and file sharing sites. They never leave the digital entirely, but the interaction between traditional forms of representations and digital platforms keeps changing as they "move." Further, events and images move geographically from and to different local and national contexts, and they move financially through different modes of (neoliberal) sources of funding. These movements do not always suggest wider dissemination; sometimes their spheres contract in one sense as they expand in another. When we talk about dissemination and proliferation of events and stories, we have to think about how such scales of reach interact with the complex human, geographic, financial, and digital moves we refer to above. Within global circulations of people, of messages, images, and activist responses, oppressive norms and structures persist; at the same time, new forms of collaboration, of support, and of meaning making appear – with a true sense of political urgency.

THE POLITICS OF (DIGITAL) CIRCULATIONS

Circulations, of course, also include acts of disappearance. Similar to the images and the narratives themselves, the role of the viewer and respondent is an integral part of these circulations and can be an intensely emotional and physical experience. In fast shifts from theory to action, from pop to politics, from fictional narratives to experience, from high-res to low-res, from Sochi to Netflix, blurry and pixelated images require the readers' direct, affective, and physical engagement. Steyerl illustrates this complex set of relations in her art. Reading the poor and blurry image is an awkward process: we might be squinting, zooming in, as we are still trying to identify an image to make an attempt to read it according to our preconceived notions. Even as we are unable to read it, we stick to the idea of the image as a stable thing to be received, as something that communicates through representation. In digital space, images appear in different contexts, and appear and disappear on image searches based on algorithms. In her recent works, Steyerl attempts to expose the politics of images. She reveals how reading images is contextual and layered, and how the image itself is a fickle product of technology and of our imagination, at times foregoing representing any "thing" altogether. We tend to fill in the blanks as images start to disappear for, just as much as it can make things appear, technology can make things disappear.

In her installation video "How Not to Be Seen: A Fucking Didactic Educational .MOV File," which was produced for the Venice Biennale Exhibition *Il Palazzo Enciclopedico* in 2013,[24] Steyerl reveals these politics. Veiled bodies that resemble women in burkas twirling and dancing are projected over what looks like an abandoned runway or airfield in the desert but, in actuality, is a photo of calibration targets in the California desert, which look like giant pixels in the ground. According to Connor (2013), they were used as a "kind of optometrist's chart for the ancestors of drones." Films of artificial-looking resorts are projected onto a large video screen that appears and disappears; people in green body suits move in and out of view. All along, the pop song ballad, "When Will I See You Again" (by the American Soul group the Three Degrees, 1974) is playing in soft and seemingly slow and distorted notes; sometimes, the singers are projected on the video screen. A film team comes into view as white outlines of people, and almost missing people appear as well. These empty outlines of people seem to cut into the landscape, making parts of it invisible as the (missing) people walk across it, which highlights this landscape as a projection while the "real" (the people crossing the screen) only exists as a void. Notes pop up on the screen that read, "camera crew disappears after invisible energy rays emanate from iPhone" or "pixels hijack camera crane." The film also masquerades as an instructional video on "how to remain invisible in the world of image proliferation" (Connor 2013), and it gives "technical lessons" on how to make things invisible for a camera. As Connor describes it: "After these tactics are outlined, the film crew making this educational video also disappears. In their absence, happy low-resolution pixels take over the production. Digital rendering ghosts dance in the desert landscape ... Silliness ensues." There is no simple political value attached to the act of disappearance. Disappearing is at the same time a defiant act in the face of constant visibility and connectedness, and a threat for and to the political voice of the subject. Acts of disappearance evoke the marginality of voices that have not (yet) been heard or remain silenced by louder voices; images that did and do not circulate; and the wish for silence, evasiveness, and invisibility in a loud and hyper-visible world. The progression of Steyerl's video project, its utterly serious and political message in combination with a playful approach to genres and form and the ultimately "silly" conclusion, mirror our search for a popfeminist methodology. Steyerl's video exposes the trappings of neoliberalism while refusing to fully comply; it creates rifts while implying communication and community.

In his conversation with Steyerl, Connor asked her about the desire to disappear. He recounts: "She pointed out that it is a highly ambivalent concept: it is something to be desired, that gives relief from the constant imaging that we are all subject to. But it is also something to be feared, evoking the spectre of mass political abduction" (Connor 2013). This quote points to the questions that we pose at the outset of this chapter. Circulation and movement are a political desire and a political danger; they create space for subversion and for exploitation. Steyerl's video, her theoretical explorations, and her previous work understand bodies as a technology in the way we define it in our introduction, which inseparably links the material to the socially and technologically constructed. The appearance and disappearance of the body in her work and the conflation and tension between the digital and the physical define the space of politics and of danger or violence – but also of "silliness." Displacement and disappearance are both physical and digital, a fact with which Steyerl wrestles in her work as she tries to address questions of social norms and transformative change. Her work is located precisely where the digitally smooth surface "cracks" open and displays its physicality or where the physical flattens out into the digital. Connor summarizes their conversation about this art installation:

> During our conversation, Steyerl proposed a model for thinking about this, suggesting that the image world is a kind of three dimensional shape that is always shifting, always in flux. The images are all on the surface, and there is no interior, no depths that harbor fundamental truths. Perhaps "lo-res" can be seen as one way of occupying this hi-res image world. Or perhaps the world is not as hi-res as we think.

The fact that Connor uses the term "occupy" in this quote infuses his suggestion with a clear political charge. We have shown that there are various ways in which such occupations illustrate how the digital image (and sound) world remains closely and affectively tied to the material world, how quickly spaces for occupations shift and how movements create a range of political effects. Political depth and maybe, however awkward, moments of "truth," where it becomes clear that this matters, flicker across our screens and are felt on our skins as images and narratives shift, migrate, and circulate.

In our reading, these circulations of Pussy Riot imagery and clips in high and low resolution highlight the process of image production, of social meaning making, and, more generally, of cultural change. Pussy Riot certainly created a new repertoire of visual meaning and also shifted existing images into new realms of meaning. It is not these shifts in and of themselves that produces political spaces for intervention but, rather, the way in which they relate to the social, spaces that are never clearly defined, that open up unexpectedly, or that are filled back up quickly – with often-familiar images. While we cannot argue that the digital realm in general generates less conventional forms of intimate relations, as Halberstam would like to see, we do show that there are moments when such unconventional forms are possible, when they even, however briefly, take over before they, yet again, might become "conventional." SlutWalks, for example, produce moments of a shifting image world and a new social context, in which a "walking slut" means freedom from violence and of sexual expression before the image again submerges in the flood of often-sexist media reporting and Internet porn. Pussy Riot activism creates a shifting world of images of bodies (covered and recognizable), images of local and global systems of violence, and of ideas of political freedom and freedom of expression. This process disturbs and reaffirms certain national(ist), conventional, and gendered notions, and it rewrites what individual freedom might mean. Tellingly, in an interview with Will Dean of the *Guardian* about her performance with Tolokonnikova as Pussy Riot at a festival in Glastonbury in summer 2015, Alyokhina claims that the decision to start a riot (i.e., a protest intervention) is a personal one and that "some of the riots can be inside riots, inside you, rather than going and attacking people." In clear contrast to the collective, anonymous, and very public activism of the initial Pussy Riot performers, in this neoliberally charged statement, one of the most highly visible Pussy Riot members puts the political charge back on the individual and thereby attempts to re-relegate feminism to the private sphere. The spaces that open up are awkward spaces since they are fleeting and often do not produce clear political statements; what they do contain, however, are frictions, disturbances, and tensions. These tensions point back to the central claim with which we began: that popfeminist circulations produce their own critique and that they undermine the evaluative stance with which we are trained to approach political activism. Snapshots of the circulations of Pussy Riot – a call for an "inner riot" by a highly popular and popularized activist such as Alyokhina or the anonymous disturbance of capitalist consumerism and patriarchy in the performances of the song "Aktsiia" – produce circular forms of critique, thereby undermining linear analysis. Rather than attempting to unravel the circular form, we turn to awkwardness as a way to describe these processes and to trace their political impacts, which are, however differently so, highly aestheticized and affectively charged.

5

The Affects of Adolescent Aesthetics: Popfeminism in Film and Literature

> To create awkwardness is to be read as being awkward. Maintaining public comfort requires that certain bodies "go along with it." To refuse to go along with it, to refuse the place to which you are placed, is to be seen as trouble, as causing discomfort for others. There is a political struggle about how we attribute good and bad feelings, which hesitates around the apparently simple question of who introduces what feelings to whom. Feelings can get stuck to certain bodies in the very way we describe spaces, situations, dramas. And bodies can get stuck depending on what feelings they get associated with. (Ahmed 2010, 98–9)

The discussions in the preceding chapters touch on questions of form and on the aesthetics of awkwardness but do not explore awkwardness *as* aesthetics or, more specifically, the affects of awkward aesthetics. When thinking of affect, we might start with the emotional discomfort – or drama – that the term "awkwardness" contains and link these emotional responses to perceptions and aesthetics since both, affect and aesthetics, are intricately tied together as ways to relate to the world that surrounds us. Therefore, and as Ahmed's quote implies, the affective and aesthetic dimensions to awkwardness open our discussion of the politics of popfeminist activism to impact, connection, and resonances. That is, affect and aesthetics matter, for it is under these terms that the awkward politics of popfeminism reach an audience, whether that audience is made up of viewers, consumers, or fellow protestors, or even if, in the most circuitous of terms, the audience becomes the mirror of the performance itself.

Perhaps the term "awkward" is such an appropriate way to address questions of the political because, like its appearance in our examples of popfeminist protest performance art, it is a word that is itself slippery and in motion: it has multiple aesthetic referents and affective charges, including embarrassment, strangeness, discomfort, breakage, humour, adolescence, and mistakes. It is also self-reflexive in that it causes us to feel self-conscious or on display while feeling. Awkwardness as affect is infused with politics of power, perception, and relation (connection and disconnect). In *Political Emotions*, Janet Staiger wonders whether "perhaps we truly encounter the political only when we *feel*" (Staiger, Cvetkovich, and Reynolds 2010, 4), which implies that politics are always also affective. This means that the affective charge of awkwardness implies process and communication that can be politically charged. It is, moreover, a negative (in the sense of critical) emotion that pokes holes in the toxic positivity (Halberstam 2011, 2–3) – or the relations of cruel optimism – of an individualized, hedonistic, and neoliberal feminism and pop-consumer culture.

Popfeminist methodology that actively attempts to grasp the political through an engagement with the awkward in cultural objects, including the ruptures, critiques, and connections awkwardness produces, offers us a way of doing critique differently (Staiger, Cvetkovich, and Reynolds 2010, 6), as we claim in chapter 3. Reading for awkwardness politicizes the object, its reception, and the very nature of the feelings it produces, but it also politicizes the research act itself. Popfeminist methodology, therefore, can be seen as highly relational and steeped in affect, for affect engages not only with emotion but also with the connection between things, subjects, and/or experiences and their impact upon one another. It does so most deliberately through the categories of corporeality and technology. That material bodies and the digital work together as technologies to communicate the place where practice and theory collide makes us sceptical of Berlant's claim that true political action is rare, particularly when seen in terms of participatory digital spaces, such as "liking" something on Facebook or sending an email, for these "continue the old model of citizenship as an event of circulating opinions" (Berlant 2011b, 261). If, however, the aesthetics of DIY activism are to become the "noise of a new politics" (262), as she suggests, and when those DIY cultures rely in their very corporeal material on the digital, this is much more complicated, not least because the location of the political is, as we argue, consistently slipping from view as these cultures are fleeting, on the move, and changeable.

It is this changeability of the performative and the digital that makes accessing the political impulse of the moment so difficult. Thus, awkwardness also describes the aesthetics of such politics as one of becoming, of process, of defiance, and of disruption. However, awkwardness is not only the search term with which to engage with these forms of activism, it is also that which, when thought in its affective dimensions, links these digital impulses through circulation to the viewer and links a variety of digital objects together. Awkwardness has a complicated and relational emotional dimension: one can feel awkward, or one can see someone feeling awkward, which, in turn, produces feelings of awkwardness. Awkwardness is contagious. Thus, awkwardness unveils two aspects of affect – that is, affect as emotion but also affect as relationality and connection – since we for the most part only feel awkward when we are perceived publicly or anticipate such public perception. Awkwardness suggests our connection – albeit via negativity – with others, including our world, experiences, events, and objects, and awkwardness has a component of power, as we discuss with regard to race and class. Awkwardness is also highly corporeal, and, therefore, when the corporeal and power are put together, it has further biopolitical dimensions.

In this chapter, we first explore awkwardness in terms of an overview of relevant affect and aesthetic theories before engaging with the affective dimension of what we call the "adolescent" aesthetics of two literary texts by German authors Helene Hegemann and Charlotte Roche as well as two related films. Hegemann published her debut novel *Axolotl Roadkill* in 2010, and Roche's surprise bestseller *Feuchtgebiete* (Wetlands) came out in 2008. Hegemann's film *Torpedo* was released in 2008, and the film version of Roche's *Feuchtgebiete* was released in 2013. The novels, and to a lesser extent the films, triggered animated public debates in Germany and beyond about feminism, postfeminism, aesthetics, literature in the digital age, sexuality, and sexual deviance. We further read Roche and Hegemann not just as authors but also as literary and cultural events that circulate, are hyper-visible, and, at times, escape into "low-res." These circulations create spheres of connectivity that are affectively charged – and often negatively so since both authors produced texts that engage with cruel optimism and its emotional trappings. Further, we turn to the implications of these texts and their associated events for thinking about female bodies, explicit sexuality, and the category of the pornographic beyond the notion of provocation and towards the inappropriate. In this manner, we suggest that the protest performance art produced by the entirety of the "moment" of these literary events – taking together text, author, and media discussion – is to be read awkwardly, not only in terms of how the texts are received or intentionally created but also as the utterance of a feminist protest in the broadest sense, an utterance that is beyond the control of the author. To read these moments as awkward allows us, yet again, to mine for the political; to read them as digitally and virally circulating will offer a way to transition to our final chapter, in which we engage with what it means when we say that (pop)feminism has "gone viral" and with the implications of a certain kind of normativity of gender discourse, also within the academy.

AWKWARD AFFECTS:
EMOTIONS, BODIES, AND TECHNOLOGIES

Using a theoretical discussion of affect to analyze cultural processes and developments is an approach that has firmly set its mark in the feminist studies of the past two decades.[1] The so-called "affective turn," which began to show itself in the humanities and social sciences in the mid-1990s, was influenced by previous work on the body and emotions coming out of feminist and queer studies, and by critical theory's approach to subjectivity, identity, and culture, following closely on the advent of deconstructionism and poststructuralism.[2] In this turn, affect is differently defined across disciplines, with a clear division between the humanities and the social sciences. Common to each approach, however, is an understanding of affect as a politically charged terminus. Ann Pelligrini and Jasbir Puar (2009, 38) write: "Recent work in affect studies – across manifold interdisciplinary and genealogical influences – points not only to different ways of conceiving bodies and subjects of politics but also, and perhaps more crucially, takes on the imperative of (re)imagining the terrain of politics 'itself.'" More so than is the case with other turns, the affective turn not only has an impact on the manner in which objects or experiences are analyzed for their political value but also goes to the very nature of how politics work or how they may work better. This is because affect reaches well beyond the analysis of representation and goes to the core of how politics might be better conceived for the present day; it means not only to do the work of critique differently but also to imagine a new political sphere of influence and to "redo" (Baer 2015b) feminist politics itself.

But the approach to the political possibilities of affect is differently skewed for the humanities and social sciences, respectively. For many in the disciplines of the humanities, affect has become synonymous with emotion or emotional worlds, and our connections to and through these. Eve Sedgwick (2003, 19), for example, writes of affect as thoroughly embodied and connected: "Affects can be, and are, attached to things, people, ideas, sensations, relations, activities, ambitions, institutions, and any number of other things, including other affects." This high range of connectivity also suggests the reconfiguration of multiple domains of experience and capacity. For Sedgwick, however, this connectivity is particularly emotional. In many of the social science disciplines, in contrast, affect relates connectivity to fields of power. For example, Michael Hardt (2007, x) defines affect as the simultaneous correspondence of the "mind's power to think" and the "body's power to act" and, along with this, the relationship between the "power to act and the power to be affected."[3] Hardt's definition suggests an openness, receptivity, and passion in the manner in which we think through and feel encounters with the other, our abilities to act and react to these encounters, and our ability to turn that receptivity into ethical, social, or political action. Thus, approaching anything through affect, be it an object or a subject, an experience or a structure, is simultaneously an intellectual and corporeal project. Further, it is also a call to arms, or at least a demand that we assess where action might be taken. It is in both of these understandings – that is, in both the humanities' engagement with emotion and the social sciences' discussion of power relations – that affect works in the feminist activisms discussed here. Through a reading of affect as connectivity that takes both emotion and power into account, the political appears simultaneously individual and systemic, internal to the object examined and placed upon that object by outward forces.

Hashtag activisms are an interesting example of multidirectional political actions that are also, partially due to their own form and partially driven by the criticism that hashtag activism is never real activism, awkward in their circulations. The German example of the #aufschrei campaign in particular illustrates how different disciplinary understandings of affect as emotion, connection, and power intersect in the corporeal. The affective charge lays within the campaign itself and the target of its critique, the prominence of sexual violence and assault, and the attempt to fight against such assault. A sense of community and solidarity emerges as more and more people (mainly women) find that publishing their experiences with sexual violence and assault is as emotionally affirming (as in, "we are not alone") as it is shocking (as in "almost all of us experience[d] such violence"). The campaign takes its political force from both of those emotional responses (Sadowski 2015). As #aufschrei achieved national attention and recognition in Germany, the affective charge shifted to a more external mode and entered political spheres of power and discourse as a call for political action and for government intervention. A facet of such campaigns circulating "beyond the hashtag," however, is that at the very point they leave the sphere of Twitter and enter discussions in other media outlets, their political effectivity is questioned. Responding to such questioning, Andi Zeisler (2014) writes in *Salon*: "Feminism that takes place online is not 'Twitter feminism.' It's ... feminism." Such questioning, one could argue, is strategically built into hashtag activism since hashtag activism often makes use of binaries and (over)simplifications, partially driven by its short digital form. In her discussion of one of the most viral hashtags to date, #solidarityisforwhitewomen, Tuzcu (2015, 9) describes this strategy as "performative binarization" that draws attention to "discursive gaps and traps."[4]

As can be seen in this reading, the divergent approaches to theorizing affect from the humanities and social sciences share an interest in the body in particular, not necessarily only as an object to be analyzed in terms of producing or experiencing affect but, rather, as a way into understanding the broader context for how reading from the perspective of affect fundamentally transforms the body and its capacities to act within a variety of contexts. Patricia Clough (2007, 2) sees in the affective turn an expression of a "new configuration of bodies, technology, and matter" in a manner that suggests a movement towards open systems "in the domain of biopolitical control." Technology becomes important in her reading because it not only reconfigures bodily capacities but also demands we rethink the representation of these capacities and, it could be argued, move well beyond representation. The notion of biopower, or biopolitics, utilized here by Clough is first introduced by Michel Foucault at the end of the first volume of *The History of Sexuality*. In it, he writes of the deployment of sexuality as one of the great technologies of power in the nineteenth century, one that became an "indispensable element in the development of capitalism" for, as Foucault (1980, 140–1) argues, capitalism was made possible by the "controlled insertion of bodies into the machinery of production" and the use of the population in "economic processes." He goes on to describe how, while the link between history and the body as a force of organization had long been established, the development of technologies that made death less ever-looming and production more profitable also expanded the demographics of control and power. "One would have to speak of *bio-power* to designate what brought life and its mechanisms into the realm of explicit calculations and made knowledge-power an agent of transformation of human life" (142–3, emphasis in original). It is this "bio-power," moreover, Foucault claims, that allows for the development of the norm as the arbiter of law.

Returning to Clough's use of the term "biopolitical" in the context of the affective turn, her claim that the approach to the corporeal through affect within structures of biopolitics points towards its increasing openness. This is also picked up on by Pellegrini and Puar, who, like Clough, define affect in terms of the body as an open system:

> Affect may anchor claims about the materiality of bodies and physiological processes that are not contained or representable by language or cognition alone ... This conception of affect poses a distinction between sensation and the perception of the sensation. Affect, from this perspective, is precisely what allows the body to be an open system, always in concert with its virtuality, the potential of becoming. (Pellegrini and Puar 2009, 37)

This is the case because affect taps into aspects of the body that cannot be addressed in linguistic terms; affect is "both a 'precognitive' attribute ... of the body as well as emotion's trace effect" (ibid.). In the context of popfeminist activism examined here, the bodies and technologies that are reconfigured as open systems under biopower, or within a structure that is motored by biopower, are accessed through thinking about awkwardness as affective. In the case of the Berlin SlutWalk, for example, (mainly) women's bodies walking on the streets mirror (even as they are intended to undo) a sexual violence that is in many cases underwritten and perpetuated by the structures of power in that such violence helps to maintain patriarchy. The over-sexed body of the woman on the street, then, is both the representation of biopower at work and its damning critique. The bodies of the protesters are charged affectively by simultaneously acting as symbols of victimhood and of political force. The suggestion is not that violence is an individual act, but that it is systemic, often condoned or ignored by the police, and generally often socially accepted or expected, as is evident in repeated cases of "victim blaming." Such forms of protests act as or replicate structures of biopower that utilize the female body as a means of control and as an open system. They emphasize the biopolitics of gendered oppression and use the body as a force to fight against such oppression. This circularity creates discomfort all along the political spectrum, for it holds up a mirror to the patriarchal system that tacitly condones gender violence as well as the activists who embody or clothe themselves in a manner that this same system implicitly or explicitly supports, thereby "becoming" that which is being criticized. Where awkwardness arises, however, is at the point at which the performance action's seriousness and lack of irony is mistaken or misread and the action is taken at face value for what, in actuality, it is criticizing – that is, it is taken as its own co-option. In 2012, for example, the Berlin branch of SlutWalk experienced sexually motivated attacks during a party held in the name of ending sexual violence.[5] While sexual violence should not be seen as awkward, what ultimately resulted in a decision to change the name of the organization and move away from the "slut" moniker leaves awkwardness in its absence. The now-absent slut continues to speak affectively. What these aspects attend to – affect thought of not only as emotion, power, and connectivity but also as a way to access the body in terms of the biopolitical structures working on its openness and potentiality – is the specificity of affect towards rethinking how we write about politics as well as about how political landscapes are formed (globally as well as locally).

Thus affect is a useful instrument for capturing the political resonances of the global reach in these digital feminist actions and for showing how their traces are embedded in bodies and emotions (or, in turn, how bodies and emotions might create transnational landscapes). This relationship between affect and the transnational has implications for thinking through the circulations of feminist protest performance art, for the relational and emotional quality of the protest action (and its reception by the public) is both bound to a national context and transformed in its travel across borders; such categories as history, language, and citizenship influence affective experience. Affect describes crucial elements of our popfeminist methodology, such as connectivity between people or things (e.g., objects, events, or spaces), action and reaction (both potential and real), and the powers and technologies working on and in emotional responses. Affect, as well as its attendant features, including emotion, feeling, corporeality, and sexuality, allows us access to the connection between subjectivity, materiality, and political action in the neoliberal economy. As Pelligrini and Puar (2009, 37) assert, "much productive critical work has been invested in how concepts like affect, emotion, and feelings aid in comprehending subject-formation and political oppositionality for an age when neoliberal capital has reduced possibilities for collective political praxis." Affect, here thought of specifically as awkwardness, offers us a vision of collectivity made up of individual corporeal experiences across geopolitical systems. If, to reiterate Clough (2007, 2), the affective turn is to be understood as an expression of a "new configuration of bodies, technology, and matter" because it offers us a way of accessing bodily capacity under systems of control, and if, moreover, bodily capacity and affect are not only the result of but also create the transnational domain as contested above, then technology is essential to that domain, including both material and digital technology. Technology demands we rethink and move beyond mere representation in our discussion of these bodily capacities. Our turn to awkwardness asks us to do precisely this: to move beyond the representational by instead asking after agency, action, and the connection of the physical-material and relational-social dimension of digital feminist activism, its form and aesthetics.

Returning to de Lauretis's (1987, ix) *Technologies of Gender*, in which she writes that gender is the product of "various social technologies," affect describes the moment of interaction between gender as a bodily capacity and that technology. In this essay, she engages with Foucault's use of the term "technology," particularly political technology, to discuss the creation of sexuality and sexual representation in order to approach moving beyond the then firm approach to gender and feminism as notions of sexual difference. Her essay wishes to answer not only "how the representation of gender is constructed by the given technology, but also how it becomes absorbed subjectively by each individual whom that technology addresses" (13). This two-part question implies an interlocutor, a receiver of both the gender and the technology constructing that gender. In de Lauretis's configuration, gender is also a product or, rather, a set of effects,[6] of the deployment of technologies, and here she focuses not only on technologies such as film but also on social and political technologies. That product is, in her understanding, representation and self-representation and, therefore, also construction (3). We borrow de Lauretis's phrase to engage with technologies of popfeminist activism; but, in doing so, the lineage from Foucault to de Lauretis to us should be clear. What is essential in today's technological field is moving away from the eternal emphasis on representation. While representation of feminist activism is one dimension (including, of course, self-representation and counter-representation), understanding the affective dimension to technology in terms of awkwardness, as well as its aesthetic form (discussed below), allows us to also take the emotional, material, circulatory, and process-based aspects of digital feminism and feminist performances and activisms into account.

This brings us back to our discussion of the manner in which awkwardness is in constant movement, circulating and slipping from view. We also emphasize that technology, not in and of itself but as a means of motion, connection, disconnection, and reconnection, plays a crucial role in trying to understand the location of new forms of activisms. Circling in and out of national, local, and global contexts, in and out of modes of neoliberal consumption and co-option, describes the way in which different forms of attachment interact and the way in which we can rethink the relationship between the digital realm and notions of difference, divisions, and connection. If we add the approach to affect offered to this reading of technology, then technology is understood not only as a conduit for motion but also as reconfiguring the very material of the activisms themselves as well as the material of their orbit. If the digital as a technology creates or configures the transnational domain in the act of circulating activist cultures, then it also fundamentally changes the very structure of the activism itself. Moreover, because of the connective aspect of affect, feminist activism also has the potential to transform technologies of gender, a transformation that results in awkward politics. In the case of Femen, for example, awkward moments emerge when Femen activism is put in relation with other forms of activisms or counter-protests (e.g., Muslimah Pride) or when the bare-breasted Femen protesters encounter German chancellor Angela Merkel and Russian president Vladimir Putin. In these cases, affective charges circulate beyond the national context and beyond binary understandings of what feminist activism used to or should look like. However, these perceptions cause political tensions that leave behind a feeling of awkward perplexity for feminist activists: against the push to evaluate the "feminism" of such actions, we are left to work with and through the awkwardness they create. As we argue, artists like Lady Bitch Ray and Chicks on Speed make this relational awkwardness their starting point for activism and harness its effects for their political messages.

POPFEMINIST ADOLESCENT AESTHETICS: BECOMINGS, PROCESSES, THRESHOLDS

Affect offers us a way to get at how political impulses come through in thinking about emotion, connection, power, corporeality, and technology. In our reading, these affective charges are awkward. However, since we are approaching the awkward politics of feminist activism in terms of popfeminism as performance, we must also engage with the manner in which these affects emerge from the aesthetic reach and form of these performances. We understand aesthetic here in, as Marcuse (2001, 132) writes, the "dual meaning of pertaining to the senses and pertaining to art." Thus aesthetic pertains to all sensual (and therefore also affective) fields, not only to those touched by creative practices.

Further, like affect, aesthetics offers us access to the contextual positioning of both object and consumer of the protest action. In his discussion of aesthetics in terms of everyday life, Ben Highmore (2010, 120–1) uses the umbrella term "social aesthetics" to describe what he calls the "cross-modal investigation" of emotions, passion, major and minor affects, forms of perception, the senses, and the body. The term describes those aspects key to the original meaning of aesthetics and connects "perception, sensorial culture, [and] affective intensities" with their social and cultural contexts (128). Using an anthropology of cleanliness as illustration, Highmore writes that social aesthetics "links the perception of cleanliness and dirt, or purity and impurity, to orchestrations of shame and comfort, to resonances of other sensual worlds, and on to the social ontology of bodies" (129). Social aesthetics describes the social utility of and cultural context behind the sensual experience. In *Ordinary Lives*, Highmore expands on this thinking through a reading of Rancière's (2004, 2009) work on aesthetics (primarily *The Politics of Aesthetics* from 2004 and *Aesthetics and Its Discontents* from 2009). He discusses how Jacques Rancière engages with the social, out of which politics emerges – here understood by Highmore (211, 47) as "the enacting of a disruption in the parceling out of allocated space, time and sense" – as containing an aesthetic dimension. Highmore, noting that Rancière engages with aesthetic as the "distribution of the sensible," quotes from the 2004 text: "It is a delimitation of spaces and times, of the visible and the invisible, of speech and noise, that simultaneously determines the place and stakes of politics as a form of experience" (as quoted in Highmore 2011, 48; in Rancière 2004, 13). For Rancière, this determination is organized and ordered by a system of policing, which is a set of bodies that decides what is seen, heard, or felt and what is not (Highmore 2011, 48). Highmore comments on this unequal distribution of the sensible: "Acts of politics and acts of art disrupt and reorder the social sensorium, making new experiences possible, making new voices heard as speech, altering the horizons of visibility" (ibid.). Thus, Highmore claims that the political aesthetics offered by his reading of Rancière is found in what he calls the "initial rip" in how the sense are distributed. Here, we can understand "rip" as a disturbance in what we are accustomed to experiencing: "Dislocations in the distribution of the sensible occur when attention is drawn (again and again) to something that had previously been deemed unworthy of attention, or when someone who was deemed as having 'nothing to say,' speaks in a way that solicits an audience and community of listeners (however small)" (ibid.). Because our senses are most often ordered – or policed – by systems of power or authority (the curatorial authority at the museum, the radio programmer, the television producer), any disturbance, or rip, in that system by new political and artistic forms opens up transformative possibility since "the rip ushers in emancipation, democracy, equality as its infinite potential" (ibid.). Awkwardness is one manner of reading this "rip" in the organization of the senses politically.

Thus thinking of aesthetics as the social from which the political emerges, and therefore speaking to the contextual position of both the aesthetic "object" and the receiving "subject," brings us back to the connectivity offered by affect – that is, how, through affect, aesthetic objects and subjects are connected to and through context. Similar to the "rip" that Highmore describes, we use the concept of "disturbance," or "rupture." Any organization of the senses and, therefore, reading of aesthetics becomes even messier, however, when the context – the social – is in constant transformation, shifting through (digital) technology and perhaps even unrooted from place or evading emplacement.

Popfeminism in particular brings these two aspects of aesthetics together – that is, as pertaining to the senses and as the context out of which the sensual experience emerges. The prefix "pop" is an aesthetic one for its immediate references bring to mind the bright colours and geometric shapes of pop art or the danceable beats of pop music. We have in many places throughout this volume attended to this aspect of pop in the activist cultures examined: the brightly coloured balaclavas of Pussy Riot that themselves spawned pop-art-inspired posters and imagery as well as their punk music; the bright pink clothing line of Lady Bitch Ray paired with the visual and sonic culture of rap; the costumes of Chicks on Speed and their poppy, electroclash music also reminiscent of riot grrrl bands. All of these visual and sonic aesthetics speak to their pop lineage. However, when feminism is added to pop, the aesthetics take on a social dimension in the manner described by Highmore. We must then read through the sensual aspect of the aesthetics of pop to reach how these are received, configured, or understood in the context or location of production and reception and, thus, read for their feminist politics.

Therefore, if, as discussed above, affect is a way of understanding or accessing open systems, then the open system itself (made up of bodies, technologies, and matter) can be read as a system of aesthetics. Our focus on how awkwardness is in constant movement, circulating and slipping from view, also means that it is in a constant mode of becoming, forever developing towards meaning that it does not yet achieve; it describes an open system. The aesthetics of awkwardness – that is, how the senses are engaged in the experience and production of or collision with awkwardness – could, therefore be called "adolescent" for a number of reasons. The so-called "awkward age" evokes gangly bodies, hormones out of whack, libidinal (or other) urges colliding with familial prohibition, the sense of sticking out while using every means necessary to conform, and the willingness to assert opinions while these are still forming. If we describe the aesthetics of pop-feminist activism in a digital age as adolescent, the invocation should not be one of teenage upstarts or immature actions but, instead, of becomings, processes, and thresholds that are intimately joined with the body and with negotiating that body within its greater context. It is this notion of *process* that is essential to seeing the circularity of the awkward moment as not merely cancelling out meaning. The political meaning is not found in a fixed result of the action (failure or success) but, rather, in the unfolding, turning back, and circulation of the intended and unintended relations and results. Awkwardness is an adolescent gesture in that it connects with the viewer through the threat of disconnection. Adolescent aesthetics are therefore also closely tied to willfulness, defiance, and impropriety.

Awkwardness helps us to tease out political moments in, for example, the activism of Pussy Riot, in Lady Bitch Ray's performances, and in the art and performance pieces of Chicks on Speed, all creative examples in which, at points in their media circulations, political interventions become murky – and are often doubted to be present at all or are subjected to rigid forms of evaluations as "good" or "bad" for politics. Approaching these examples by considering questions of affect and (or even as) aesthetics in the stricter sense allows us to highlight the fact that, regardless of how one might evaluate them as effective (or not), their aesthetic interventions make a lasting political impression in the circulations of images. The black boots and colourful stockings, short dresses, and balaclavas that became the brand-marker for Pussy Riot activism openly play with riot and teenage girl aesthetics. This playfully defiant gesture is not just a performance: it is that very gesture that goes viral in the reception of Pussy Riot activism, the aesthetic form that appears to be applicable to other political contexts, that travels, that can be marketed, but that can also morph and change, appear and disappear in new guises, even duplicating itself. The tension between certain elements that seem to carry the same meaning regardless of location, and elements that morph all too quickly and willingly, is what we describe as awkwardly adolescent. The digital enables and becomes such a process, which, in some cases, describes the process of an event, a clip, a hashtag, or an image "going viral."

The creative act, then, is not an isolated event but always thought of as part of event culture, particularly when understood within the framework of pop and feminism. In the following sections, we explore how awkwardness is a useful concept for the analysis of literature and film as it allows us to mobilize their political gestures and to connect these to the broader activist context. We look at two contemporary artists, known for their scandalous appearance within the German literary market and located at the intersection of commercial success, ideological agendas, and digital proliferation in and for the twenty-first century, and they are equally subject to the fickle ebb and flow of popular interest. Specifically, both authors triggered heated discussions about whether or not their works were feminist or political and both were consumed within and by neoliberal market mechanisms but also positioned themselves, in however complicated a manner, within and against these mechanisms. Their cultural products and author personas circulate through various mediated forms and are adapted, a process that allows us to describe further the affective and aesthetic dimensions of awkwardness. They also illustrate facets of what happens when pop-feminist literary events go viral, which, in the German context, triggered broader public discussions about body politics, (post-)feminism, female adolescence, sexuality, and porn. The texts and the films rely on affect at the level of form and narrative, and count on affective audience responses – and successfully triggered such responses. They work, intentionally, with awkwardness as a key feature of their aesthetic form and in the way in which they relate to narrative forms, the body, and reception. By examining the production of affective awkwardness and its aesthetic implications in the texts and films of these two publicly contested writers, we exemplify further facets of our larger political considerations of awkward activisms, particularly the manner in which these politics reach their audience and what happens when they get there.

We begin with a discussion of Helene Hegemann's film *Torpedo* (2008) and her novel *Axolotl Roadkill* (2010) in terms of the unwieldy material form of the text itself and her person. We then turn to *Feuchtgebiete* (2008) by Charlotte Roche and the challenges this text made to the reader's preconceptions or emotions. *Feuchtgebiete* has been adapted to film (2013, dir. David Wnendt), which allows us to uncover the awkwardness of adaptation into visual forms and the "mainstreaming" of a certain affective response to explicit female sexuality, particularly when placed into the (here safe) rubric of female adolescence, sexuality, madness, and feminism – aspects often found together as literary tropes. We describe these textual moments as events because Hegemann and Roche are not merely literary authors but also creative entrepreneurs; the literary is but one aspect of their popfeminist political intervention. The success of and controversies around Hegemann's works, themselves fairly alternative, catapulted her for a short while and uncomfortably into the mainstream. Alternative music-TV moderator Roche became a public authority on all things postfeminism after the surprise success of her novel, though its highly successful adaptation did not spark the same kind of discussions. Like our other examples, popfeminist texts and literary events are found (or consciously place themselves) in the middle of affective relations that uphold cruel optimism; however, they also engage with and exploit the assumptions that underlie these relations. Feminist causes remain at the centre of their narratives, but emotional attachments are mainly formed via critical negativity towards those causes, particularly in their reception. These discussions illustrate how our theorizations of awkward politics in the digital realm also apply to analogue forms, and they reconfirm how content moves between analogue and digital economies.

CUT/PASTE:
HELENE HEGEMANN'S *TORPEDO* AND *AXOLOTL ROADKILL*

The manner in which aesthetics function as an open system made up of bodies, technologies, and matter that produce an affective charge in the texts at hand is best seen in Helene Hegemann's approach to the visual field in her film *Torpedo*, an approach that is mirrored in poetic form in her novel *Axolotl Roadkill*. As we argue, awkwardness emerges in circularity, where we read the complicated and messy positions of the political. Here, this messiness can be seen in a type of cut-and-paste technique utilized by Hegemann. This brings us back to this notion of the "rip" in the distribution of the senses discussed by Highmore in his reading of Rancière. By creating rips, or disruptions, in her textual material, Hegemann engages the senses in a direct but confusing way. On the formal level, it is this rip that creates awkward affect. This technique, further, links her to her German pop forbearers, beginning with Rolf Dieter Brinkmann in the 1960s. He utilized what he called a cut-up

5.1   *Torpedo*, Dir. Helene Hegemann, 2008

technique in his writing, reconfiguring language by connecting disparate material together in the manner of a cinematic cut, thus heightening the sensorial quality of text. He writes: "I broke out of the imprisonment of the film's plot and while I concentrate on my fingertips, I experience the cuts / in the fierce tremor that goes through my body as soon as a cut happens, an event stops, quivering light" (Brinkman 1982, 286).[7] The cut found in film is, for Brinkmann, highly corporeal and experienced personally.[8] This cut-up technique describes the visual and sensual field of the film *Torpedo*; moreover, the cut in the material offers a visual match to the developmental threshold that describes the position of the adolescent, in between worlds of childhood and adulthood.

Helene Hegemann was fourteen years old when she wrote the script for and directed the film *Torpedo*: a film about a teenager, the fifteen-year-old Mia. The film evokes the term adolescence in its aesthetic approach and, of course, because its main character is an adolescent girl. She depicts herself as a traumatized and psychologically disturbed teenager who struggles to find a "new" mother figure after her mother, who appears to have been a drug addict, committed suicide. The mother figures she encounters along the way, however, are also "adolescents" in that they appear lost, searching, and failing. Mia's aunt Cleo, who has accepted Mia into foster care, is an aspiring actress and single mother

to a younger son (Fritzi), and Cleo's friend Elise is a trained computer
scientist but works in a school cafeteria and seems to be preoccupied
with finding a partner. In connection with the presentation of these
characters, the film creates a vague narrative tension between a traditional search for stability and family and the depiction of this very
search as misdirected.

The forty-minute film is a youth drama that offers a portrait of a
life similar to the one Hegemann will later describe in her novel *Axolotl Roadkill*, a life of affluent neglect. Aside from a few scenes in the
middle part, where the camera shifts to either Elise's or Cleo's perspective, the film mainly depicts Mia's defiant and snippy perspective on the
world and the people who surround her, contrasted with her deep emotional desire for a "mother." Except for the beginning scenes in the park
or a few connecting scenes in which she roams the city streets, most of
the film is filmed indoors, inside apartments, through doors, and with
the main characters in front of random art objects. The only brightly
lit rooms – except for the very final scene described below – are institutions: the school and the room for Mia's therapy. When Mia roams
the streets or finds herself in dark spaces, it is not clear whether she
is in danger or whether she poses a danger to the people she encounters. In – possibly cliché – adolescent fashion, she appears vulnerable
and dangerous, out of control and wise, detached and attached at the
same time.

Mia's perspective and her search for emotional connection are undermined aesthetically and narratively in the creation of awkward tensions. The first two-thirds of the film are made up of snippets out of
what is possibly just a day of Mia's disjointed and restless life. The final
one-third of the film develops a storyline that culminates in a few dra-
matic scenes and an awkward ending. After a failed theatre premier of
a play in which Cleo is the main character, she sends her son off in the
middle of the night to his father so that she may go on what appears
to be a drug and alcohol binge to drown out her disappointment. Mia
comes home, where she dances and parties with Cleo until Cleo starts
to scream, hold her head, and collapse to the floor. An emergency team
picks up Cleo, but it appears to be too late: in the following scene, Elise
and Mia visit Cleo in her (dark and gloomy) hospital room, and a doctor informs them that Cleo has been pronounced brain dead and will
not wake up from her coma. The two women travel home together
via subway and, in a sudden moment of emotional vulnerability at the
apartment door, Mia confesses to Elise: "I don't want to lie any more.

I have gone crazy and I think I know why." After a strange pause, she continues, "I have started to dream about my mom,"[9] recounting her surreal dream about her mother, which she describes as the most beautiful moment of her life, only to confess that, even though she tries to be responsible for herself, she cannot take this responsibility. She concludes with a plea for help: "I did not want this. I survived all of this and I shouldn't have ... Because one does not die easily when one is young ... You have to help me. I have never said that to anybody before."[10] After this (melo)dramatic monologue in the dark staircase, music starts playing and Elise tries to pull Mia into the apartment. There is a sudden cut, the music stops, and Elise and Mia stand face to face, very closely, inside the apartment, which appears flooded with sunlight. They hug and kiss intimately, and Elise asks, "do you want to marry me?"[11] to which Mia answers "no" (nein). The film cuts to the final credits and the music appears to pick up where it left off, rather abruptly. The viewer is left to wonder whether, somehow, the two women found love or family in the end, whether the film tries to uncover the cruel optimism of such a search for belonging, or whether it offers an alternative, however vague.

The film has an equally confusing and confused relationship to its main character. Mia is unreliable at best and mentally ill at worst. She confesses to having seduced her father, for example, and appears to have an abusive or sadistic (but not clearly sexual) relationship with a nearly middle-aged man she met in the park after jumping on his car. At the same time, in the concluding scenes, Mia appears as the most self-reflexive and only reliable character in the film. In a popfeminist move, the film reverses the relationship between generations of women and the search for the mother and queers the family structure by, repeatedly, clashing notions of parenthood with sexual desire. In the film, this works less as shock-effect and more as a further "cut"; the film cuts up, thereby dissolving, any sense of progress, generational logic, or familiar structure.

Both on the level of the narrative as well as with regard to its main character, the film is built on a tension between the desire for unobtainable happiness and a defiant gesture against any such desire. The combining of depictions of emotional distress and cruelty with awkward humour further fuels this tension. The scene in which Elise tries to record a professional film for a dating website or in which Mia arrives at the therapist and is set up in a children's therapy room filled with toys and with furniture that is too small for either Mia or the therapist to sit are awkwardly funny. The camera emphasizes this awkwardness in the therapy scene, for example, by cutting the frame low so that, while the therapist sets up the room, her head is outside the frame.

Thus *Torpedo* offers a thematic, visual, and material point of entry into popfeminist adolescent aesthetics as well as the potential for the emergence of politics from these aesthetics. The cuts between scenes that bring together jarring or thematically mismatched moments, particularly in the first two-thirds of the film, create a rip, here a disruption of the viewer's sensual experience of the film, which mirrors the disconnect in the main character's sensual experience of her context in the final one-third of the film. The cut (as a rip) erects the aesthetic threshold at which the protagonist finds herself. If, as Highmore contests, political aesthetics emerge from this rip, for it offers the potential for the development of social concepts of democracy and equality, that potential is made awkward by the abrupt negative ending: "no" (nein). The affective resonance of the "no," however, in all of its awkwardness, perpetuates that political potential; it is the defiant *no* of the adolescent who refuses systemic control and disrupts power structures, including those of narrative and form in which she finds herself.

The film, therefore, acts as an open system that offers a process-based sensual experience. If *Torpedo* offers a visual portrayal of Hegemann's aesthetics as adolescent, one that also mirrors the content of the film itself, then *Axolotl Roadkill* takes these adolescent aesthetics to narrative-poetic turns. Further, the novel displays what the collapse of standard theoretical frameworks enacted by the awkward moment looks like in literary-aesthetic practice.[12] When the novel hit German bookstores in late January 2010, it was praised by journalists in regional and national newspapers, in magazines, and in a variety of literary blogs as the great coming-of-age novel, on par with *The Catcher in the Rye*, applicable to an entire disillusioned generation of millennials,[13] not the least because its author, who had already written a short story and a play and directed a film, was then only seventeen years of age. The hype was exacerbated and complicated on 5 February of that same year, when Hegemann was revealed to have plagiarized content from a selection of pop-cultural and digital sources. Thus the "cut" in the film is also a "paste" in the novel. Despite the final tally of one "mere" plagiarized page out of the novel's over two hundred pages, confirmed by an extensive source-list provided by the author and publishing house in a second printing run, the scandal raged on well into the spring, fuelled by the author's and the novel's participation in and disturbance of the literary establishment, including a clear questioning of the publishing industry and masculine critical tradition.[14]

The implications of the firestorm of debate for the literary establishment come jarringly together with the novel's aesthetic quality. The novel follows Mifti, a girl of sixteen – self-described as a victim of affluent neglect – who lives with her two elder half-siblings in well-to-do squalor in an apartment in Berlin, their leftist artist-father residing with his girlfriend in a separate apartment nearby. The novel is without plot, narrative arc, or clear direction, and, instead, may be described as a loose collection of vignettes made up of Mifti's drug use, the Berlin club and party circuit, demeaning and often violent sexual encounters, emotional confusion and pain, familial dysfunction, and snide attacks lobbed at the thirty-something cultural, artistic, and intellectual scene that makes up Berlin Mitte, Friedrichshain, and Prenzlauer Berg. Aesthetically, the novel is awkward; both narrative voice and poetic form occupy a threshold in between text forms and media varieties, a threshold that also describes the position of the adolescent. This same quality becomes charged in a feminist-political sense when one takes into account the implication that the narrator, like the film's protagonist and by extension the author, is an emotionally distressed and sexually empowered no-longer-child and not-yet-adult. The narrative-poetic awkwardness emanating from the novel consistently disturbs any clear-cut reading of abuse, misguidance, or naiveté on the part of the author, thereby questioning the motives of the literary establishment in the scandal.

The novel is written in an angular, bristly, and unwieldy language, the building blocks of which reference, cite, and intersect with a variety of textual styles and media. Both the terms "intertextuality" and "intermediality" offer potential interpretative frameworks for understanding this aesthetic construction. However, neither suffices on its own: while intertextuality is interested in the communication of symbolic meaning as text references collide,[15] intermediality takes into account the materiality of that collision.[16] In *Axolotl Roadkill*, the symbolic and material interactions are at odds. The novel's language is created from a mixture of symbolic text and material media forms, ranging from invented compound words, e-mails, text messages, letters, dialogues, and found prose, which, in turn, might include television taglines (such as the channel Pro7's "We Love to Entertain You"), song titles and lyrics (including riot grrrl band L7's "You've Made My Shitlist" or lyrics by Leonard Cohen), as well as media sound bites (from soccer star Franz Beckenbauer, for example; Hegemann 2010, 7, 13, 44, 172). Aside from suggesting that reading is a form of pop cultural consumption, such text and media sources have no internal relationship to the novel. The disconnect between the symbolic and material level of the novel's language resonates also in its construction of adolescent narrative subjectivity: Mifti's descriptions veer off course, her prose is interrupted, and her communication with other figures is often stilted and broken (Hegemann 2010, 14, 16). In her discussion of intertextuality, Julia Kristeva identifies a threshold that is crossed when texts and subjectivities interact within a narrative. This threshold, Kristeva (2003, 9) notes, in keeping with Hannah Arendt, is an "in-between zone" that creates a "social melting pot, a political openness and most of all a mental plasticity." The threshold is essential to understanding the disconnections and their effects in *Axolotl Roadkill*. The novel produces seams and cracks over which the reader trips. The "inter" here is not a unifying concept but, rather, a divisive one.[17]

This threshold, or "inter," also describes the adolescent, who is standing at the developmental precipice that is adulthood, and mobilizes this position accordingly, for the narrator of *Axolotl Roadkill* is very aware of her self-positioning at this threshold as culturally constructed. For example, she describes adulthood as buying sofa covers, understanding Foucault, and "being ashamed to death of everything I ... bang into this computer here" (Hegemann 2010, 17).[18] If adolescence is a state of "being or becoming," as well as a time of heightened sexuality, rebellion, volatility, and freedom from norms, then here that state also includes cultural production – and textual self-creation – even as this is playfully and self-referentially disregarded (Burt 2007, 3–4). Adolescence, as the so-called awkward age, thus has a direct impact on the text's narrative poetics. In its language, the text, like its narrator, is awkward, struggling for its unique voice: "I was given a language that is not my own" (Hegemann 2010, 49).[19]

While we do not see here the same types of cuts between scenes as is the case with *Torpedo*, the jarring integration of the variety of text forms and Mifti's creation of new words can be seen as rips in the sensual experience (the reading act) out of which new political forms emerge. As is the case in the film, these aesthetics build open systems made of technology, text, and narrative that write and project onto bodies and the material world. In the novel technology is found not only at the level of content, poetics, and narrative construction but also in reception, marketing, and critical debate.[20] Mifti's experiences taking drugs, hitting the club scene, and stumbling through sexual encounters are constructed out of snippets of quotations from mass media – many of which are in English, e-mail exchanges, and text messages. But technology in the text is not reserved solely for recognizable media forms. Bodies and language (as material) also act as technologies. The text begins with the body as a disorganized technology turned into language: "Ok, nighttime, grappling again with death ... Only the claviature of absolute darkness, the screeching in my head, this unrhythmic drumming, shit. That all used to be beautifully pubescent vomit, and now it is laborious literature" (Hegemann 2010, 9).[21] The sounds (screeching, drumming), both engineered and primal, coming from the post-pubescent body create the literature at hand. Further, in response to the contestation that she has destroyed language, Mifti says: "Later, when the blood just circulates around technoplastictically, everything will be super again" (52).[22] The term "technoplasticity," linked here to language and blood, suggests a technological basis to life forces and thus a non-specific locality to the textual construction. However, it also references the techno-scene around the famous club Berghain, anchoring this broken language firmly in Berlin. The word also nods towards digital circulation: technoplasticity is one of those phrases Hegemann copy-pasted from the blogger Airen.[23] The word thus directly points outward to the ensuing media circus of Hegemann's plagiarism and, further, transnationally to the moralizing intellectual property discussions spurred on by the open access movement.[24]

The political implications of the resulting awkwardness become clear when we turn to the cultural meaning of adolescence, thus thinking of the popfeminism of this text in terms of its social aesthetics. Carsten Gansel (2003) reminds us that, because the physical and emotional signs of adolescence occur as a process contained within culture, it is important to interpret the (affective) relationship between adolescence and culture. Mifti seems cognizant of this fact, as seen in her self-introduction to readers:

1. I have lost my patchwork history that was written by anal sex, tears, and corpse defilement.
2. I have an open sore in my throat.
3. My family is a heap of random people with an addiction to self-performance stuck in omnipotent fantasies of early childhood. In the extreme case, they might write a pop-cultural text on the question as to why the avant-garde NEVERTHELESS belly dances, but that would be about it.[25] (Hegemann 2010, 12)

These disjointed statements display the narrative voice's self-positioning at a threshold that is located between childhood and adulthood, is rebelliously textual, and is wrought with cultural expectations surrounding childhood. The narrator comments early in the text: "Oddly, I know exactly what I want: not to grow up" (7).[26] This positioning of the no-longer-child and not-yet-adult at a desired-for eternal threshold references the neotenic salamander, the axolotl, in the novel's title. That the "Roadkill" of the title appears toward the end of the book with reference to Mifti's writing style ("You write like a roadkill"; 190, English in original), further cements female adolescent development within the textual aesthetics in an awkward, self-referential manner.

The childish yet self-aware voice collides in the novel with sexual precociousness, which ranges from anal sex to same-sex desire. In the introduction to *Curiouser*, Steven Bruhm and Natasha Hurley (2004, ix) write of the dominant cultural narrative that children are innocent of sexual desire: "People panic when that sexuality takes on a life outside the sanctioned scripts of child's play." That panic is felt acutely with the queer child, who conforms neither to asexuality nor to the "blissful promises of adult heteronormativity" (ix). In *The Queer Child*, Kathryn Bond Stockton (2009, 5) claims that all children are queer children for they are foreign and strange to adults, and their assumed "innocence is queerer than we ever thought it could be." When we examine where the child has grown sideways, as Stockton calls it, away from the narratives of innocence and asexuality but not up towards adulthood, then we see the political implications of our "cultural ideals" (13). Mifti's refusal to grow up is not classically childish, a la Peter Pan, as our cultural ideals would have it. She has grown sideways: Mifti is not innocent, is decidedly sexual, and is also depressively exhausted. The text thus presents readers with their own cruelly optimistic stance towards the societal expectations for girls, a stance that also counters lifestyle feminism's positive coding of empowerment. Further, it also uncovers the titillated desire on the part of the literary establishment to participate in the plagiarism scandal: the condemnation from older authors and the outrage of literary critics spoke as much to the desire to consume the event as it did to their potentially outmoded understanding of publishing in the digital age. That much of this condemnation and outrage was couched in sexualized, gendered, and age-driven terms in the national newspapers returns that consumption circuitously and uncomfortably back to the author/narrator.[27] The awkwardness associated with adolescence becomes political in both the textual aesthetics and the affective resonances of its reception.

THE AWKWARDNESS OF RECEPTION: CHARLOTTE
ROCHE'S *FEUCHTGEBIETE* IN LITERATURE AND FILM

The question of politics and, specifically, of feminist politics defined the initial reception of Charlotte Roche's novel *Feuchtgebiete*;[28] the fact that Roche's literary event in many ways *is* this question often leads to rather circular discussions. To approach Roche's text as an awkward literary event couched in adolescent aesthetics allows us to discuss not if but how it engages in feminist politics and to read the text as a form of feminist critique. In its awkwardness, it pokes holes into the toxic positivity of the idea of feminist progress and postfeminism, and positions itself clearly against feminisms' cruel optimisms. In that sense, the gesture of the text is one of defiance; however, the novel also facilitated a sense of a new feminist community during Roche's highly popular reading tour and other public appearances. With its frantic reception, the text most certainly also triggered public discussions about things that were deemed unworthy of attention, a further example of Highmore's "rip." As a voice that took on a measure of authority within the discussions about postfeminism, Roche's text transformed a depoliticized discourse and introduced new affective charges, including discussions about "gross" bodily fluids, raunchy pornography, autoeroticism, and female sexuality. Like *Axolotl Roadkill*, Roche's novel is a first-person narrative told from the perspective of an emotionally disturbed young woman who tries to come to terms with her familial past, sexuality, and various physical ailments; however, unlike Hegemann's novel, it does so within conventional aesthetic and formal structures. Thus, in contrast to Hegemann's aesthetic awkwardness, the collapse of any clear discursive framing of Roche's literary text happens when uncomfortable encounters at the level of plot collide with expectations, both those produced by the text and those brought to the text by the reading public, in the process of reception.

The text creates plot-based tensions by combining disturbing psychological experiences with embarrassing or disgusting physical conditions. These emotional and physical disturbances are narratively intertwined with explicit (and in some cases raunchy or pornographic) descriptions of sexual encounters and sexual fantasies. While these tensions in and of themselves might produce uncomfortable feelings in the reader, the fact that the text directly addresses, and thus creates expectations around, traditional feminist questions related to physical norms, motherhood, sexual liberation, and sexual self-realization politicizes this awkwardness. Added to this is the receptive awkwardness: *Feuchtgebiete*, which became a bestseller within a month of publication, was understood as a phenomenon – a true event – leaving the reception process to produce a broad variety of conflicting emotional responses. The reception finds itself rubbing up against the text's intended politics: *Feuchtgebiete* engages the audience's emotions by inciting, for example, feelings of disgust, arousal, amusement, or celebration, but it fails the reader on all these emotional accounts by explaining away the experience and thereby questioning the legitimacy of the emotional responses it triggers. These affective connections to the audience via moments of emotional disconnect or instability can be described in terms of adolescent aesthetics, for the distribution of the senses and the social context continually shift, are continually in process.

Feuchtgebiete is narrated by eighteen-year-old Helen Memel, speaking from her hospital bed, where she is recovering from surgery due to an anal fissure. The story is told entirely from her perspective as she obsesses over her body, remembers sexual adventures, and plots ways to subvert hygienic conventions or bring her divorced parents back together. In the media, the novel was discussed mainly for its subversive approach to female hygiene and Helen's experimentation with bodily fluids and smells. Praised by some as a new feminist manifesto and critiqued by others as pornographic trash, the text triggered strong reactions across Germany. Roche's readings of *Feuchtgebiete* were extremely popular, especially among young, educated women, and almost every major newspaper reported about the novel or her readings or printed interviews with Roche; she was one of the most popular talk show guests on almost any show on German television that year.[29] In the process of this production of awkward moments in media reception, a rather strange emotional relationship forms among text, author, and readers' bodies. Sentences like the very first of the novel, "as long as I can remember, I have had haemorrhoids," phrases like "back to ass-shaving," or hygienic strategies such as the use of vaginal fluid as perfume trigger confused reactions (Roche 2008, 8, 10, 19) that feel "too close" for comfort.[30] These range from amusement, to sexual tension, to embarrassment due to their blunt, matter-of-fact, or dirty flirtatious tone; such reactions read alternatingly as amusingly politically subversive, obsessive, or even disgustingly psychologically disturbed.

Such a reception puts readers and audience members, together with the author and her character, into the confused but nonetheless political position of the self-challenging, questioning feminist. At times, it appears as though Helen's actions and thoughts are subversively political – she explores her sexuality, expresses her desires and needs, and rebels against conventional notions of female body image or appropriate female behaviour – and at others they mimic those of a hurt, insecure, and psychologically disturbed young woman. Further, *Feuchtgebiete* plays with the neoliberal notion of individual self-realization absorbed by mainstream and lifestyle feminisms by showing a young woman who exaggeratedly tries to attain self-realization and, for the most part, seemingly fails. In this way, Roche reveals the optimistic cruelty of such notions and their often pseudo-feminist positions while at the same time embracing them. For example, when Helen describes her relationship to motherhood by explaining her sexual games with avocado pits, which she calls her "Biodildo" (organic dildo), and then ends this reflection just as her mother enters her hospital room, the text creates a tension by connecting the validation of individual sexual self-exploration to traditional questions of motherhood:

> Thanks to my well-trained vaginal muscles I can shoot the avocado pit back out ... I can't come closer to a birth ... I've really always wanted a child as long as I can remember. But in my family there's a pattern that keeps repeating. My great-grandmother, my grandmother, Mama, and I. All first born. All girls. All weak-nerved, disturbed, and unhappy. I've broken the cycle ... been sterilized ... When I open my eyes, I see Mama leaning over me.[31] (Roche 2008, 40–1)

In this paragraph, Roche combines the tensions inherent in neoliberal forms of feminism – the tension between the sexual power of her masturbation experiments and her self-identification as weak and disturbed, the desire for motherhood and her decision against procreation – with a strange concept of motherhood that is located somewhere between popular readings of Freud and second wave feminists' rebellion against their mothers. In such examples of sexual experimentation, but also in psychological explanations (75), Roche's text functions as a complex commentary: it reaffirms goals of both second wave and lifestyle feminisms but exaggerates and deconstructs these, locating them squarely within and against the cruel optimism of feminist self-realizations.

Helen's choice to be sterilized not only playfully refers to the "our bodies, ourselves" motto central to the feminist waves (and puts a twist on body-modification discourses that usually circle around the beauty industry) but also implicitly attacks the biopolitical and highly classist, racialized, and gendered discussions about the importance of reproduction for the future of Germany (see chapter 2). Helen refuses to participate; she explains her refusal in a highly personalized manner, but since Helen is a rather unreliable voice, especially in relation to offering rational explanations, the text allows for a more general reading of her actions as forms of social commentary and critique. What Helen does is often fairly political in that she willfully defies norms; Helen is, in all her vulnerability and hurt, the willful subject of the text. Her explanations, however, often fall back onto vague and worn out notions of psychologized feminism, as is seen in the above quote. The text neither questions nor validates Helen's perspective. *Feuchtgebiete* does not offer a clear position from which to evaluate the text and its voice; on the contrary, the novel and its narrator create an insecure position for readers.

The awkwardness in this literary event originates in the (author, character, reader) position of the self-directed, self-challenging feminist and emerges in the process of reception as well as in Roche's media circulations. Roche exploits the cruel optimism of feminism mainly by questioning the legitimacy of any emotional responses that her texts might produce; she exploits the cruel optimism of pop by making entirely uncomfortable the object or scene that promises participation in the consumer event (the books themselves but also her readings and media appearances). Popfeminist readers are invited to identify with the painful, physical, and sexual emotions the texts describe; they must ask why they are feeling aroused, disgusted, or amused as they confront the cruelty of the optimistic claim that bodies are our own and that sex can be whatever we as women want. This freedom of sexual and physical expression, or simply the idea that one is in control of one's own body and one's physical and emotional well-being, appears as desirable and impossible – thus awkwardly political. The literary body in this novel is written as an open system in the most pleasurably and painfully literal sense (it bleeds, oozes, is cut into, and self-penetrated), and, on a narrative level, the text remains with this open, evolving body, watching and describing it without evaluation. Helen can or will not pass out of adolescence; there are no suggestions in the text that growing up might be a solution to her problems. On the contrary, narratively and aesthetically, the text remains with the trouble of feminism.

Similarly, the text seeks neither to resolve nor to ironically deconstruct the melodramatic moments it depicts. When, in an interview with Dana Luciano in *Social Text*, Berlant asserts that "most politically-engaged critical work is still super-melodramatic and cruel optimistic in its hope that a strong emotional noise performs the importance and authority of something, a view or a situation," and that such political work "still uses rhetorics of catastrophe and exceptionality to describe the ordinary of subordination,"[32] she describes Roche's text and the initial emotional response it triggers. *Feuchtgebiete* is a crisis text not only in terms of the state of the narrator and her body but also with reference to the state of feminism and feminist causes that are attached to bodies as open systems for neoliberal self-realization or for the capitalistic whims of the beauty industry. There is no sense of authority or progress that might resolve the crisis. Here, the notion of the body as an open system finds itself at the level of sexuality, where the overused and misogynistic image of the female body as grotesque is transformed into an affective landscape of potentiality. The political potential arises not mainly from the critique of the larger systemic orders attempting to organize, tame, or contain the open body but, instead, from Helen's defiant and willful voice. The seriousness with which Helen attacks systems of physical control clashes awkwardly with her playfully defiant gestures.

Both *Feuchtgebiete* and *Axolotl Roadkill* provide interesting cases for our larger discussion of global popfeminist protest actions because, as Baer argues, both novels can be understood as transnational texts. Baer underscores this claim through an examination of precarity. She writes that these two novels

> investigate key facets of life in neoliberal capitalism, including sexual deregulation, privatization, and new configurations of the family. By emphasizing precarity, they also open up spaces for thinking about statuses such as gender, sexuality, class, race, and ethnicity, that no longer form the basis for an oppositional politics today, and yet continue to inform the subjective lives of individuals and their ability to survive or thrive in the present. (Baer 2015a, 163)

This returns us to how affects connect to the broader reach of global flows and, further, to the manner in which the circulations of these texts and their reception find their place in the larger landscape of popfeminist activism. Baer claims that these two texts, due to their engagement with neoliberalism and precarity, must be considered "aesthetically sophisticated and politically meaningful works of contemporary transnational literature" (163). This is, in part, due to their stunning success on the literary market, their ability to be seen as what Baer calls "traveling texts" (181), which would include not only the success of the translations but also their use of language in an inventive, popfeminist manner. One additional aspect of this, it could be argued, is the manner in which they come into dialogue with their cinematic counterparts. While we do not wish to go so far as to claim that *Torpedo* is the adaptation of *Axolotl Roadkill* (or vice versa), it is in a sense the novel's prequel and, as discussed above, thus comes into dialogue with the aesthetic form and affective resonance produced by the novel, including its awkward political invocations. Thus, it is also the depiction of the body as an open system that enables such travel between texts and films and beyond, into different aesthetic and affective terrains of politics.

Feuchtgebiete was adapted for screen in 2013 by David Wnendt, released in North America in 2014, and made available in the United States on Netflix. The surprise success of the novel *Feuchtgebiete* already indicates the potential for exploiting this kind of awkwardness for financial gain; the film version certainly commercially and rather successfully markets the adolescent aesthetics and affective charges presented by the novel. Despite being intended for a mainstream audience, the film does not turn the novel's awkwardness into comedic ridicule but, instead, calls for an emotional attachment to the unstable and nonconformist character of Helen and her body politics. This might be in part credited to the actress (Carla Juri), who plays the main character, and in part to the fact that there are no other characters in the film that become possible targets for identification. Helen's body politics show the body as an open system in the most literal sense, which not only includes germs, bacteria, and objects in exchange with her body but also refers to her fluid understanding of her sexuality, bodily integrity, and identity in general. In both book and film, there is an awareness that neoliberal bodies can or must be controlled and consumed; Helen's body is, at least within the world of the film, located outside of this consumption, which creates an interesting tension with the film's own marketing of this outside position for ticket sales. The film achieves emotional attachment to an unstable and non-conformist kind of body politics in a popfeminist manner and undermines neoliberal bodies and biopolitical systems in a way that is, despite the potential for the experience of disgust on the part of the viewer, accessible. Instead of replicating the awkwardness of the novel, the film plays with the viewers who expect to feel awkward while watching the cinematic adaptation of the text. The awkwardness is instead on par with what might be best termed a commercial awkwardness, one seen in such pop-cultural uses of the term as MTV's television series *Awkward*, a comedy about the life of a teenage girl. This accessibility or glossy awkwardness continues to contain popfeminist implications.

Part of the accessibility is the film's play with its own self-produced expectations. This is already clear from the outset. The film opens with a shot of an indeterminate crease of flesh, meant to raise the expectations of the wily viewer who remembers that the book version starts with haemorrhoids. Paired with the driving beat of the opening drums from the Peaches song "You Love It," the camera swivels to reveal the crease to be not Helen's backside but, rather, a close-up of the fold at the knee of her bent leg. As the camera pulls back she stands up and the song's refrain, "you love it when I'm bad," accompanies her as she whizzes down the street on a skateboard, absent-mindedly scratching her behind. This refrain seems thus twofold: while the implication is Helen's badness, which is set up by viewers' knowledge of the book and the film's hyped release, the phrase also implies the film itself and its coquettish relationship with viewer expectations.

However, this is not to say that the film smoothes over the uncomfortable moments of the book. In fact, it heightens some of the less sexual scenes. Following Helen's barefooted skateboard ride down the street as an introduction to her character, with all of its implied freedom and popfeminist, willful irreverence, we follow her down the stairs of a public washroom, which is an exaggerated representation of a dirty and neglected space; it is littered with garbage and flooded with murky water. And we watch as Helen picks her way – still barefoot – through the muck to arrive at the toilet, its seat stained with urine. The voiceover speaks the first lines of the book as we watch Helen squirt and insert haemorrhoid cream into her anus with her finger, the extreme close-ups of the cream and the camera's almost-but-not-quite tracking of her finger to her anus heightening both the potential for disgust in the viewer and humour in the last-minute avoidance of that disgust: the film, again coquettishly, does not go there, at least not quite – just enough for the viewer's imagination to complete the scene. This technique is reminiscent of many adolescent boy movies, such as *American Pie*, that rely on the humour produced by the viewer's relief from the (near) awkward moment. The sequence continues towards the overdrawn, or "too much," as the camera's ever-increasing close-up peers with Helen at the dirty toilet, and we shift into a cartoon-like world of swirling bacteria, still to the tempo of Peaches's music. When the camera pulls back, the viewer is finally given the "release" in the fulfilment of disgusted expectations: we watch as Helen joyfully sits on the toilet seat, swiping the seat clean with her exposed vulva.

The film is not true to the novel in the sense of replicating its narrative arc. This opening scene, for one, combines the addition of character traits (Helen as a skateboarder) with a scene that comes slightly later in the book (the public toilet; Roche 2008, 20), with the opening lines of the book itself. A further aspect transformed in the film is the development of characters. For example, the expansion of the role of female friend, who in the film receives her own plotline, offers depth and sympathy to the figure of Helen. Robin, Helen's nurse and love interest, is given a fiancée and we watch him struggle with his fascination with Helen. Most notable is the manner in which the figures of the mother and father have been transformed. Helen's desire to use her injury in the hospital as a front to bring her divorced mother and father together creates a tension on the level of the plot between Helen's playful sexual experimentation and her melodramatic and childish emotional state.[33] This plot device in the novel could be seen as a manner of unsettling the otherwise powerful call to free women from the constraints of the beauty industry and other social expectations around the body and sexuality. By radically expanding the figures of mother and father, which are fairly underdeveloped in the novel, the film gives space to important discussions around cycles of abuse, verbal violence, and depression, whereby these discussions can – if not entirely unfold – then at least begin to emerge.

The film provides background regarding Helen's mother's depression and the ensuing divorce. In one very telling scene around the table with dinner guests, the father cuts open a turducken (the chicken, inside a duck, inside a turkey that has become a culinary pop legend of sorts), which his wife has slaved over, and makes the comment that, when Helen was born, the doctors had to cut the mother's perineum. The resulting look of the mother's vagina following the episiotomy, he says to laughter, was much the same as the stuffed turkey, presumably referencing the crowning of the infant Helen inside her mother. The mother, in response to her husband's quip, raises her dress to the dinner guests, revealing her naked genitals, and points: "They cut right into there."[34] Helen watches throughout the scene from a position on the stairs. This scene connects the mother's inappropriate reaction to verbal abuse directly to Helen's later exhibitionism, thus politicizing Helen's actions and creating a sense of physical solidarity between the two women, even though that solidarity is never explored in the film in feminist terms.

The resulting attempt at suicide and matricide, for the mother attempts to kill herself and her infant son with the same oven in which she cooked the father's meal, is no longer merely an event to cause Helen to despise her mother, as is the case in the novel, but, instead, brings up questions of abuse and postpartum depression. These scenes that are emphasized in the film also ask viewers to question Helen's devotion to her father. Further, while Helen's mother is indeed depicted as at times cruel, primarily in flashback form, where we see Helen as a young girl scrubbing the toilet or jumping into waiting arms that are pulled away at the last minute, this depiction is balanced out with scenes of loyalty. For example, when Helen's doctor is introduced to her mother, he makes a quip about being able to cope with difficult personalities and offers her child-rearing tips. The mother responds in true schoolyard fashion by fiercely calling the doctor's own mother a difficult personality, not her daughter. However, like the book, any clear-cut reading of the mother figure is subverted by the film's ending: as Helen and Robin get into his car to leave the hospital, we see the mother and father arrive at the same time and unite in an embrace. This pseudo-resolution (not offered by the book) makes any positively charged reading of the mother throughout the film politically awkward.

The opening scene discussed above illustrates a set of key aesthetic transformations in the film's adaptation of the novel that produces interestingly similar affective charges to those found in or produced by the written text, even if these are less confrontational. These charges move beyond the narrative world of book and film: for example, the soundtrack matches in tenor the book's bright pink cover, and the spunky wardrobe and mannerisms of the actress match the manner in which the author Roche held herself in television interviews and in her earlier appearances as a music TV moderator on the music television channel Viva 2. Thus, what is adapted quite faithfully is the book's adolescent aesthetics and, further, the affective landscape of the greater public debate, or the event of the book itself. The text works with viewer expectations by disappointing pornographic expectations, coherent character psychologies, and plot resolutions. The film uses the expectations built up by the novel's reception in its own popfeminist manner: it uses pop as its aesthetic language and politicizes this pop with feminist content while at the same time pushing feminist concerns into the popular. It uses the popular appeal of the novel and its wide reception to propel discussions about body politics, sex, and normativity further into the mainstream and leave them there – without resolving any of the questions it poses and without offering any alternatives. The film

itself does not work with and through awkwardness; the viewer of the
film takes part in an event created around and by the author Roche, her
novel, and its adaptation, and it is here that awkwardness arises.

RECEIVING SEX: THE AWKWARD BODY POLITICS
OF POPFEMINIST EVENT CULTURES

The process of the reception of *Feuchtgebiete* in its various circulations
emphasizes the reader's role as part of an *Erlebnisgesellschaft* (liter-
ally, experience society, though more broadly known as event culture)
as defined in Gerhard Schulze's 1992 study (republished in 2005). In
this case, the event culture is infused with messy forms of feminist politics. In his study, Schulze (2005, 24, 52) argues that audience and self
are integral to the experience or event. It is, he claims, no longer the
exchange of goods that drives the market but, rather, the exchange of
experiences, whereby the person consuming an experience also contrib-
utes to its production; the audience consumer is essential (423). When
thought in terms of cultural products such as the novels and films discussed here, or the popfeminist actions, protests, and performances discussed throughout our study, the readers and viewers effectively insert
themselves as creators, as textual subjects, and as activists into the
object's story and its political trajectory. In the contemporary period,
this insertion also happens as digitally shared experience, as comment
or blog post, or as digital manipulation. In this way, *Erlebnisgesellschaft* has become increasingly prolific – or viral – in the digital age.

What these discussions illustrate is that the readers or consumers
of the event become part of it, along with the activist-performers. In
terms of the texts discussed here, which all share a certain explicit take
on sexuality, that "sexiness" (both in terms of the content as well as
the hype around the content), however awkwardly adolescent, is harnessed and circulated in the reception of these works, something that
also most notably occurs in the case of Lady Bitch Ray but is also
implicit in all activist performances that utilize the female body, including especially Pussy Riot and Peaches, Chicks on Speed, and SlutWalk
as well as actions such as #aufschrei or #RegrettingMotherhood. The
body is present here as perception, representation, and manipulation:
there is no "real" body outside of the mediated body, and the mediated
body is always also physical. In these texts, bodies become hyper-visible as sites for emotions, whether as pain, pleasure, lust, or depression;
at the same time, bodies are the main objects for playful negotiations

of connection and pleasure. The pop-body becomes an event to be consumed by an *Erlebnisgesellschaft* that is spectacular in its pseudo-pornographic appeal and that is political through its infusion with, however messy, feminisms.

Popfeminism, therefore, flows into the mainstream through the media circus of the reception. This media circus triggers a range of affective responses, one of which is the (here sexually coded) awkwardness that we describe as politically productive in these novels, films, performances, and protests. It is by looking more closely at this relationship with the sexualized adolescent body that we can describe how such a relationship is political precisely by not taking a distant or ironic perspective on the body and body politics (which often produces, albeit sometimes unintentionally, rather arrogant and privileged kinds of politics) but, instead, by politicizing our close relationship to the body as an open system and as a socially constructed technology, which, at the same time, transforms and is transformed by its (digital) circulations. As readers and analysts of texts, we are constantly thrown into a close, physical, and affective relationship with the fictional characters we read about and view only to be troubled by the awkward relationship between the playful immaturity and the serious political charge of the narratives, and between these bodies and the world that surrounds them – a world that is inevitably also our own. This troubling can be thought of as a rip or disturbance in the organization of the senses, here in the affectively felt expectations of clarity of meaning around these relationships. The trouble we experience therefore writes awkwardness onto our own political perspective.

The political female body in popfeminism is caught in the push and pull of feminism and pop, taking traditionally feminist body concerns – abortion rights, contraception, eating disorders, pornography – to a media-oriented level that also includes traditionally antifeminist approaches such as glossy images of highly stylized, normative, sexy, and even pornographic female bodies. While an understanding of the body as raw matter (Stöcker 2007, 47) – a place of individual formation and play and for individual self-stylization, as some neofeminisms would argue[35] – could produce a rather apolitical understanding, awkwardness complicates this notion of the body. Bodies matter not only as individual expression of troubled adolescents but also as producers and reproducers of social and political technologies, power structures, and forms of oppression. Bodies are technologies that are also always simultaneously textual, social, and material – and digital.

In this way, popfeminism recognizes, but also manipulates, the traditional feminist belief that the body makes meaning and that it is representative of a masculine dominated system. In some way, Roche's and Hegemann's works could be understood as the contemporary, awkward, and adolescent response to popfeminist manifestos like *Wir Alphamädchen*, which, as we discuss in chapter 2, have often been criticized as depoliticized. In that text in particular, Haaf, Klingner, and Streidl define body styling as the woman's decision; no longer is body styling a response to male-dominated beauty culture but, instead, it becomes an expression of individual liberties, which includes also the defiant, the negative, the injured, or otherwise imperfect body.[36] These popfeminist events politicize the body and body styling by presenting and embracing sex as awkward, as immature, and as adolescent, a strategy shared by the other artists we discuss, such as Lady Bitch Ray and Chicks on Speed. Emphasizing the body as sexual, or, to go one step further, depicting the female body as always and only sexually coded, popfeminism mirrors (and messes with) the politics of pop culture. In Hegemann's and Roche's texts, such body styling is revealed as a sometimes painful, and most definitely negative process that is culturally coded. In the case of *Axolotl Roadkill* and to some extent *Feuchtgebiete*,[37] this cultural coding is related to the randy sexual body of the adolescent. Such approaches to the body (re)politicize body politics by illustrating the role physical bodies play in the mechanisms of circulation and the production and reproduction of affective attachments. They confirm the continuing, if very different, entanglement of the personal and the political, the private and the public. Butler (2009, ii) argues that "gender norms have everything to do with how and in what way we can appear in public space; how and in what way the public and private are distinguished, and how that distinction is instrumentalized in the service of sexual politics." In their depictions and writings of bodies in different and new public contexts, these authors as well as the other performers and activists discussed here break down essentialist ideas of femininity, natural beauty, and sex – including those solidified in earlier forms of feminism. They also question what feminist body politics might mean in the contemporary setting, yet emphasize again, infused with a new sense of urgency, that there is no strategy of writing (about) the body that places it outside of cultural norms and material contexts.

The political charge of these depictions of the sexualized body as at the same time caught within and pushing outside the normative offers us a new approach to writing and thinking about sexuality in the contemporary period. In "Homonationalism as Assemblage: Viral Travels, Affective Sexualities," Puar discusses two modes for understanding sexuality within queer theory. The first strand she understands in terms of deconstruction that emphasizes

> social construction of sexual difference for which language dominates the political realm through an insistence on the endless deferral of meaning. The other way of understanding sexuality can loosely be defined as the multiplication and proliferation of difference, of making difference and proliferating creative differentiation: the becoming otherwise of difference. (Puar 2013, 41)

While deconstructionist understandings of sexuality wish to "think against and through binaries in hopes of undermining and dissolving them," the second form, which Puar terms "affirmative becomings," wishes to "read and foster endless differentiation and multiplicity in hopes of overwhelming those binaries" (41). The difference between "undermining" and "overwhelming" seems also to be one of technology, the latter comprehensible as data "flooding" the (digital) system made of binary code. The second manner of approaching sexuality does not wish to make sense of representational form but, instead, "solicits sense, the creation of potentialities of emergence" (41) and pays attention to the "multiplicity of affirmative becomings" (42). This formulation returns us to the claim made at the start of this chapter, that focusing on affect and aesthetics in the manner outlined here offers us a way out of the representational trap. Instead, thinking in terms of affirmative becomings – a statement that in a sense addresses both affect and aesthetics as understood in its two-part phrase, the "affirmative" relating to the emotional dimension of affect and "becomings" a part of adolescent aesthetics – goes to the very fabric of creative differentiation.

The two-part phase of affirmative becomings also defines our position as consumers, readers, and scholars as always trying to think against and, at the same time, trying to solicit sense from text or performance sources with which we ourselves are intimately entangled. The notion of affirmative becomings as a way to read the sexually coded body in popfeminism applies to the body politics discussed throughout this book, to their aesthetics and affects. The sense that some of the popfeminist activisms we describe here are searching for new forms of doing politics in the face of impossibility is captured by the notion of becomings: something is in the process of emerging; there is a sense of ongoing experimentation, always on the threshold. And while often coded negatively and defiantly, it never loses its ultimately affirmative affective impulse – even if that affirmation should not suggest a return to the evaluative mode of thinking feminist actions as success or failure. Affirmativity is not to be understood as synonymous with positivity for it communicates no sense of linear progress, but it does suggest confirmation and joy. Affect and aesthetics are crucial to this discussion for they refer to communication, relations, and reception, and the social or political sphere, in the most direct ways, thus (too) closely implicating the reader-viewer-participant in the awkwardness of it all, thereby forging – an at times strange or uncomfortable – solidarity.

6

On the Contemporary: Materiality and Virality of Feminism from Mainstream to the Academy

Throughout *Awkward Politics* we discuss the manner in which pop-feminism utilizes both feminist and anti-feminist codes to rewrite pop culture and feminist culture, and we show how both of these codes are part of a digital moment. This is true for a wide variety of popular appearances of feminism in the mainstream beyond explicitly activist interests. Pop events have generated viral discussions about feminism, as, for example, illustrated in Beyoncé's (2014b) "feminist" declaration and her short film *Yours and Mine*, which explores her own subject position, her feminism, and her "humanism." Or they have produced their own pop moments, as seen in MTV's October 2014 launch of "Braless," a YouTube channel devoted to, as the tagline says, "all things pop culture and internet," but which, with the title's reference to the second wave feminist movement and its being hosted by sex-positive activist Laci Green, clearly wishes to ride the current popularity of feminism in the mainstream.[1] But these popfeminist moments have also been triggered by the use of digital means to pursue more traditional forms of activism, such as is seen in hashtag activism or street protests, and the performative, as is the case with Pussy Riot, Femen, or Lady Bitch Ray. Digital forms expand literature and film into feminist event cultures; the digital and the analogue are never closer than they are in these actions for, both being mediated spheres, they feed into one another and inform one another. At each turn, however, the event or object itself as well as its reception contains feminist- and anti-feminist moments, which, in their simultaneity, point to the central claim with which we started this book: that, in popfeminist circulation, the evaluative stance itself needs constant undermining.

The preceding chapter addresses the affects emerging from what we term the adolescent aesthetics that describe this type of popfeminist activist work. These aesthetics are made up of the open systems of bodies, technologies, and materials in a neoliberal society that function in the dual aspect of aesthetics – that is, engaging the senses, on the one hand, and motivating or motivated by the social, on the other hand. These two aspects are encompassed in both parts of the term "popfeminism." The affective reach, both in terms of emotional power as well as in terms of connectivity, of these aesthetics as awkward allows for a political reading of the structure as well as of the reception of popfeminist performance art activism, a reading that has broader implications. These implications are related to the immediacy of that impact and the manner in which contemporary feminist actions comment on, or even create, a sense of the present.

If one attempts to compare these examples of feminist protest cultures to other partially digital protest events of the twenty-first century – for example, the "Occupy" movements – the difference not only in speed and temporality but also in "attachment" becomes clear. While Occupy had a decidedly political attachment, a goal, and a message (to fight against – or draw attention to – the "1 percent"), which might have contributed to its initial "success" (if media attention equals "success"), this attachment ultimately also led to the swift end of the movement. The goal could not be achieved and the movement appeared as unsuccessful, either because it was eaten or overwhelmed by "the system" or because it simply "lost steam." What we show in the messy and murky circulations of popfeminist activism, however, is that, without a clear "goal," protest events manage to constantly slip in and out of sight without losing their political currency, maybe by constantly shifting their political target.

In this chapter, we turn from the relational and impact-specific aspects of affect and aesthetics to their usefulness as a means of harnessing the immediacy of these digital feminisms in terms of their constitution. Through affective aesthetics, we find traces of the awkward as readable for the transformations and trappings of capitalism – within feminist discourse but also in other political contexts – which allows us to understand how history, in the form of the historical present, is central to understanding the current moment. Furthermore, reading for affective aesthetics also suggests that bodies – in the digital sphere and as digital bodies – continue to act as technologies of popfeminist activism that bring together the historical present of past actions with the affective experience of the presentness of the politically urgent moment.

This chapter revisits issues discussed throughout *Awkward Politics*, but it also addresses the central urgency evoked by awkwardness as a politics. We turn that urgency into an ethical call for action not only on the streets and in the digital sphere but also in the feminist academy in an age of neoliberalism. Through this it becomes apparent that we talk about "digital feminisms" not because our examples are found only in the digital sphere or have a digital component to them (though they do, most often in circulation or reception) but because the awkward politics that originate in and go viral through the digital offer essential dimensions to non-digital contexts, thus "digitizing" the non-digital in a theoretical manner and asking us to approach "data mining" in a political – and awkward – way.

Popfeminist activisms work to create a sense of the contemporary, one that is always also quite aware of its pasts. We begin by cycling back to Chicks on Speed as an example for just such present historicity. Their combined use of material and technologies also allows us to reexamine the link between affect and aesthetics. But this contemporary is also temporary, as the title of this chapter implies, which returns us to the discussion of circularity. This temporariness leads us to take a closer look at the conception of the viral and virality, which is not only a way to think about the temporary but also to return to connectivity and collaboration. The second example in this chapter is our popfeminist reading of the Barbie Dreamhouse Experience, the protests that accompanied the exhibit while in Berlin, and its travels. The Barbie Dreamhouse appears to pose a challenge to feminist politics in its excessive display of neoliberal consumption, body norms, and the blatant exploitation of the cruel optimism of living the dream. Popfeminist readings for awkwardness start with this very challenge not by creating ironic distance to Barbie but, instead, by mining for levels of affective charges, of viral proliferation, and of circulations of Barbie as a doll, a digital projection, and an idea that incites protest. Finally, this discussion of the contemporary and the viral brings us, through a return to Lady Bitch Ray/Reyhan Şahin as well as a look at the "Professx" discussions in Germany, to academic discourses and thus back to our own positions as scholars within the North American academy, where, strangely but maybe not surprisingly, feminism and pop are simultaneously marginalized and mainstream. In these final considerations, we risk a proposal that asks feminist scholars, teachers, students, and administrators to employ a version of our popfeminist methodology and thus engage with awkwardness as theory and practice in the spaces of the academy.

EMERGENCE AND CONTEMPORANEITY

Chapter 5 ends with the notion of "affirmative becomings" that focus on the "creation of potentialities of emergence" (Puar 2013, 41).[2] Like becomings, emergence suggests process; however, it does so in a manner that is temporally grounded in a sense of the present. In *Cruel Optimism*, Berlant (2011b, 4) speaks of the present as "perceived, first affectively: the present is what makes itself present to us before it becomes anything else," and, further, as "a thing that is sensed and under constant revision," emerging from how we individually and collectively experience situations and events. Affect is key to grasping the immediacy of the present, or the "now," in that common experience. Ben Anderson also sees affect as central to theorizing the contemporary; however, he grounds this centrality in the political. He writes: "Affects are an inescapable element within an expanded definition of the political," and, for this reason, "attention to affect in cultural theory is not only necessary but contemporaneous" for it "provides a way of understanding and engaging with a set of broader changes in societal (re)production in the context of mutations in capitalism" (Anderson 2010, 164–5). He lists these changes as new forms of labour, biopolitical networks of discipline, and digital developments. For our purposes, we might slightly alter this list to read: new forms of protest, feminist networks of neoliberalism, and the technologies of the digital and the corporeal.

Taken together, the social changes we see here and that are found under, or even expose, the mutations in capitalism tell a story about how feminist action, creative work, and political engagement is defined in interaction with the contemporary moment and at the same time defines our sense of immediacy and the present. Berlant (2011b, 5) further discusses the present in her development of what she terms genres that describe "the activity of being reflexive about a contemporary historicity as one lives it." On her research blog, Berlant (2011a, 2) explains her understanding of the term "genre" as utilized here further: "A genre is a loose affectively-invested zone of expectations about the narrative shape a situation will take. A situation becomes-genre, finds its genres of event." Because she identifies these new genres of the present as genres of crisis – crisis that is sustained because it is not exceptional but ongoing and ordinary – they describe forms of living within contemporary structures of politics. In identifying that genre that Berlant (2011b, 5) sees as "tracking the sense of the present" in her study, she settles on the term "impasse," in which the individual experiences the present as "stretched-out," as if living in an "extended crisis" (7).

This sense of the present produced in the impasse, or rather its affective charge, Berlant calls emergent (6). This implies that the affective experience of the present is one of process, continual recalibration, and situation. The person experiencing the impasse will continue to find ways of living on in what is seen to be a situational crisis, redefining her actions, habitus, or relations in order to keep going (ibid.).

"Genre" might be one way of talking about the narrative of a politics of contemporary (German) feminism that is developed through these digital actions. This narrative is positioned both as part of and against other narratives of the present (such as mainstream postfeminism, historical lineages of second and third wave feminism, and neoliberalism). Indeed, crisis, a term we use at various points in this book, is central to the story of feminism in the present and to neoliberalism because it is based on many of the forms of discourse produced simultaneous with or in the wake of the financial crisis, the production of precarity and alternative protest forms, and the ever apparent impact of global structures of power on experience. Further, the term "impasse," as one such genre, describes well the experience of the circularity of the political in popfeminist activism and performance work. At each evaluative turn, the failure/success binary erects an impasse. However, this impasse does not erase the critical urgency around feminism, or the need to do feminism in the face of its impossibility, which, particularly in the digital age, is ever increasing. The impasse found in the circularity of the political asks us to recalibrate towards new attempts to do feminism. The awkward does not recalibrate but, instead, makes that impasse visible by harnessing the emergent moment as containing creative potential.

Chicks on Speed provide an example of how our archive of awkwardness, or the variety of moments and actions discussed in this book, visually and performatively enacts that genre and aesthetically, affectively, and materially emerges from the impasse of the circular narrative of contemporary feminisms. In many ways, their work is not of the present but of the historical present for they engage past discourses, visual cues, and tensions in a manner that suggests ongoing immediacy. Chicks on Speed link second wave feminist concerns with popfeminist aesthetics and a sense of cyberfeminist disturbances. Their most recent album project, *Artsravaganza*, illustrates this mixing. On their website they describe their work as "a collision between pop music, art, activism and data," "the culmination of the transdisciplinary ideal," which includes "an album and a collection of music apps." The combination in the description between performance art and the digital sphere is mirrored in the list of collaborators who offered their musical

contributions, including Julian Assange, Princess Francesca von Haps-
burg, Yoko Ono, Peter Weibel, Angie Seah, and Anat Ben David.[3] Visually, the font on the cover of the album makes a clear historic reference
to the prolific pop artist Andy Warhol and his Campbell Soup series,
which, again, connects to the historical dimensions of their work but
brings this history into the contemporary moment by using digital
forms to create a new and appropriately messy and playful claim for
a *Gesamtkunstwerk*.

As discussed in chapter 3, in their works, the body becomes a hyper-
real instrument and a cyber-feminist machine, while, at the same time, it
continues to be the physical locus for political negotiation. In this sense,
their approach to the performative body could indeed be described as
"cyberpopfeminism" (Kuni 2007) for their works often include technology attached to and controlled by their bodies, as, for example, in
the case of the "Supersuit" that contains Neopreen pouches into which
sensors are slipped, allowing the wearers to control the audio-visual
aspects of the performance through their bodies (Chicks on Speed et
al. 2010, 069). The manner in which the cyber-body is endowed with
pop and feminism becomes clear in their performance piece "Objekt
Instruments," the description of which is reprinted in ~~Don't~~ Art Fash-
ion Music. In it, they include a Theremin Tapestry that combines a traditionally woven tapestry with Theremin technology (the theremin is
an electronic musical instrument that was invented in Russia in 1920)
(014). During the performance, the tapestry plays an audio loop controlled by the bodies of the performers, the words of which are inspired
by Butler's (1997) *Excitable Speech* (Chicks on Speed et al. 2010, 015).
In the handwritten text outlining the performance, working in a sense
as "found" performance notes, the Chicks write: "This instrument is in
no way under controle [*sic*!] of the player but neither is it out of controle [*sic*!]. Are the performers the instrument of the Theremin or the
other way around? Is this performance a demonstration of Technology,
a craft exhibition? a concert? a theater play? a voodoo train? Don't
Answer!" (013). In the photograph that accompanies these words, we
see a performance that mixes outmoded electronic technology and traditionally female handiwork with their own awkwardly contorted bodies, clothed in bright, pop-art inspired costumes: high heels in primary
colours, capes with cartoon-style lettering,[4] and shiny leotards (016–
017). These visual elements are tied together by the use of an audio
text referencing Butler's political understanding of performative language. Connecting the mediated but physical bodies of the performers
directly to a political-theoretical agenda creates different possibilities

for an audience response that is built into the performance as a somewhat unpredictable factor. This is clear in their questioning of the audience quoted above and their command: "Don't Answer!" The questions are intended to stand unanswered. Such a performance ultimately asks after the role of mediation for popfeminist politics or politics in general, but it also creates emotional responses to the physicality of the body in the digital realm – responses that thus act politically.

The body on stage or in the performance piece is the locale where political and feminist tensions play out. The bodies of the performers are simultaneously coded as authentic, or "real," in a traditional feminist way and are excessively mediated through cyber-invasions and alterations. Photographs taken from performances throughout Europe and the United States starting as early as 2001 and printed in ~~Don't~~ *Art Fashion Music* visually exemplify these awkward tensions between the authentic and the cyber body. In an image taken during a performance in Frankfurt, Germany, in 2009, for example, we see one of the members sawing the heel off of a pair of purple pumps (Chicks on Speed et al. 2010, 146–7). The authentic feminist message is clear: high heels unnaturally hyper-sexualize the female body in a manner that is uncomfortable. By severing the heel with a handsaw Chicks on Speed appropriate masculine tools to destroy a man-made object designed to harm women. However, as discussed in chapter 3, Chicks on Speed elevate the high-heeled shoe to the status of an art object that is simultaneously a musical instrument and can be worn, theoretically, by the artist to turn her foot into a guitar. But this object is further complicated by a performance from 2007, entitled "Shoe Fuck" (the reprinted image is attributed to a performance in London, England). Here, we see a woman, presumably one of the Chicks, vaginally penetrating herself with the heel of a high-heeled shoe to obvious (staged) pleasure (159). The implicit reference to the shoe guitar here doubles the affective resonances of the self-pleasure of masturbation; it is not only the fashion industry that is implicated in the performer's repurposing of the object but also Chicks on Speed's own musical creations. The willfulness of the object out of place is here heightened in a joyfully inappropriate manner.

In a further photograph taken in Malmö, Sweden, in 2010, we see another band member wearing a pair of stretch capri pants with the crotch removed (Chicks on Speed et al. 2010, 137), part of the performance "Girl Monster." Here the authentic is simulated not in the performance of a clearly feminist message but in the explicit citation of the historical legacy of feminist performance art in the form of Valie

Export's "Aktionshose: Genitalpanik" (Action pants: Genital panic).
Returning to the photograph from the Frankfurt performance, the awkwardness arises when the audience is taken into account, for the viewer
of the photograph is placed in a strange position at close range to the
performer, whose face is covered with her hair. We are left to inspect
the performer as excessive and even unsightly, lingering over her hairy
arms, her hands grasping the saw and shoe, and her green-clad breast.
Indeed, the breast, with its clearly defined nipple, takes up the left fore-
ground and provides visual counterpoint to the saw in the right side of
the frame. In the Swedish example, the performer creates the awkwardness for the photographer – and, repeatedly, for each viewer of the photograph – who has captured her standing, hands-on-hips, in the middle
of a backstage changing area. Surrounded by the informal and everyday chaos of such a space with casually dressed people in the background, the performer's body and her aggressive stance are awkwardly
out of place.

The fact that Chicks on Speed have developed apps around the release
of their new album, meant for their audience to engage with during the
performance, pushes this work firmly in the realm of digital circulation, but a circulation that is also different from the circulation seen on
social media sites. Though online and digital, the app is unlinked from
the "Web" (in that it needs no browser) and highly personalized (car-
ried around on individual device screens, for example). The absolute-
ness of this process seems to be mirrored in the song "Wir sind Daten"
("We are data," with Peter Weibel, based on an original song by Hotel
Morphilia Orchester), streamable on the Chicks on Speed website and
licensed under a Creative Commons Licence, where we hear a long
string of phrases – in German and English – connecting our everyday
world to digital data. Similarly, the song and video "Utopia," under collaboration with Yoko Ono (and available in multiple remixes), offers
a vision of freedom from gentrification in a digital realm: "Virtual vs.
real space. No place. No space. / The world is a theater. We each have
a role. But art's not the answer. We are not social workers, you know.
Let's go on strike. It's arts for art's sake! / ... [F]eminism gave us para-
dise, a perfect place." While these lyrics contain a vision for a feminist
digital utopia, they also suggest a "strike," a form of political refusal to
provide an "answer."

The aesthetic reach of Chicks on Speed is citational and playful, but, as
we claim, also awkward in the use of the material. Revisiting Chicks on
Speed under this perspective illustrates how this kind of awkwardness,

as we discuss in chapter 5, has an adolescent aesthetic form, one that is described by words that suggest emergence, such as "processes," "becomings," and "thresholds." As we have noted, we understand aesthetics as both engaging the sensual field (sight, sound, taste) and being born of a social and historical context. Highmore's "rip" in the organization of the senses from which the political is generated makes a claim for awkwardness within the aesthetic field as political. These theoretical conceptions come together and are put into practice in the art of Chicks on Speed and in their collaborations. Returning to Berlant (2011b, 7), she writes that new genres of crisis create an "emergent aesthetics" that return us to "older traditions of neorealism, while speaking as well to the new social movements that have organized under the rubrics of 'precarity' and the 'precarious.'" Emergent aesthetics describe how we make sense of the experience of the world (in terms of the narrative being developed, here about contemporary feminisms) and how we measure what impact our emotional and sensorial engagement with the material or with experience has on our immediate development of self. Emergent aesthetics could be another way of capturing the adolescent impulse of popfeminist creative work, continually finding its form, or, rather, utilizing process as form, for the narrative and impact of experience are process-based – that is, in a state of constant emergence. In the case of the Chicks on Speed example, it is precisely this constant search for form and genre that resonates with the viewer and causes affective charges as well as a sense of action and community (an affirmation) as being part of an event, albeit an event of "crisis."

FEMINIST VIRALITY: A BARBIE DREAMHOUSE

While it was erected in Berlin, the Barbie Dreamhouse Experience, an actual pink house filled with mainly digital objects, displayed an event of crisis while at the same time creating community by offering a time and space for rebellious gestures. The way in which practice and theory, digital and corporal, crisis and joy, pop and feminism, collide in the travelling exhibit itself and the protest events surrounding it, of course, works much differently than is the case in the art events of Chicks on Speed. If affect is how we perceive the present and its genres of crisis, then thinking of affect in response to the increasing technological dimension of activism and its transnational reach opens us to expansive, unlimited, and self-reproducing relations in the collision of the digital with the corporeal, creating an openness that also speaks directly to what it means to be political in the present moment. Puar uses her discussion of affirmative becomings in thinking about sexuality as "assemblage and not identity" to approach viral theory that understands virality not simply as mere replication but also as mutation: virality addresses transmission to multiple contexts, a concept that further links digital circulation to the biological workings of the body. Virality simultaneously suggests "speed and reach of information transit, especially in relation to the internet" as well as "bodily contamination, uncontainability, unwelcome transgression of border and boundaries while pointing more positively to the porosity, indeed the conviviality, of what has been treated as opposed" (Puar 2013, 42). Virality reproduces affective tendencies that themselves virally reproduce; as Brian Massumi (2002) claims, affect becomes autonomous through its becoming virtual.

The flows of technology across borders are embodied and affective, but they are also process-based (as in part of the immediate moment) and future-oriented for they show, in the form of the bio-mediated body, what the body is becoming and can become (Clough 2010, 211). Puar (2013, 43) describes the viral form in terms of circularity, a motion we refer to continually throughout this book: "The beauty of virality, of course, is that it produces its own critique" (ibid.). Because, however, it creates its own criticism, virality – not only the motion or description but also the viral object, person, or event – is also "altered through that encounter" (ibid.). Here we see a similar self-reflexive motion that is engendered by popfeminism. She continues, explaining that

> what is reproduced is not the human subject, identity, or body, but affective tendencies, ecologies of sensation, and different ontologies that create new epistemologies of affect. When we say that something has gone viral, it's another way of acknowledging everything that is opposed to the virus, or the viral, can be circumnavigated. Viral theory, then, as a post humanist intervention, also begins before the species-like divide of the activism versus theory binary, an opposition that is foundational to the production within the fields of Women's Studies and Gay and Lesbian studies. Viral theory is immune to such divides and divisions. Virality indicates not so much the portability of a concept but a measure of its resonance. Thus virality might also be a way of differently thinking geopolitical transversality that is not insistently routed through or against the nation-state, providing an alternative to notions of transnationalism. (ibid.)

Puar's approach to virality, which we like to think of as another and force of power, allows us to again pair theory and practice in the awkward politics of popfeminism. Indeed, we make a claim for utilizing popfeminist methodology to approach popfeminist objects, a methodology that – like its own object of critique – is circular but also searching. Although it turns back on itself and reproduces much of the circular impulse that it wishes to examine, popfeminist methodologies offer readings that do not directly replicate the impulses emerging from the objects at hand but, instead, produce mutations. Therefore, while we cannot and perhaps should not speak of productivity in terms of what is produced by such methodology, we may speak of virality.

In her essay, Puar engages specifically with how her term "homonationalism" has gone viral and is used in a variety of ways and contexts. While we are not discussing homonationalism here, her posing of this question – of how a theoretical term goes viral – as a springboard to further thinking around corporeality, theory, and geopolitical divisions is helpful. This viral moment disengages transnationalism not only from conceptions of nationhood but also from the distinction between local and global, routing it instead through digital embodiment. Of course, many images and discursive strategies discussed in our study have gone viral in the most basic of senses, crossing multiple cultural and national boundaries, being usurped (even as there is a sense of shying away, as from a virus) by many different causes. We see this most particularly in the case of Pussy Riot, where the term "Free Pussy Riot" became a viral call to arms of all sorts, but also in #aufschrei, among many others. The question then arises: Do we currently find ourselves at a moment when feminism itself is viral, has gone viral, and displays virality? (Pop)feminism is contaminated and speedy, travels fast, and infects things as it goes. This disturbs any notion of historicity or waves, and, like the digital, it suggests instead simultaneity in the contemporariness and geopolitical reach, or in the time and space, of the term. "Awkwardness" or "the awkward" as terms, too, have a viral component, for they are quickly taken up in everyday speech and appear in mutations of pop culture from television to internet.

We turn now to an unlikely example of the viral dissemination of contemporary feminist activism's imagery through not only digital but also material corporeal means in the form of the Barbie Dreamhouse Experience in Berlin. This example, at least as a playful reference, circles back to chapter 1 and The Julie Ruin video *Girls Like Us* (Harris and Gribbin 2013), which prominently features Barbie dolls. It also shows well the temporal collapse and spatial boundary crossing, the

6.1   Protests at the Barbie Dreamhouse Experience
(Berlin), 2013

simultaneity of multiple competing discourses, and the awkwardness of
feminism's virality that we are now discussing. The process-based aesthetics of awkwardness identified above are related to the present and
to affective relations, and they link up with and disrupt the popular
sphere. With this example, we attempt to make awkward attachments
visible as a political method by appropriating the Barbie Dreamhouse
Experience for our cause to talk about awkward digital circulations;
about the body, aesthetics, affect, the digital, gender, race, and feminisms; and about activism. Again, we highlight that the story of new
forms of appropriations, digital activism, and defiant disruption in the
neoliberal context is a complicated one, whereby specific national contexts and geographic movements, material cultures and their digital
projections, normative body politics and their subversions, and financial interests and political actions collide in awkward ways. We also

6.2   Protests at the Barbie Dreamhouse Experience (Berlin), 2013

take joy in playfully approaching the pink plastic and digital world as it is constructed, and circulates, as an "experience."

It certainly appears paradoxical to claim exhibits of digital and plastic Barbie dolls in a pink house and events such as the Barbie Dreamhouse Experience – and the protests surrounding this exhibit in Berlin – are playfully subversive since, as soon as we do that, we affirm our neoliberal and affective attachment to these images. We want to show, however, that popfeminist moments of disruption can also, and maybe have to, be found in what might be considered the centre of a, in this case, Western and white, gender and consumption regime. In this example, it is not so much the event itself as thinking and writing about the event that we consider to be popfeminist. Our readings of the Barbie Dreamhouse Experience in Berlin and its travels produce popfeminist stories that attempt to highlight the awkwardness that emerges from such forms of display, experience, and circulation.

The Barbie Dreamhouse Experience kicked off its tour in Berlin,[5] steps from Alexanderplatz, in late spring 2013. Barbie Dreamhouse Experience is a theme park of sorts, complete with a pink kitchen, pink display cases, and pink wardrobes offering children (girls) "experiences," from trying on Barbie's clothing and make-up to baking virtual cupcakes. Its two-thousand-and-five-hundred square metre plastic and pink appearance in the middle of East Berlin vies for attention with grey socialist-era high-rises. It thus aggressively positions its presentation of the neoliberal, capitalist, Western commodification of the female body as individual self-discovery within soaring unemployment and rising social welfare costs in continuing difficulties around German reunification and the Eurozone crisis. In Berlin, Barbie Dreamhouse was met with immediate and ongoing protest from primarily three groups: the anti-sexist group PinkStinks, a branch of Occupy, and representatives from Femen. A journalist describes the event:

> The scene was almost idyllic. Leftist demonstrators, feminists and other anti-Barbie protesters sat peacefully on the artificial grass or on pink chairs enjoying the warm May sun while small children crawled around in front of the display tent. And then, Barbie was burned on the cross.[6]

Femen activists brandished a Barbie on a cross, which they subsequently burned, while sporting on their bare breasts the words "life in plastic is not fantastic" and their signature Ukrainian wreath on their heads. The naked and burning body of the plastic doll that has come, for so many, to symbolize the capitalist proliferation of sexist messages to young girls is directly related to the blond, white, and naked body of the female, on "fire" with the wild emotion of her protests. Here, we see aesthetics and affects of awkwardness produced in or by political feminist creativity transnationally for competing local contexts (United States, Unified Germany, former East Germany, Ukraine). Moreover, it clearly shows the central position of the digital in form, content, circulation, and reception of feminism: "Occupy Barbie Dreamhouse" has close to three thousand followers on Facebook and, in collaboration with PinkStinks, is a self-sustaining protest group against sexism in the media.

The protests around the Barbie Dreamhouse and the Dreamhouse itself produce a range of awkward moments and circulations. While claiming that they do not want a "life" like the plastic Barbie Doll, who, in turn, "lives" mainly as a nostalgic exhibition object and as a digital projection inside the Dreamhouse, the Femen protester, in line with Femen's common presentation, looked somewhat like a Barbie Doll. The half-naked blond protester who, through writing on her own body, created an analogy between herself and the plastic doll, displays eerie self-aggression and self-destruction when she burns the naked body of

a look-alike doll on a cross. This tension is, of course, intentional, and it
produces a range of possible political responses. On one level, the protester identifies with the Barbie and is identified with her. On another
level, she aggressively burns the Barbie in an act of sacrifice that, simultaneously, has blasphemic undertones. It is common for Femen protesters to use religious icons in their protests and to critique traditional
religions (mainly Christianity, Orthodoxy, and Islam) as part of patriarchal oppression. By burning the Barbie doll on a cross, however, the
protester aligns herself with what she critiques as a sexist toy fantasy
and protests by making a range of messy references to Christianity: it
is unclear whether the female body (in plastic doll shape, in this case)
is aligned with Christ as a sacrifice or is meant to ridicule Christianity. These kinds of ambivalences point precisely to where this protest
is at its most awkward: it creates a confusing set of imagery around
female vulnerability, victimhood, and sacrifice whose images, by themselves, are very aggressive. It is only because of an assumed knowledge
of the history and form of Femen protests, and the combination of this
action with the Dreamhouse exhibit and even in anticipation of the
arrest of the protestor, that the political meaning of this act is legible as
"feminist." Of course, one can simply argue that this act of protest is
an intentional mess that is meant as nothing more than a way to draw
attention to the fact that certain feminist groups "disagree." It is, however, not in the protest act of the Femen protester and her act of burning
the Barbie on the cross itself that we see popfeminist politics emerging.
It is in the interchange or relations among these acts, the exhibit itself,
the appearance and disappearance of the exhibit and the protests, the
shifting meaning, and the circulations of and in between forms that
political moments surface.

The exhibit itself and its attendant objects or artefacts, not only the
protests it sparked, create a range of possible awkward moments, or, at
least, moments that can be read for awkwardness. For example, images
of the Dreamhouse circulating digitally show girls exiting giant plastic high-heeled shoe slides in what appears to be neon-pink-lit rooms.
These rooms look creepy, tinted in red and pink with a dark purple
night sky outside the big window; the shape of the shoe is surreal and
distorted and could be in a pop art exhibit and most certainly be a
prop in a Chicks on Speed or Lady Gaga video. Further examples are
the webisodes of the Barbie Dreamhouse as well as the video game
"Barbie Dreamhouse Party" (Nintendo 2013), which further contribute to the viral spread of Dreamhouse imagery. The game includes a
part in which dance postures are rated based on the digital images of

Barbies of various skin tones on screen. The scale ranges from perfect, to good, to "oops." The different skin tones of the Barbies attending the Dreamhouse Party together with their clone-like bodies relate to Barbie's historical colour-shifting. In response to market demands, over the past few decades, Mattel "diversified" the originally white, blond, and blue-eyed doll with clearly Caucasian features by selling it in various skin tones from white to brown, though without changing body type or significantly altering its facial features. Barbie's clone-like postracial appearance is awkwardly political in the context of discussions about, and the hope for, a "postracial" age following the election of President Obama, which were quickly countered by heightened racial tensions in the United States, in Germany, and globally, thus sparking the activist movement #BlackLivesMatter. When embedded in the context of the "experience" of the Dreamhouse, such imagery points towards the complicated collision of persisting narratives of sexism and racism in consumerist cultures, even as these become playful, popularized, and eventful – much like the protest cultures surrounding the event.

Thus, the Barbie Dreamhouse in Berlin is an important example in the context of our argument because it so clearly illustrates that certain commercial forms, such as Barbie, work together with popfeminist movements like Femen in ways that are certainly not intentional, while clearly also politically awkward. Mattel and the Barbie franchise might, in fact, have profited from the publicity the protests in front of the Barbie Dreamhouse Experience in Berlin gave the exhibit. Further, popfeminist activisms against the exhibit (and associated protests) certainly rely on the very existence of the commercial cultures they deconstruct to be politically productive. In the case of Barbie, this deconstruction in the feminist context is so par for the course that it requires little engagement or media back-story to go viral. This protest relies on a history of Barbie controversies and the fact that Barbie is an all-too-obvious object for feminist discourse; a popfeminist perspective, however, sheds a different light on where to locate the political in this relationship.

The Barbie Dreamhouse Experience came to Berlin and went.[7] The plastic house started to travel physically: the next stop was Sawgrass Mills in South Florida before a further exhibit opened in the Mall of America in Minneapolis. Both locations closed in August 2015. While in Berlin, the object of protest (the Barbie Dreamhouse) could be understood as the object of cruel attachment, that which, from the perspective of the protesters, must go in order to obtain "the good life," a life that is free of gender-biased marketing and toy manufacturing. This sense of a clear political goal echoes previous feminist discourses about

Barbie, in which the critique is focused on her "unnatural" appearance and the kind of "unhealthy" body image this doll conveys to young girls. When thinking about virality and the kind of imagery that circulated around the Barbie Dreamhouse and the protests, however, the political impact of these protest actions shifts significantly. Certainly, once the Barbie Dreamhouse, containing its plastic and digital, not only good but perfect "life," disappeared from Berlin Mitte and was re-erected in a much more protected space – a mall in Florida – the object of discontent and attachment disappeared as well. With it left the stage for the protest, the pink landscape into which the Femen protesters effectively inserted their own "non-plastic" bodies. The overall conclusion would be a cynical one: capitalist consumerism creates its own spaces for marketing upon which political protest can never have an impact. The Dreamhouse did not move because of the protest: its time was merely up and Barbie's dream went on to make more money elsewhere. The space where the pink house once stood and where the colourful protests took place is empty and the grey housing blocks once again dominate the area.

While the protest performances themselves can be awkward, which was most certainly true in the case of the Femen protester burning the Barbie doll on the cross in front of the pink exhibit house, such protests produce awkwardness in their messy circulations. Nothing is detaching from the logic of neoliberal capitalism, and neoliberalism can co-opt such forms of protest into its logic. But the discomfort inspired by both events, the Dreamhouse exhibit itself and the protests outside of the house (and, further, their connection to the travel of the Dreamhouse, the doll, the set of fantasies and affective attachments that the doll stands for and the doll franchise trigger) has political currency. The meaning of "Barbie" shifts, awkwardly and uncomfortably. This awkwardness extends to how both of these events, the Dreamhouse and the protest, relate to the actual Barbie doll, to the webisodes of the Barbie Dreamhouse, and to the presence of Barbie on all kinds of products.

No Femen protesters appeared at Sawgrass Mills in Florida, a gigantic mall complex with shops and entertainment venues, described on its own website as "the largest outlet and value retail shopping destination in the United States."[8] The Barbie Dreamhouse was listed on the mall website under "Dining and Fun." The move from Berlin, Germany, to Fort Lauderdale, Florida, and the fact that the exhibit moved from a public urban, into a private commercial, space certainly plays a role in the absence of protest. The main factor, of course, is that the active protest culture in Berlin has no equivalent in suburban Florida. The protests in Berlin did not travel to the United States; the actual plastic doll and the Barbie image on all kinds of (plastic) products continues to exist in a global marketplace. All the while, Barbie's "life in the Dream-house" has departed from her plastic existence. Barbie in the Dream-house, in the exhibit, but most certainly in the webisodes of "Barbie Dreamhouse," is digital animation. As a digital presence, Barbie is made to look like a plastic doll, and she seems to be aware of the fact that, "in reality," she is made out of plastic.[9]

In many ways, this is as much a question of circulation as it is a ques-tion of material, form, and scale. This becomes clear when we return to The Julie Ruin video *Girls Like Us*, in which a seemingly large group of Barbies take position in the real world, which is much too big for them. In the end, they do not burn themselves, but they burn the life-size women's magazines in a bonfire, and, as we describe in chapter 1, the video concludes with an image of a few of the Barbies as they look at a photograph – in digital replica – of themselves sitting around the bonfire with the burning magazines. The Dreamhouse Barbie is a "girl like us," engaging in all sorts of mischief as well as doing "Bar-bie things," like going to the hair salon, nail studio, and the beach. Bar-bie's viral presence is affectively charged in all events, The Julie Ruin video, the Dreamhouse, and the associated protests. The viral Barbie, her imageries, narratives, and circulations, stands for the contemporary impasse (the tension produced in the collision of consumerism with protest, girlishness with riot grrrls, racialization with neoliberalization, among others) as well as for all possibilities that can or could emerge from the impasse.

(Pop)feminism has gone viral in this contemporary moment, but we continue to struggle with the question of what this mean for the politi-cal; the struggle, so we argue, is critique and contains its own critique. In order to work politically, popfeminism counts on virality as central to the contemporary and the critiques it contains and produces. Chicks on Speed and Lady Bitch Ray, for example, as we argue in chapter 3, make this the starting point for their art – for example, the shoe gui-tar, the sonic carpet, the feminist porn-rap, and/or the popfeminist pin-up girl. The viral, with its physical, bodily, infectious connotations that could also include forms of feminist art and activism that were not yet digital in the 1990s, is a precondition for popfeminist activism to do its political work. Virality also illustrates how momentary and contem-porary some of this activism is and how it must have the flexibility to react to momentary flows as well as to impasses (like a virus, it can also disappear, run rampant, and then vanish or hide). While some of the forms of activisms, such as Femen, SlutWalks, and aspects of Pussy Riot activism, thrive on this virality and only in their viral circulations produce awkwardness that is politically legible, others, such as Chicks on Speed and Lady Bitch Ray (specifically) but also more recent Pussy Riot events, thematize this virality and thus illustrate and politically crack open the process of "going viral." They show how things circulate, repeat, and change, how they appear and disappear, how they appropriate and vanish.

Our popfeminist readings of the Barbie Dreamhouse Experience illustrates an impasse and/or a moment of transition not only "between modes of production and modes of life, but between different animating, sustaining fantasies" (Berlant 2011b, 261). They mess with fantasies and these economies. It is not in any single protest or performance event itself that one can locate a "threat[] to detach from what is already not working" (263), or, to rephrase this in our terminology, politically disruptive awkwardness, but it is in the circulations through different modes of dissemination, adaptations, and translations of these events. This means that we are not really talking about "one" event or a specific "moment" of feminism but, rather, of a process and of narratives that constantly slip into new interpretive contexts. When it comes to such feminist protest cultures, digital spaces are not only spaces of convergence but also of divergence; the digital space, as it interacts with other spaces, is a transitional space, a space in motion, a space in question. While we might often assume that digital disseminations increase visibility, some of our examples show that, in the digital realm, events appear and disappear, create hyper-visibilities as well as different forms of disguise; they expand and contract. Rather than converge, paths diverge, meander, and circle. None of these examples moves at any point entirely outside of the realm of neoliberal economies – that might be impossible by definition – but, in their awkwardness, they threaten to detach from what they reveal to be fraught neoliberal logic. In their article on normativity and materiality in digital culture, digital anthropologists Heather Horst and Daniel Miller (2012, 107) write of the study of how innovative things become mundane or normative: "The most astonishing feature of digital culture is not the speed of technical innovations, but rather the speed at which society takes all of them for granted and creates normative conditions for their use." And later: "What we experience is not a technology *per se*, but an immediate culturally inflected genre of usage or practice ... The word *genre* implies a combination of acceptability that is simultaneously moral, aesthetic and practical" (108). If, as they contest elsewhere, there is very little

difference in terms of mediation and material between the digital and
analogue worlds, then we might expand this reading to include the very
"objects" being disseminated on and off-line (105). When their reading
of genre is merged with Berlant's discussion above, then digital technology is also a genre of the present, both enabling (in its normativity) and
exposing (in its narrativity) the impasse. The word "feminism," moreover, itself threatens to become normative; awkwardness continually
interrupts the process of normativity, on all fronts.

A POPFEMINIST ACADEMY?

The entanglement of theory with practice that we emphasize throughout *Awkward Politics*, the manner in which our popfeminist methodology often mirrors the methodology of the performers and activists we
are discussing, and the way in which we write ourselves into this book
brings us to the academy. The academic mode and the academy itself,
as a space and as an institution, also depends on, and implicitly and
explicitly demands, normative genres and categories for and of evaluation. This applies to writing, teaching, lectures, grant proposals, and
conference presentations. At our own workplaces and in our writing
we are securely located within these genres while knowing that their
workings are constantly considered in (financial and intellectual) crisis;
we are acutely aware of working inside an impasse. A certain kind of
academic feminism, a feminism that has also defined and enabled our
careers, has entered the mainstream in North American institutions and
has become a normative genre in itself. At the same time, feminism and,
with it, gender studies in the academy are also marked by the genre of
impasse, are at an impasse. As a discipline, its own (supposed) success
questions its necessity. In the German context, because of a postfeminist argument in conjunction with questioning the "scientific" validity
of gender studies, the existence of these programs is threatened before
they have even been securely established. Rather than lamenting these
(often affectively charged) attacks on feminisms and feminists within
the academy, our popfeminist perspective suggests reading the genre of
impasse, with Berlant, as a genre of emergence.

As we imply above, pop culture is part of university curricula in the
humanities and arts disciplines, either as an object of critical analysis
or as a way to infuse (particularly) introductory classes with more relevance to the students or with "fun," even as a selling point. Popfeminism, however, remains an awkward fit in this context. In the German

6.3 "Dr Bitch," Lady Bitch Ray

university, where the establishment of gender studies in the academy
has a much shorter history than it has in North America and where the
discipline is still openly contested, Reyhan Şahin/Lady Bitch Ray has
been at the forefront of a new academic feminist pop culture and a new
pop-cultural genre of "doing" academic work.[10] Rather than having
to beg students to attend academic lectures, her "Bitchsm" seminars,
such as the one she gave at the University of Cologne in May 2015, are
massively popular events. The German tabloid paper, the *Bildzeitung* –
a long-time follower and unlikely (due to its often antifeminist and
misogynistic objectification of women on its pages) supporter of Lady
Bitch Ray's career – reported on the seminar in Cologne, where, after
close to seven hundred people had crowded the lecture hall, no more
could be allowed to enter. While Ebru Ugurlu from the *Bildzeitung*

refs to the seminar as a "lecture" (Vorlesung), the event was a combination of a reading from the book *Bitchsm* (2012), a lecture about
Şahin's (2014) recently published dissertation, and a performance of
her most recent rap song, all with a view to popfeminist empowerment.
In an interview by Alexandra Spürk, published in the local paper *Kölner Stadtanzeiger* and on the university's website, Şahin gave a description of what she was planning to do at the event:

> I will talk about "Bitchsm" and my dissertation about the headscarf.
> It will be about sexuality, language, Lady Bitch Ray, politics, and
> the headscarf. The Bitchsm-seminar is a mixture between lecture,
> reading, and performative acapella-rap-inserts.[11]

The sensationalist language used in the *Bildzeitung* report suggests surprise (the reporter claims that Şahin, too, was speechless, "baff," at its
success) that "scandal rapper" Lady Bitch Ray is giving a lecture at a
university. This surprise is in itself awkward since Şahin is a successful academic and currently holds a prestigious funded postdoctoral
position at the University of Hamburg. She is therefore firmly located
within the normative structures of the academy. This "lecture" created
a sense of community among students who wanted to hear, learn, and
talk about these topics regardless of the "scandal" appeal that mainstream media seem to emphasize. Being awkward – or being an awkward fit or disturbance – within the academy appears to resonate with
student audiences in a different manner. In a rather direct way, Şahin
brings pop to (academic) feminism and offers a loud and popular kind
of willful disturbance. Her work in and the reactions to the seminars
engage directly with the social, material, and theoretical forms of both
feminism and pop.

Understanding Reyhan Şahin/Lady Bitch Ray's lecture in terms of
the genre of impasse might seem to be a stretch in light of an event that
could be described as a clear success. Defying the success-failure binary,
the impasse, here, is not in the event itself but in its awkward positioning in the academic, feminist, and pop contexts; indeed, the event – in
its awkward position – makes the impasse visible. After such a "successful" – or popular – event, the university would certainly claim the
lecture to be truly academic, thereby claiming it as its own. At the same
time, and in line with German understandings of pop as political as
defined in the 1990s, Şahin infuses her pop with political and academic
language. In this sense, Şahin's seminars remain in a troubling position
of neither-nor and both, pop and academic, pop and political.

This lecture took place in the months following a short but heated media debate concerning a proposal by another linguist within the academy. Humboldt University professor Lann Hornscheidt suggested introducing a gender-neutral form of address for professors into the German language. The German language clearly denotes gender through the ending "-in" for women (in this case, Professor*in* to denote a female professor, in contrast to Professor for the male counterpart). Hornscheidt offered the form "Professx" as a neutral alternative, beginning by personally asking to be referred to in such manner. Academic debates on gender-neutral language are familiar, particularly from the second wave feminism in the 1970s.[12] Further, the proposed "x" was not the first linguistic intervention in the contemporary period in Germany: the addition of the capital "I," the asterisk, or the underscore to denote gender-neutrality (for example, StudentInnen, Student, or Student_innen for the combined male and female form of student) have long been part of feminist academic writings as well as left-leaning mainstream news sources (such as the Berlin daily *Tageszeitung*). Hornscheidt's proposal, however, quickly left the strictly academic or feminist-queer context and mobilized a public backlash that attempted to marginalize and isolate Hornscheidt. The viral outrage against Hornscheidt's proposal might originate in the manner in which, unlike the previous changes, the "x" does not build on male or female endings but, instead, offers a trans alternative.

The proposal mobilized a certain section of the public against the attempt to change "our" language. In the German context, such language discussions are closely tied to national identity, heritage, and pride, and, because of this, those attempting to "preserve" the language are also often seen in ways tainted by Germany's historical past.[13] Other attempts to not appear opposed to a more inclusive language in general resulted in arguments that stressed that, if "reality" were to change, the language would surely follow but that language cannot force social change: "Should there be enough people who would like to be called Professx or Studentx, then one would have little scientific evidence in hand to oppose such a proposal."[14] The reference to scientific proof is an intentional attack on and attempt to undermine Hornscheidt since it implies that such research is not scientifically sound. This line of argument further reproduces the circular question of social and linguistic change familiar from political correctness debates (whether language changes opinions and actions or vice versa) while at the same time participating in this very change. In this twist, pointing out Hornscheidt's privileged position at one of the most prestigious universities in Germany becomes a way of further undermining academic authority in general.

The mobilization of negative affect is a common anti-feminist strategy that relies heavily on digital dissemination. Hornscheidt's website responds to these discourses and threats by asking for the following:

> If you want to contact Lann Hornscheid, please use respectful language that does not imply gender binaries, such as, for example, "Hello Lann Hornscheidt," "Good Day, Lann Hornscheidt," or "Dear Lann Hornscheidt" [original in English] and avoid binary gender language such as "Mr. _____", "Ms. _____", "Dear_____" [in German with gender endings]. There is no right and good language but we require respectful new forms – I look forward to your creative anti-discriminatory ideas.[15]

What follows is Hornscheidt's institutional e-mail address, and then the following recommendation:

> In case you do not want to communicate but only throw your irritation at me instead of using it as an impulse for yourself to think about your own norms and world views, please use the following email address: hatemail.an.hornscheidt@gmail.com
> Or – you take the time to write something nice and respectful to a person of your own choice instead – and see what such an action would feel like.[16]

Hornscheidt acts here as the professor, reasserting professorial authority. The first request is pedagogical as it expresses hopes for discourse and seems interested in further fostering linguistic and social change. In addressing the second group, equally pedagogically, Hornscheidt acknowledges the many negative and even virulent responses to the suggestions for a gender-neutral x-ending but expresses the hope for positive affect instead of viral hate. The way in which any form of negative affect is dismissed as a refusal to think about one's own position, of course, might be perceived as highly arrogant, which, again, fosters a clear stereotype of the (gender studies) professor.

These two examples of academic feminist and pop-cultural debates in the German context hint at how willfulness works within and against the neoliberal academy, and how awkwardness could play a role in formulating a politics out of that willful gesture. The debate sparked by Hornscheidt very clearly shows this willfulness, as language itself becomes something clumsy, something to stumble over, and awkward.

But when that language over which we stumble explicitly references transgender politics, the impulse to say or do the "right" thing comes to be about existence, being, and safety.[17] What we observe here are moments of transition and impasses that also enable the emergence of a new kind of (popfeminist) politics. While a position of authority and privilege enables us and our colleagues to speak and act in these scenarios, this very same position also potentially awkwardly undermines our own agency and academic forms and/or genres in general. At least in the North American context, academic feminism has entered the mainstream in the last decade, which arguably also contained certain forms of theoretical feminism within the academy. The contemporary, the collaborative, and the viral, however, create moments of impasse and emergence that work against such established containment. Awkward politics that often originate in or are triggered by the digital spill over into other, non-digital contexts. This also implies a way of thinking about digital feminist humanities as a way of working against the containment of knowledge, of politics, and, in this context specifically, of feminism and gender studies.

If, as we argue above, awkwardness is a way of making the impasse visible, then it is also a way of making the researcher who is entangled in this impasse visible. Thus awkwardness also describes us as researchers. Awkwardness is a method of reading and analyzing – that is, of doing political feminist work, of choosing to read awkwardly, and of making things awkward. Feminist academics must understand (not make, but understand) their work as politically meaningful and as politically feminist, as theoretical and interventionist, not in spite of, but in the face of, this sticky mess that defines the spheres of feminist political influence in the twenty-first century. Direct attacks on feminism in the academy highlight the urgency of this claim, as do ongoing discussions around the ever-increasing neoliberalization of universities themselves.[18] It is precisely in the face of such attacks that we see how feminist work, including the search for feminist methodologies, remains crucial.[19]

We pose this challenge in light of Berlant's argument in the final chapter of *Cruel Optimism*. She ends her chapter on politics as cruel by describing the current political moment as one of transition (perhaps even as adolescent) – a transition that we want to harness for feminist politics. This transitory moment is the reason for the political bind we are in, but it also challenges us to make this precise moment productive. The defiant gesture of engaging in politics in spite of ridicule, cynicism, or despair and in spite of the messy challenges posed by the contemporary political landscape is what Berlant (2011b, 263) describes as new political forms that are "in the middle of detaching from the fantasy of the good life," as we discuss above. To reiterate, these political forms, as Berlant understands them, aim to "produce some better ways of mediating the sense of [this] historical moment ... so that it would be possible to imagine a potentialized present that does not reproduce all of the conventional collateral damage" (ibid.). Awkwardness highlights precisely those processes of collision that we see happening across feminist activist work in the digital sphere. Awkwardness is also a mode of challenging our scholarship about such activism in order to create new political forms. The call to be awkward, to address awkwardness, and to collect awkward moments is essentially a call to be self-aware as researchers, writers, teachers, and administrators – and as feminists. This self-awareness must be slightly uncomfortable, stick out, and be a bit ugly, thereby pointing towards and remaining within the trouble of circular politics, not as a mode of authority or a new -ism but, instead, as a strategy for building a collaborative and intimate public approach to the mainstays of power found throughout the language of our disciplines and institutional authority – a model that itself might be described as DIY. Awkwardness, then, does not describe the private politics that were the hallmark of earlier feminist and queer movements but, instead, the radical publicness of our academic work and the manner in which all forms of public spaces in the academy – whether these are virtual, written, classroom, community, administrative, or conference spaces – are also intimate spaces and, therefore, consciously and unconsciously involved in the project of making, doing, and undoing critical subjectivities, including our own.[20]

For feminist academics, staying with the trouble invokes what we might see as an awkward answer to the question of what feminist ethics are today, perhaps even to be understood as an awkward ethos. Much like the awkward forms described above, an awkward ethos offers us not only a manner of describing the potentials of a feminist academy but also the form and trajectory that our ethical positionality vis-à-vis that academy must take. To emphasize awkwardness means to stick with the process and to deny ironic distancing, but it works politically only when it is understood as an ethical position that implies self-reflective, engaged involvement, compassion, solidarity, and connection. Again, this awkwardness neither signifies failure nor implies success; instead, it demands a multivectoral approach. It is, to return to Ahmed (2014b, 51), the bumpy ride that cannot and should not be smoothed out. Using the image with which she begins *Willful Subjects* – the image of the willful (female) child in the Grimm Brothers' fairy tale who, after death, continues to raise her arm stubbornly and willfully out of the grave and in the air – she ends with the following:

When arms come up, they disturb the ground. Can we learn not to eliminate the signs of disturbance? Disturbance can be creative: not as what we aim for, not as what grounds our action, but as the effect of action: disturbance as what is created by the very effort of reaching, of reaching up, of reaching out, of reaching for something that is not present, something that appears only as a shimmer, a horizon of possibility. (204)

This call to raise our arms – a call for, not to, arms – does not focus on the cause or the goal of action but, rather, on the potential of the process and the act, the potential for conversation, argument, connection, disruption, and engagement. We read the examples in this book as part of such a process of disturbance. Similarly, our collaborative process of writing this book, thinking through these examples, struggling with the theory, and developing our methodology has been a – at times disturbing but mainly joyful – process of reaching out and reaching up. For us as feminist teachers, the image of the raised arm used in Ahmed's quote also evokes feminist pedagogy. In feminist pedagogy, the very effort of reaching, the act of reaching out, and the creation of a horizon of possibilities are crucial concepts. This also implies that awkwardness, as a perspective and as a politics in and for the classroom, makes power dynamics visible, highlights the multiplicity of voices, and the difficulty of conversation by, at the same time, emphasizing connection and community since "awkward moments remind us that we are never isolated individuals ... Awkward moments are, by definition, relatable" (Batuman 2014). In rather different ways, the success of Şahin's seminars and the media outrage against Hornscheidt's proposals illustrate that academic (pop)feminists are not isolated, neither from the public nor within the academy. This non-isolated position creates connection and community, but it also puts them in a potentially vulnerable position where they are exposed to attacks and threats. That might be awkward, but it is taken up with conscious agency.

EMERGENCE AND ACTION

Thus we return to community and to collaboration and, with these concepts, to the sense of urgency emerging from the present moment, with which the impulse for *Awkward Politics* began. Emergence, as the discussions above illustrate, is not a solitary act. Further, emergence – and with it process – is essential to understanding the aesthetics of popfeminist activism. Because of this, the impasse – that is, the genre describing our experience of the present, the contemporary – must be understood aesthetically. In *Ordinary Lives*, Highmore (2011, 11) claims that aesthetics posit "our most subjective experiences as social." Because of this, aesthetics do not define the exceptional and beautiful but, instead, how the ordinary resonates in our senses and emotions and turns these into collective experiences (21). The political realm is, like aesthetics, pervasive and shapes all aspects of our collective present. Berlant (2011b, 12) writes of aesthetics:

> Aesthetic is not only the place where we rehabituate our sensorium by taking in new material and becoming more refined in relation to it. But it provides metrics for understanding how we pace and space our encounters with things, how we manage the too closeness of the world and also the desire to have an impact on it that has some relation to its impact on us.

We argue that the years following the financial crisis in 2008 in particular are the moment when we see these new forms of popfeminist political interventions emerge. Thus, what threatens feminism, what puts it in crisis, are its very successes. The impasse is erected. Simultaneously, in the era that has been termed the awkward age, irony no longer has a place.[21] Global political and economic crises require us to seriously and non-ironically rethink notions of difference, connection, community, and solidarity. The clear sense that something is at stake, that something matters politically, but the inability to express clearly *what* matters in advance of the viral, and before the "event" happens or goes viral, is at the core of these forms of activism. This, again, defines their contemporality.

Thus we can claim that the awkwardness that comes from popfeminist activism *is* the manner in which the political takes its contemporary form. The awkward is not only a descriptor or a search term: it is at the very heart of the present moment. The "affirmative becomings" Puar sees as creating potentialities for emergence also describe, then, the awkward politics of popfeminist creative actions, according to which we do not see a neither or a nor, a failure or a success, but, instead, the creation of a space of multiplicity and emergence where acknowledgments of difference can become a starting point for developing a sense of political solidarity.

Towards an Awkward Ethos: Conviviality, Joy, and Feminist Ethics

Together we can create a pushy riot.
Sara Ahmed[1]

We end the first chapter of this book with "trouble" and return to this word at key points (sometimes in the form of crisis). We state that not only is feminism "in trouble," it also *is* "trouble," and doing feminist politics in the face of its impossibility – "staying with the trouble" (Haraway 2014) – is where our thinking and our trouble begins. For Haraway, staying with the trouble, as we describe in chapter 1, offers a way to push back against cynicism, despair, and denial to engage with the destruction we inherit by practising joy and embracing pleasure, collectively and individually. We, too, put out a call to stay with the trouble. The trouble is that feminist politics are part of the double bind of cruel optimism, which often results in cynicism and despair in the face of our political (second and third wave) inheritance.[2] In order to push back against such cynicism, we must stay with the trouble by embracing the circularity of feminist politics today as producing an awkwardness that communicates not only joy, collaboration, and community but also hyper self-awareness, disturbance, and subversion. For us, trouble also refers to the troublesome positions and perspective feminist politics take in popular culture and to the difficulty feminists seem to have in working through this trouble. The circularity we begin with in our description of pop, popfeminism, activism, and digital cultures and our readings for awkwardness brings us, therefore, full circle to the academy. Indeed, if we are in agreement with Berlant and Edelman (2014, xvi) when they write, in *Sex, or the Unbearable*, that theory needs to be thought of as a type of social practice, then theorizing the awkward as we do here must be seen as social practice. And, furthermore, the rips created in our own aesthetic language in this book might give rise to their own sort of politics. By staying with the trouble, we argue with Haraway that, if we understand our position as politically engaged, we can neither avoid nor deny the trouble by retreating into cynicism, but we also cannot attempt to solve or work through the trouble. The assertion that "this is trouble" becomes the starting point for political engagement.

One part of this trouble, as our discussions throughout this book show, is that the digital age forces us yet again to revisit certain binary notions – for example, of inclusion and exclusion, of self and other – and find new language(s) to describe them, not because these binaries have ceased to exist (indeed, the digital is per definition a binary system) but because their politics have shifted. The question of how, for example, we think about differences in the digital age as simultaneously heightened and levelled out weaves itself through our discussions.[3] Related to this, how do we theorize the tension among (digital) images as overly sharp, as endlessly reproduced, as prolific, but as also, in this process, losing their resolution, fading into pixels, or disappearing altogether? How do we understand the digital as simultaneously so widely and openly accessible but also so exclusive and divisive; as a technology that so many people today access on their phones but that, if we want to participate actively in shaping and changing its surfaces, requires so much labour and know-how, labour that often remains invisible?

Since we stress the importance of finding a position beyond evaluation, we do not even attempt to draw any conclusions about what the "right" or the "wrong" tools or avenues for digital activism might be. What we do want to suggest, however, is that such avenues constantly open up within processes of dissemination and in and through the viral. These strategies include not only hyper-visualization, appropriation/co-option, and citation but also flattening out and disappearance, becoming blurry and, yet again, setting things into motion. Certain tropes, threads, images, or topics leave and re-enter digital spaces as their political targets move, as the example of Pussy Riot that weaves throughout this book illustrates. There is a new kind of (hi)story to be told, one about digital traces, one about objects and forms that emerge with urgency and disappear from sight, that reappear as blurry and out of focus, that are forcibly or absentmindedly removed – deleted, dropped from memory, disappeared from the algorithm of the search engine, or simply not archived or captured. Throughout *Awkward Politics*, we identify moments when gender, class, and racial differences level out or disappear, and other moments when such difference is highlighted and sharpened – painfully so and politically so – as moments of transition. All of these moments offer chances to find new ways to think about these politically urgent issues. This process of finding new ways of doing politics and acting politically is a messy one that, per definition, cannot follow a straight path to "success" but, rather, needs to struggle against the notion of being evaluated based on a quantifiable scale of success and failure of "feminism" as a monolithic project. This means that we have to be pushy feminists in spite of and in defiance of the fact that we might not always know what we are pushing up against or what we are pushing for.

Ahmed, in her blog post entitled "Pushy Feminists," describes this process in which we have to push back against forms of evaluation – or judgment – as pushed on us but as something that we need to confront in our activisms in order to "push" beyond it. She describes the starting point for her book *Willful Subjects* in this research blog as follows:

> You have to become what you are judged as being to survive that judgment. So you might have to push against the judgment of being pushy; you might have to do the thing they say you are in response to what they say you are. Thus even if the judgment eventually catches you, even if that is so, even when it is so, it misses so much. It misses you, the history of you becoming you: and it also misses its own sharp edges; its own role in forming what it finds. (Ahmed 2014a)

In order to get beyond the judgment of being pushy or willful (or even awkward), Ahmed claims we must embrace pushiness, that is, fulfill the judger's expectations. But as she says further, this circular moment, even as it contains a sense of emergence, misses the history of getting to this moment. Ahmed thus describes circularity and the notion of becoming, core elements of our discussion of awkward popfeminist activism. Solidarity begins when we work together to unveil the process of judgment and show how such judgment works to "form what it finds." In many instances – and this is what Ahmed's previous book, *The Promise of Happiness*, is about – this means to be a (feminist) killjoy, to be pushy, but, possibly, joyfully and collectively so. Ahmed (2010, 87) writes: "There is solidarity in recognizing our alienation from happiness, even if we do not inhabit the same place (as we do not). There can even be joy in killing joy. And kill joy, we must and we do." Further, that joy turns, in *Willful Subjects*, towards a sense of hope that "there is a point" (Ahmed 2014b, 173), or even an optimism that simply manifests itself as the insistence that we are "not giving up" (174). Therefore, when we call for joy in this process, we talk about a complicated process that includes being pushy, stubborn, and awkward but that also contains a sense of community, hope, and optimism – affirmation – despite itself.

To emphasize that this is a complicated process and not an individualized notion, this joy might also be described as "convivial." Or to speak with Hardt (2014, 221), "a joyful encounter always indicates that there is something in common to discover."[4] When we think about popfeminist activism in the digital realm, we do not describe joy or pushiness as solitary but as a new way of finding a, however complicated, sense of community and solidarity. Puar (2009, 168) uses the standard definition of conviviality as coming together with companions for merriment when she writes: "As an attribute and function of assembling, however, conviviality does not lead to a politics of the universal or inclusive common, nor an ethics of individuatedness, rather the futurity enabled through the open materiality of bodies as a Place to Meet." She reminds us that this coming together or meeting is not always, or rarely, comfortable but rather "entail(s) forms of eventness that could potentially unravel oneself but just as quickly be recuperated through a restabilized self," thus inviting "political transformation" by embracing the difference of the other (169). Conviviality offers a way of moving away from thinking about sexuality, gender, race, and feminism in terms of identity politics and, instead, as she writes, thinking of them as "events" or "encounters" (ibid.). In this, then, conviviality recognizes that "political critique must be open to the possibility that it might disrupt and alter the conditions of its own emergence such that it is no longer needed – an openness to something other than what we might have hoped for" (ibid.). The awareness that political critique is temporary, that it may be discarded or forgotten, is central to our understanding of both popfeminist methodology and awkwardness. The searching approach of popfeminist methodology suggests that this search will not end. Furthermore, this search is itself awkward, circular, and threatens to detach or self-consume, but it is also festive and joyful in its sociality.

This internal instability brings us back to the trouble. As we state at various points, the trouble we find ourselves in is being faced with the necessity of doing feminist politics in the face of its impossibility. The trouble, in short, is circularity of thought that consistently undoes any measurement of productivity. This circularity, however, is exactly where we must begin and with which we must stay. Awkwardness is a way to use this circularity, to use the trouble, without attempting to get out of it, solve it, or to explain it away. It is inherent to and simultaneously intentional and unintentional in many of our examples. This circularity and its attendant awkwardness are most obvious in the crossing of activism with pop and popfeminism. Pop culture is, by definition, cruelly optimistic. As consumers of pop culture, we are constantly reminded of that which we cannot achieve; pop culture's work is based on unfulfilled and unfulfillable desire. This desire is coded as playful, performative, and, by definition, popular. Because pop is reflective of broad-based desires and optimisms in a community it also reflects the elitisms, classisms, racisms, and the violence or gender imbalance of that community. Popfeminism as understood in Germany and as implemented throughout this book starts with the assumption that, due to its wide sphere of influence, including its concern with sex, body politics, and identification, pop is the perfect playing field for feminist activism. Popfeminist activism produces an excess of meaning through an excess of awkwardness – awkwardness that, we argue, is politically legible and productive, especially as affect and critical agency.

What we show with Chicks on Speed, Lady Bitch Ray, Pussy Riot, Femen, Barbie Dreamhouse Experience, the events of Helene Hegemann and Charlotte Roche, and other examples in the messy and murky circulations of popfeminist activism is that, without a clear "goal," protest events manage to slip in and out of sight without losing their political currency, maybe by constantly shifting their political target. One could also argue that, for that precise reason, these protest events are not actually *working* – and we might agree – but they certainly seem to continue to trigger moments when politics are *at work*. The task then is to create a space where we can play through scenarios, theories, and pedagogies of awkwardness and, ideally, experience joy in doing so. We cannot stay with the trouble without the practice of joy: "The practices of joyful collective and individual pleasure are essential to the art of living on a damaged planet" (Haraway 2014). If part of that damage is the neoliberal cruel optimism that is rampant throughout the above spheres of influence, then we must find forms of "making, doing, thinking" (ibid.) together publicly and intimately that harness the joy inherent in the manner in which we use the awkward. The trouble is worth it.

Notes

INTRODUCTION

1 For further reading, see also Coleman (2009).
2 For a discussion of cyber-feminism and contemporary digital feminism, see Tuzcu (2015).
3 The first book-length study on Pussy Riot is Gessen (2014).
4 This could be seen in their appearance at the Amnesty International concert in New York City in February 2014. See also the open letter from Pussy Riot members printed, for example, in the *Guardian* (Pussy Riot 2014).
5 In their attempt to read for the politics in Pussy Riot's performances, Heinrich and Segschneider (2013) also use Kristine Stiles's definition of performance art.
6 In keeping with Ahmed's (2014b) spelling of "willful" in *Willful Subjects*, which we discuss at various points, we use the American spelling "willful" instead of the Canadian "wilful" in order to highlight the notion of "will."
7 As Lady Bitch Ray, Reyhan Şahin published *Bitchsm* in 2012, followed by her dissertation *Die Bedeutung des muslimischen Kopftuchs* in 2014. Chicks on Speed published various books about their work, such as ~~Don't~~ *Art Fashion Music* in 2010 and, prior to that, *It's a Project* (with Walter Shönauer) in 2004, and *Cultural Hacking: Kunst des strategischen Handlens* (with Thomas Düllo)in 2005.
8 See, for example, Masha Gessen's work on Pussy Riot, academic articles, and an HBO documentary.

CHAPTER ONE

1 We are thinking here of T.L. Cowan's claim on the FemTechNet Facebook site on 4 November 2014 that "collaboration is a feminist technology."

2 Interestingly, much writing on collaboration and feminism in the academy places emphasis on pedagogical practices, such as collaboration in the classroom or between mentor and student. These readings might seem to fall back on this maternalist line of thinking. Other books do emphasize intellectual and philosophical relations to feminism. See Peck and Mink (1998). York analyzes much of the work in Peck and Mink's volume as leaning towards the valorization of female and feminist collaboration, reading the term "common ground" in its title as that which the chapters suggest the differences in the authors' voices are working towards. However, as York claims, a notion of fusing differences is not always desirable.

3 In academic collaboration such as we find here, York does underscore the aspect of risk, which seems to also be context-specific, certain countries and intellectual communities favouring the collaborative mode over others. While, at the time of this writing, things have already changed to some extent since the time of York's writing in 2002, the aspect of risk for tenure and promotion considerations in the Anglo-American context she discusses in relation to collaboration by women is considerable. The awkwardness of the collaborative mode has its own political implications for the feminist academy. See, in this context, our article (Smith-Prei and Stehle 2014) for the *Women in German Yearbook*.

4 See Williams (2010) in *Ms. Magazine* and Hughes (2013) in *Thought Catalog*. Of course, Lady Gaga is not alone in this, and many international superstars are also held up to such yard sticks. See "10 Celebrities Who Say They Aren't Feminists" (Huffington Post 2013) in *Huffpost Celebrity* or McDonough (2013) "I'm Not a Feminist, But ..." in *Salon*, both of which offer numerous ambivalent quotations from celebrity women, ranging from Beyoncé to Sarah Jessica Parker to P.J. Harvey.

5 In January 2014, Beyoncé (2014a) had already penned a short essay for the Shriver Report on gender equality and feminism. See http://shriverreport.org/gender-equality-is-a-myth-beyonce/.

6 See Stokowski (2014). See Gottschalk (2014) for a discussion of the *Emma* controversy. Of course, Beyoncé's performance occurred the year after Miley Cyrus's twerking performance at the VMAs.

7 This protest sparked also numerous reactions from mainstream news sources (each using the word colonial or neocolonial in their titles), such as Nagatajan's (2013) article "Femen's Obsession with Nudity Feeds a Racist Colonial Feminism" as well as Al Jazeera's (2012) "The Future of Feminism?" a live discussion on Al Jazeera's English show *The Stream*.

8 See Al Jazeera's (2014) "Anti-Feminist Campaign Targets German Gender Quota Proposal" for an English-language discussion of the story.

9 This is seen in the feminist response to the May 2014 shooting at UCSB in the form of hashtag activism #yesallwomen, which reached its peak on 25 May with 61,500 tweets per hour. See Nutter (2014).

10 For an academic study on Occupy, see Mitchell, Harcourt, and Taussig (2013).

11 In their introduction to *Digital Anthropology*, Horst and Miller (2012) offer a very thorough discussion of the digital, which also includes the material.

12 See Emspunk (2007). For a discussion of the 1970s feminist extremist group Rote Zora in the context of contemporary digital feminisms, see Karcher (2015).

13 "Staat und Macht und Geld, vide-vide-vit und Bullen-Schweine, alle groß und klein, kriegen eine rein; wir machen unsere Welt vide-vide-wie sie und gefällt, Kampf dem Kapital, illegal, legal ist scheiß-egal."

14 The album and booklet can be downloaded here: http://web.archive.org/web/20071012180014/http://www.freetofight.org/

15 See *Free to Fight: An Interactive Self-Defense Project*, http://web.archive.org/web/20071012180200/http://www.freetofight.org/MP3s/03%20Definition%20Of%20Self%20Defense.mp3.

16 See the riot grrrl manifesto written by Kathleen Hanna of Bikini Kill, first printed in the BIKINI KILL Zine 2 in 1991 and reprinted here: http://onewarart.org/riot_grrrl_manifesto.htm. It is this consciousness that also drives Chicks on Speed, whom we discuss later.

17 In the English-language context see, for example, Feree (2012); Adelson (1993); or Frevert (1990).

18 The reference to Hall's (1992) important essay "The West and the Rest" is, of course, intentional here.

19 See Tumblr, awkwardtaylorswiftdancing.tumblr.com.

20 See Stampler (2014).

21 Think here of such LGBTQ movies as *But I'm a Cheerleader* (1999), which is entirely dependent on camp and irony, particularly towards its audience, as the driver of its politics.

22 Of course, there will always be exceptions to such broad-brushing of artistic production of a certain generation. See Fox (2010) for a discussion of precisely this as anti-feminist in performance art.

23 For a discussion of this lineage, see Dreher (2001).

24 For a summary of female performance artists, see Potkin (2000).

25 While this is not the space to go into performance history in detail, or into the history of feminist art in Germany, it does serve to mention that not only art of this period can be seen as performative and that, like much of the actions of feminists today, many protests by radical feminists can be seen as similar to performance. For example, actions by the Rote Armee Faktion (Red Army Faction, RAF) in the 1970s were staged much like performances. Other specifically feminist groups, such as the Rote Zora (Red Zora), also engaged in acts to protest violence against women in ways that mimicked performance art. See Karcher (2015).

26 See Export's own personal website for documentation: http://www.valie-export.at/.

27 See Labelle's (2001) review of the performance in Issue 60 of *Frieze*.

28 Adorno (2005) explains in "Juvenal's Error," originally published in 1951, that satire can only be recognized as such when the audience, or receiver, of the satire clearly understands the satirical referents.

29 For some of these artists – certainly in the case of Jelinek – an extensive body of secondary literature exists. The reception of others remains largely within their respective niches or genre. Peaches and Beth Ditto comprise more recent examples.

30 For Elfriede Jelinek, this most clearly applies to her text *Lust*, published in 1989; and for Cindy Sherman, this refers to some of her work from the early 1990s, in which she used plastic body parts for her photographic displays (e.g., "untitled #264" and "untitled #250," both 1992). See http://www.moma.org/interactives/exhibitions/2012/cindysherman/#/6/.

31 For a full video of all seven pieces, see http://www.ubu.com/film/abramovic_seven.html.

32 For the official lyric video, see http://www.youtube.com/watch?v=5wmL97Ape70.

33 Here, the relationship of Pussy Riot to the riot grrrl movement and Bikini Kill in particular is already obvious in the semantic connection to this album.

34 Mostly, such critique focuses on Butler's emphasis on identity formation over structural inequalities. Famous debates include those with Martha Nussbaum and Nancy Fraser. For definitions of intersectional analyses, see the work of Patricia Hill Collins (e.g., Collins 2004). Gayatri Spivak coined the term "strategic essentialism" to further complicate identity politics and performativity in feminist activism (e.g., Spivak 1999).

CHAPTER TWO

1 See Standing (2011).

2 Germany still has one of the lowest per capita birth rates in Europe. A recent study published by the BBC (2015) even suggests that Germany has the lowest birth rates globally. See http://www.bbc.com/news/world-europe-32929962.

3 It is most certainly true that the third wave had firmly taken hold in Austria simultaneous to or slightly later than the riot grrrl movement in the United States. See, for example, Baldauf and Weingartner (1998).

4 This moment would lead to a radical restructuring of early childhood education and care in West Berlin that quickly spread throughout West Germany and still dominates today. See Smith-Prei (2013, chap. 4).

5 For a more in-depth discussion of this, see Smith-Prei (2009).

6 "Wir wollen wieder Feministinnen sein." For a critical discussion of these contexts, see also Baer (2012a) and Scharff (2014a).

7 "Ja, alles klar, Schwestern, ihr müsst eure eigenen Erfahrungen machen, aber: Bitte fangt nicht schon wieder von vorne an."

8 See McCarthy (2011); Baer (2011); and Scharff (2014a). This is particularly the case for the text *Wir Alphamädchen* (2008), in which the authors themselves draw very clear generational lines from the second to the third waves.

9 "Die Zeit hat sie eingeholt, ihre Rhetorik ist oll, Alice Schwarzer und ihre Frauen sind Historie geworden."

10 "Wie es ist, heute eine Frau zu sein."

11 See, for example, Henry (2004).

12 In the German context, texts like *Wir Alphamädchen: Warum Feminismus das Leben schöner macht* (2008) and *Das F-Wort: Feminismus ist sexy* (2008) are often criticized for ascribing to lifestyle feminism. For a critical discussion of the term in the American context, see, for example, Groeneveld (2009).

13 An important publication in this context is the collected volume *Farbe Bekennen: Afro-deutsche Frauen auf den Spuren ihrer Geschichte* (Oguntoye, Ayim, and Schultz 1986). Subsequently, and in close contact with Black US feminisms, initiatives and further publications led to a wider discussion of the intersectionality of race and gender in German feminism. See also organizations like ADEFRA http://www.adefra. de/, an organization for black women in Germany, or Initiative Schwarze Menschen in Deutschland http://isdonline.de/links/.

14 We are thinking here about a wave of comedians who perform racialized subjects, with Kaya Yanar being the most well known performer in Germany. While their performances are complicated in the way in which they uncover racisms, in their reception by mainstream TV audiences they often convey a rather superficial message of a post-racial society. For critical discussions of the discourse of "post-racialism," see, for example, Lentin (2011).

15 See also McCarthy (n.d.).

16 For detailed discussions of these discourses, see Weber (2004, 2015a, 2015b). Weber emphasizes, for example, the innovative force of women of colour feminists in the 1990s and the importance of Muslim feminist activists for current feminist discourse in Germany.

17 "Popkultur [sollte] durch feministische Strategien perforiert und erschüttert werden."

18 A more extensive definition is found in Smith-Prei (2011).

19 "Pop ist ... eine Strategie, eine Haltung, eine Attitude."

20 "Nur [in Deutschland] ist Pop immer auch ein Problem."

21 "Definitionen permanent zu unterlaufen – gegebenfalls auch in vermeintlich gegenläufige Richtungen."

22 See Wolfson (2014).

23 In her article "Cyberpopfeminismus? Nutzen und Nachteil des Popfaktors von/für Cyberfeminismus," Kuni (2007) suggests the term "cyberpopfeminismus" to help in the investigation of this process. While published in 2007, the opening questions of this article continue to resonate. Kuni traces the history of cyberfeminism and pop from Sadie Plants's 1996 use of the former word for the first time and the resonance for the German-speaking realm. About the history of cyber feminisms, see also Wilding (1998).

24 In some ways this question echoes Baer's (2012a) starting point in "German Feminism in the Age of Neoliberalism," where she positions pop-feminism as part of, but also acting as an orientating point within, neoliberalism.

25 The first book-length study on Femen is Tayler's (2013) "Topless Jihadis: Inside the World's Most Radical Feminist Movement."

26 See Femen's official website at http://www.femen.org.

27 See also Zychowicz (2011, 222), who argues that "ten minute street-performances in real-time were traded for five-second photo ops that the group could frame with comments and disseminate in virtual space. With the rise of Femen's global popularity corresponding directly with the rise of Internet use in Ukraine, I would suggest that the group has adapted their format to fit the shifting nature of their audience."

28 See Elgot (2014).

29 For references, see, for example, Pape (2013) and Gümüsay (2013).

30 For extensive discussions of these media discourses, see the work of Beverly Weber.

31 See the discussion of this event in Smith-Prei (2013).

32 See, for example, Nasman (2014).

33 See, for example, Traister (2012) in the New York Times.

34 "Geschlechter abschaffen – Männer zuerst abschaffen."

35 See the flyer Diskussion bei Slutwalk Berlin – "umgedrehter Sexismus?" (2011).

36 See interview by Matteoni (2011) as well as the interview with Sona (2012).

37 See Horak, Rudiger, and Susemichel (2008). See also the discussion of Lady Fest and digital culture in Groß (2006).

38 "Die Lage von Mädchen und FrauenLesbenTrans in Deutschland sowie weltweit."

39 "Missy ist ein Magazin für Frauen, die sich für Popkultur, Politik und Style interessieren – für Frauen wie uns halt."

40 "All das passiert mit einer Attitüde, die beständig den Status Quo mit einem Grinsen in Frage stellt. Weil wir (noch) nicht in einer gleichberechtigten Gesellschaft leben … Feminismus ist passé? We don't think so. Deshalb *Missy*."

41 See *Spiegel Online International* (2010) for an English-language overview of the debate.

42 "Manche Feministinnen sehen in der Geburt eines Kindes auch die Chance der 'Geburt eines feministisches Bewusstseins': So kann die Annahme, bereits gleichberechtigt zu sein, durch die Mutterschaft und damit einhergehende Beschränkungen infrage gestellt werden."

43 See http://mombloggersforsocialgood.com/ for an example of this type of large-scale social organizing through the mommy blog.

44 "Um dieses Ideal zu verunsichern und destabilisieren, möchte *Fuckermothers* die Perspektive, wie man/frau heute Mutter sein kann, erweitern und die Vielfalt an möglichen Lebens-, Körper- und Gefühlsentwürfen zeigen."

45 "*Fuckermothers* möchte deswegen auch nach den verschiedenen Möglichkeiten feministischer Mutterschaft(en) fragen, nach den queeren Müttern, den hetero-Müttern, den hippen Müttern, den nicht-Müttern, den Anti-Müttern … den trans-Müttern, den VäterMüttern, den sexy Müttern, den marginalisierten Müttern, den pro-sex Müttern, den cripple moms, den traditionellen Müttern, den kritischen-Müttern-die-trotz-dem-in-traditionellen-Beziehungen-leben, den männlichen Müttern, den mütterlichen Männern."

46 The article was published by Anja Maier in advance of the book on 9 October 2011. See http://www.taz.de/!5110280/.

47 This is something also discussed at length in many publications and volumes edited by Andrea O'Reilly. See, for example, her edited volume, O'Reilly (2014), as well as O'Reilly (2008).

48 See Halberstam (2011).

49 See http://maedchenmannschaft.net/tag/selbermach-sonntag/page/2/ "Auch diese Woche freuen wir uns auf eure Links: was habt ihr gelesen oder selbst geschrieben? Auf welche Veranstaltungen möchtet ihr gerne hinweisen? Welche Fragen sind übrig geblieben? Wie immer: ab damit in die Kommentare, und wir wünschen einen schönen Sonntag!"

50 For a critical perspective on these models, see also Berlant (2011b, 261–2).

51 See Kämper (2014).

52 "Ich liebe das Internet und dessen Möglichkeiten! Ich habe es wachsen sehen (und tue dies noch) und erlebt, wie immer mehr und andere Möglichkeiten hinzukamen. Und schließlich habe ich nicht zuletzt

durchs Internet gelert, dass das, wofür ich stehe, feministisch ist – kein großes 'ABER,' sondern nur ein 'Fuck yeah!'"

53 See the announcement posted under "Third World Bunfight/Brett Bailey Exhibit B" at http://www.barbican.org.uk/theatre/event-detail. asp?ID=1622.

54 See the website *Buehnenwatch.com*.

CHAPTER THREE

1 The full issue can be found here: http://socialtextjournal.org/ periscope_topic/cruel_optimism/.

2 "(Post-)Punk entlehnten Guerilla-Gestus"; "postmodernen Glamour des Fake."

3 See the Chicks on Speed official website at: http://www.chicksonspeed. com/.

4 They might also reference the postures of the performance band the Clichettes. For a more detailed discussion of their politics, see Wark (2006, 152–3).

5 For a fairly recent example, see ZKM Karlsruhe, "IMA Lab No. 12 – Chicks on Speed," 25 January 2015.

6 See Ibid.

7 See Citygallerywgtn (2013).

8 "Feministisch ausgerichtete Studien und Konzepte, Bitch-Rap-Musik, Votzenkunst, bitchige Kliteratur und Mode."

9 "Morgen der BitchWalk von Lady Bitch Ray auf der Frankfurter Buchmesse. Eat this, Bitch!"

10 "Zieh dich aus, setz dir ein Koptuch auf oder gehe in Dessous auf die Straße!"

11 For the 2012 video (posted by Rap Vita) see: https://www.youtube.com/ watch?v=q7r6q4K5Nac

12 The following discussion of *Bitchsm* draws on a discussion in Smith-Prei and Stehle (2015a).

13 *Bitchsm* website and blog: http://www.lady-bitch-ray.com/tx-bl/tag/ bitchism/

14 For a more detailed academic discussion of the headscarf debates, see, for example, Weber (2004).

15 "Für emanzipierte Bitches, deren Muschi nicht genug kriegen kann und andauernd juckt – steht auf, wenn ihr Fotzen seid! Bitchsm 2012, yeah!!"

16 "Original-Votzenabdruck von Lady Bitch Ray."

17 "Liebe Hunde und Hündinnen, genießt dieses mutterfickende Werk! Bitchsm for Bitches, Bitchsm for Live [*sic*], Biaaaaaach!!! Ihr könnt es nicht mehr ignorieren. Endlich kann ich Bitchsm veröffentlichen und

kein Schwanz redet mir dazwischen. Geschrieben von Mushido – der buschigen Muschi von Lady Bitch Ray."

18 "Ich hatte Frau ALICE SCHWARZER gefragt, ob sie das Vorwort für dieses Bitchsm-Werk schreiben will, sie hat mir leider nicht geantwortet, dann hat's meine Fut verfasst. Ist doch viel fotziger geworden!"

19 See their song "We Don't Play Guitars" (Chicks on Speed, feat. Peaches 2015). See the version featuring Peaches at: https://www.youtube.com/watch?v=pO8MvjiIGko.

20 This is particularly well illustrated, for example, in the 2014 so-called "Gamergate" surrounding sexism in the gaming industry after Anita Sarkeesian spoke up against misogyny. As a result of her speaking out she received death threats. For more details, see Parkin (2014).

21 See https://vimeo.com/74614251 for the video of "Utopia" (Chicks on Speed 2013).

22 See First Supper Symposium (2014): https://www.youtube.com/watch?v=BXbx_P7UVtE

23 See Pham (2014, 2011).

CHAPTER FOUR

1 This can be seen, for example, in invitations to events such as the First Supper Symposium, where they shared the stage with Judith Butler and Rosi Braidotti.

2 "Vermeindliche Geschwindigkeitszunahme." See Röggla (2013, 14).

3 For a detailed discussion of race (in particular) in global activism and the issue of the privilege of "whiteness" in protest, see Mahrouse (2014).

4 Whenever we discuss Pussy Riot we do attempt to distinguish between the actions engaged in by the group and those enacted by Masha Alyokhina and Nadia Tolokonnikova. However, at times we use the blanket term "Pussy Riot" to discuss activisms pursued by these two members, primarily because, despite their ejection from the group proper in early 2014, they continue to protest under the moniker Pussy Riot and therefore continue to be – at least in the eyes of the Western consumer – synonymous with it.

5 See, for example, Schuler (2013).

6 In this article, Hall first offers a history of neoliberalism and then focuses on the specific case in Britain.

7 For other relevant discussions of neoliberalism, capitalism, and globalization, see also Cazdyn and Szeman (2011).

8 See, for example, Caspari (2014) and Reinbold (2013).

9 Tuzcu discusses this complex mechanism in relation to the #solidarityisforwhitewomen campaign in her 2014 online lecture at https://www.artsrn.ualberta.ca/feminism/?page_id=41.

10 For a more detailed exploration of the performative in the digital age, particularly in relation to race and gender, see Nakamura (2002).

11 For these examples, see Al Jazeera (2014).

12 For a rather detailed account of Pussy Riot's actions before their performance in the Cathedral of Christ the Saviour, see Heinrich and Segschneider (2013).

13 Gradskova (2013) offers statistics from a detailed attitudes survey reflecting on the Pussy Riot reception in Russia. Kendzior (2012) talks about the perception of Pussy Riot in general and how many misrepresentations and misunderstandings there are about the band. See also Miller (2012).

14 For a detailed description of views on Pussy Riot in Russia, see Miller (2012).

15 For Butler's reading of Pussy Riot as political performance, see her talk following the podium discussion at the First Supper Symposium: https://www.youtube.com/watch?v=QeHPfXUmY3g. See also https://www.youtube.com/watch?v=BXbx_P7UVtE. See http://www.thefirstsuppersymposium.org/index.php/en/ for more information on the event, conceived also as art project.

16 See Gradskova (2013).

17 See the video posted by Sky News on 19 February 2014 at: https://www.youtube.com/watch?v=eiwofw_sJOk.

18 See Pelly (2014).

19 See the video here: https://www.youtube.com/watch?v=qmuZwBuEIyI (2015).

20 Translations by Olena Hlazkova.

21 See, for example, the television documentary "Party, Protz und Putin. Rätselhaftes Russland," which aired on the German channel Vox on 22 November 2014.

22 "Durch die mediale Verharmlosung – sie werden zumeist als 'Mädchen,' nicht als Frauen, oder eben als Punk Girls bezeichnet – bieten sie sich als Projektionsfläche und Identifikationsfiguren für Menschen verschiedenen politischen und sozialen Hintergrunds an. Das bürgerliche Lager kann sie als Beispiel zivilen Ungehorsam, die radikalere Linke als Widerstandskämpferinnen betrachten. Ihre mediale Verwertung eignet sich folglich, um einem breiten Spektrum westlicher Rezipienten ein das eigene Selbst- und Weltbild nicht gefährdendes, Identifikationsmoment anzubieten. Auch ihre kremlkritische Haltung ist für die westliche Presse prädestiniert, um die Geschichte um die 'Mädchen,' die lautstark Putin und den russischen Staat kritisieren und dafür inhaftiert werden, zu skandalisieren."

23 See Heinrich and Segschneider (2013): "solange sie also nicht im Kontext der Performance-Kunst einer ernsthaften Betrachtung ihres politischen Potentials unterzogen werden, eignen sie sich für den medialen

Kampf um diverse politische Interessen und können gefahrlos auch Eingang in den Mainstream-Diskurs finden."

24 See Connor (2013).

CHAPTER FIVE

1 Some of the following section on affect appears in an earlier and much altered version in Smith-Prei (2015).

2 See Hardt (2007m ix). Clough uses the term "affective turn" in the title of her chapter in the volume *The Affect Studies Reader* as well in the title of a collection of essays she edited in 2007. See Clough (2010, 2007).

3 Each contemporary take on affect theory draws on a long and differentiated history of thinking about affect. For a discussion of the important tensions found in this legacy, see Pelligrini and Puar (2009).

4 See also the online lecture at https://www.artsrn.ualberta.ca/ feminism/?page_id=41 (2014). This argument could probably also be made for more recent campaigns, such as #BlackLivesMatter.

5 See SlutWalk Berlin (2012).

6 Here she uses Foucault's (1980, 1:127) phrase "set of effects produced in bodies, behaviors, and social relations," from *The History of Sexuality*.

7 "Das Gefangengehaltenwerden durch die inhaltliche Abfolge des Films habe ich durchbrochen, und während ich mich auf die Fingerspitze konzentriere, erfahre ich Schnitte / an dem heftigen Zucken, das durch meinen Körper rinnt, sobald ein Schnitt erfolgt, ein Vorgang abbricht, zuckendes Licht."

8 Later pop authors, particularly coming out of the resurgence of pop literature in the unified Germany of the 1990s, utilized a different sort of cut-up technique, one that would, however, also engage with a variety of materials due to the reconfiguration of those materials in literature. These included anything from placing snippets of music and advertising in text (in the case of Christian Kracht and Benjamin von Stuckrad-Barre) to quoting from phone books and gender theory (in the case of Thomas Meinecke).

9 "Ich will nicht mehr lügen. Ich bin verrückt geworden und ich glaub' ich weiss woran das liegt ... Ich träum' jetzt auch von meiner Mama."

10 "Ich wollte das nicht. Ich hab das alles überlebt und ich hätte nicht sollen ... Weil man nicht so leicht stirbt wenn man jung ist. Sie hat gesagt, dass ich das Beste bin, was ihr je passiert ist ... Du must mir helfen. Ich hab das noch nie zu jemand gesagt. "

11 "Willst du mich heiraten?"

12 Our discussions of the literary texts are, in parts, also published in Smith-Prei and Stehle (2015a).

13 See Delius (2010).

14 For example, it was nominated for the prestigious Leipziger Book Prize, prompting a host of established authors to sign a declaration decrying intellectual theft.

15 See Kristeva (2003). For a good summary, see also Irwin (2004).

16 On theories of intermediality, see, for example, Paech (1997).

17 For another interesting reading of Hegemann's work, see Jeremiah (2013).

18 "mich zu Tode schämen für alles, was ich hier … in diesen Computer reinhacke." See also Rachael McLennan's summary in McLennan (2009).

19 "Mir wurde eine Sprache einverleibt, die nicht meine eigene ist." See also Burt (2007) for a discussion of poetics and individuality.

20 See also Biendarra's (2012) discussion of digital dimensions of transnationalism and literature.

21 "O.k., die Nacht, wieder mal so ein Ringen mit dem Tod … Nur die Klaviatur der absoluten Dunkelheit, das Kreischen im Kopf, dieses unrhythmische Trommeln, scheiße. Früher war das alles so schön pubertär hingerotzt und jetzt ist es angestrengte Literatur."

22 "Irgendwann, wenn das Blut so technoplastizitätsmäßig durch die Gegend zirkuliert, ist alles wieder super."

23 See Pirmasens's (2010) blog.

24 The Public Knowledge Project, for example, claims to wish to "improve both the scholarly quality and public accessibility and coherence of this body of knowledge in a sustainable and globally accessible form" (http://pkp.sfu.ca/about). Creative Commons, on the other hand, notes its vision as "universal access to research, education, full participation in culture, and driving a new era of development, growth, and productivity" (http://creativecommons.org/).

25 "1. Ich habe meine von Analsex, Tränen und Leichenschändung geprägte Patchworkgeschichte verloren.
2. Ich habe eine offene Entzündung im Rachen.
3. Meine Familie ist ein Haufen von in irgendeiner frühkindlichen Allmachtsphase steckengebliebenen Personen mit Selbstdarstellungssucht. Im äußersten Fall wird von deren Seite aus mal ein popkultureller Text über die Frage verfasst, weshalb die Avantgarde TROTZDEM bauchtanzt, aber das war's auch schon."

26 "Ich weiß komischerweise genau, was ich will: nicht erwachsen werden."

27 This produced such headlines as Hammelehle's (2010) "Axololita Overkill" and Radisch's (2010) "Die alten Männer und das junge Mädchen" (The old men and the young girl).

28 Charlotte Roche's *Feuchtgebiete* was first performed as a play at the Neues Theatre Halle under the direction of Christina Friedrich in 2008; subsequently, the text was performed at the Theaterforum Kreuzberg in Berlin, at the Brandenburger Theatre, and at the Theater Liga in

Hamburg. Charlotte Roche published a second novel, *Schoßgebete*, that was also adapted to film (dir. Sönke Wortmann, 2014). We discuss the two texts together in Smith-Prei and Stehle (2015a). See Roche (2008, 2011)

29 As we argue elsewhere, these television appearances produced a specific kind of awkwardness as the often male talk show hosts engaged in discussions of the book that, due to Roche's clever media strategy, turned the pornographic gaze from her text and author personality to the talk show hosts themselves, challenging them to confront their own preconceptions about female sexuality. This meant that awkward passages in the text that are based on detailed and exaggerated descriptions of the female body, its smells, and fluids were transferred to the male body. See Smith-Prei and Stehle (2013).

30 "solange ich denken kann, habe ich Hämorrhoiden"; "zurück zum Arschrasieren."

31 "Dank meiner gut trainierten Scheidenmuskeln kann ich [den Avocadokern] nachher wieder rausschießen lassen ... Näher komme ich an eine Geburt nicht ran ... Ich will wirklich seit ich denken kann, ein Kind haben. Es gibt aber bei uns in der Familie ein immer wiederkehrendes Muster. Meine Urgroßmutter, meine Oma, Mama und ich. Alle Erstgeborene. Alle Mädchen. Alle nervenschwach, gestört und unglücklich. Den Kreislauf habe ich durchbrochen ... habe mich sterilisieren lassen ... Als ich die Augen aufmache, sehe ich Mama über mich gebeugt."

32 See Berlant and Luciano (2013).

33 See Stehle (2012).

34 "Da haben sie reingeschnitten."

35 See also Haaf, Klingner, and Streidl (2008, 66).

36 See ibid., 53.

37 For a reading of both Mifti and Helen in terms of youthful rebellion, see Schlaffer (2011).

CHAPTER SIX

1 See the MTV Braless YouTube channel here: https://www.youtube.com/user/mtvbraless.

2 For a discussion of how this might also be furthered by queer theory, see McCallum and Tuhkanen (2011).

3 See Chicks on Speed website at: http://www.chicksonspeed.com/.

4 A close-up shot of the fabric of their costumes reveals cartoon-inspired words, such as "Bang," "Crash," and "Boom" mixed with slogs "Fluxus for all" or "Create under all difficult circumstances" and German "Kultur des Scheins." See Chicks on Speed et al. 2010, 118–19.

5 See http://barbiedreamhouse.com/, masterminded by Event Marketing Service Entertainment for Mattel.

6 See Leurs (2013).

7 For an illustration of the deconstruction, see https://www.facebook.com/photo.php?fbid=501822276570748&set=a.440130382739938.107374 1831.424632290956414&type=1&theater (2013).

8 See the website of the mall here: http://www.simon.com/mall/sawgrass-mills.

9 See episode 41, "My Plastic Feels Warm," and episode 45, "Trapped in the Dream House" at: http://dreamhouse.barbie.com/en-US/.

10 See, for example, Schaschek (2014) on the most recent turn of hate and violence towards gender studies in Germany.

11 "Ich werde über 'Bitchsm' und meine Doktorarbeit zum Kopftuch sprechen. Es wird um Sexualität, Sprache, Lady Bitch Ray, Politik und das Kopftuch gehen. Das Bitchsm-Seminar ist eine Mischung aus Vortrag, Lesung und performativen Acapella-Rap-Einschüben."

12 Most famously in the German context is Verena Stefan's 1974 novel *Häutungen* (*Sheddings*), which utilizes lowercase letters and other feminist subversions of the German language (see Stefan 1974).

13 This pairing appears in an article in the online edition of the weekly newspaper *Die Zeit,* in which the author Detje uses the phrase "Schlussstrichdebatte Nationalisozialismus" (the final debate on National Socialism) shortly followed by "Schlussstrichdebatte Feminismus" (the final debate on feminism). See Detje (2014).

14 "Sollten sich also ausreichend Menschen finden, die gerne *Professx* oder *Studierx* genannt werden möchten, dann würde man diesen Wunsch mit rein wissenschaftlichen Argumenten wenig entgegensetzen können."

15 "Wenn Sie mit Lann Hornscheidt Kontakt aufnehmen wollen, verwenden Sie bitte respektvolle Anreden, die nicht Zweigeschlechtlichkeit aufrufen, wie z. B. 'Hallo Lann Hornscheidt,' 'Guten Tag Lann Hornscheidt' oder 'Dear Lann Hornscheidt' und vermeiden Sie bitte zweigendernde Ansprachen wie 'Herr ___,' 'Frau ___,' 'Lieber ___,' oder 'Liebe ___.' Es gibt nicht die eine richtige und gute Anrede, sondern es bedarf respektvoller neuer Anredeformen – ich freue mich auf Ihre kreativen anti-diskriminierenden Ideen."

16 "Falls Sie nicht kommunizieren, sondern nur Ihre Irritation zurückwerfen wollen, statt sie als Impuls für sich zu benutzen über eigene Normen und Weltbilder nachzudenken, dann schicken Sie dies bitte an folgende Mail-Adresse: hatemail.an.hornscheidt@gmail.com
Oder – Sie nehmen sich die Zeit, um was Nettes und Respektvolles stattdessen an eine Person Ihrer Wahl zu schreiben – und schauen mal, wie sich eine solche Handlung anfühlen würde."

17 Internal critique of Professx focused on race with reference to Malcolm X. Current form is "professecs" (ak forschungsHandeln 2015).

18 See Sachaschek (2014) in the German context or Wingfield (2014) in the US context. Of course, such attacks and threats are not limited to these two national contexts. For an opinion piece on the neoliberal university and public intellectuals, see Giroux (2013).

19 We are not alone in this assessment. See Wunker's blog post "Once More, with Feeling: Why Feminist Methodology Is Crucial" (Wunker 2012). See also the most recent paper published on Academia.edu entitled "For Slow Scholarship: A Feminist Politics of Resistance through Collective Action in the Neoliberal University" by members of the Great Lakes Feminist Geography Collective, in which they propose, in order to counter the neoliberalization of the academy (which demands ever more output from scholars and devalues pastoral or care work and service), activities often coded as feminine. See Mountz et al. (forthcoming).

20 One way of doing this is engaged by FemTechNet, who have developed a feminist answer to MOOCs in the form of the DOCC. Pedagogy, and specifically digital pedagogy, is collaborative and political.

21 See Batuman (2014) and our arguments in earlier chapters.

CONCLUSION

1 See Ahmed (2014a). See also http://feministkilljoys.com/2014/11/16/pushy-feminists/.

2 We discuss this in more detail in Smith-Prei and Stehle (2015a). The thinking began in an earlier version, in Smith-Prei and Stehle (2015b).

3 For detailed discussions of race and visual cultures of the internet, see Nakamura (2008).

4 Hardt (2014, 221) goes on to write: "Once we recognize those common relations, we can compose a new, greater body, which contains the cause of our joy." This constitution of a new body he relates to the transformation of "passive into active affections."

References

Abramoviç, Marina. 2015. "Seven Easy Pieces by Marina Abramoviç (2007)." UbuWeb. n.d. Viewed 16 January 2015. http://www.ubu.com/film/abramovic_seven.html.

Adelson, Leslie A. 1993. *Making Bodies, Making History: Feminism and German Identity*. Lincoln: University of Nebraska Press.

Adorno, Theodor W. 2005 [1951]. "Juvenal's Error." In *Minima Moralia: Reflections from Damaged Life*, trans. E. F. N. Jephcott. 209–12. London: Verso.

Ahmed, Sara. 2010. *The Promise of Happiness*. Durham, NC: Duke University Press.

– 2014a. "Pushy Feminists." *feministkilljoys.com*, 16 November.

– 2014b. *Willful Subjects*. Durham, NC: Duke University Press.

ak forschungsHandeln. 2015. interdependDenken! Berlin: w_oreten & meer.

Al Jazeera. 2012. "The Future of Feminism? Ukraine's Protest Group Femen Takes Their 'Sextremism' to the Streets." Stream.aljazeera.com. 25 October. Viewed 13 August 2015. http://stream.aljazeera.com/story/201210250016-0022381.

– 2014. "Anti-Feminist Campaign Targets German Gender Quota Proposal." Stream.aljazeera.com. Viewed July 2015. http://stream.aljazeera.com/story/201404012147-0023610.

AllMusic. 2015. "*Artstravaganza* – Chicks on Speed: Songs, Reviews, Credits, Awards." Viewed 9 August 2015. http://www.allmusic.com/album/artstravaganza-mw0002673432.

Anderson, Ben. 2010. "Modulating the Excess of Affect: Morale in a State of 'Total War.'" In *The Affect Theory Reader*, ed. Melissa Gregg and Gregory J. Seigworth, 161–85. Durham, NC: Duke University Press.

Arnold, Heinz Ludwig, and Jörgen Schäfer. 2003. *Pop-Literatur*. München: Edition Text + Kritik.

Bachmann-Medick, Doris. 2007. "Cultural Turns: Neuorientierungen in Den Kulturwissenschaften." *L'homme* 18 (2): 123–38.

Badinter, Élisabeth. 2011. *The Conflict: How Modern Motherhood Undermines the Status of Women*. Trans. Adriana Hunter. Toronto: HarperCollins.

Baer, Hester. 2011. "Introduction: Resignifications of Feminism," *Studies in 20th and 21st Century Literature* 35 (1): 8–17.

– 2012a. "German Feminism in the Age of Neoliberalism: Jana Hensel and Elisabeth Raether's Neue Deutsche Mädchen." *German Studies Review* 35 (2): 355–74.

– 2012b. "Sex, Death, and Motherhood in the Eurozone: Contemporary Women's Writing in German." *World Literature Today* 86 (3): 59–65.

– 1015a. "Precarious Sexualities, Neoliberalism, and the Popfeminist Novel: Charlotte Roche's *Feuchtgebiete* and Helene Hegemann's *Axolotl Roadkill* as Transnational Texts." In *Transnationalism in Contemporary German-Language Literature*, ed. Elisabeth Herrmann, Carrie Smith-Prei, and Stuart Taberner, 162–86. Rochester: Camden House.

– 2015b. "Redoing Feminism: Digital Activism, Body Politics, and Neoliberalism." In *Digital Feminisms: Transnational Activism in German Protest Cultures*, ed. Christina Scharff, Carrie Smith-Prei, and Maria Stehle. Special issue of *Feminist Media Studies* 16 (1). New York: Routledge. doi:10.1080/14680777.2015.1093070.

Baldauf, Anette, and Katharina Weingartner. 1998. *Lips, Tits, Hips, Power: Popkultur und Feminismus*. Wien: Bozen.

Barbican. 2015. "Third World Bunfight/Brett Bailey Exhibit B." barbican.org.uk. n.d. Viewed 14 August 2015. http://www.barbican.org.uk/theatre/event-detail.asp?ID=16226

Batuman, Elif. 2014. "The Awkward Age." *New Yorker*, 9 September. http://www.newyorker.com/culture/cultural-comment/awkward-age.

Beck, Ulrich. 1999. *World Risk Society*. Malden, MA: Polity Press, 1999.

– 2013. *German Europe*. Trans. Rodney Livingstone. Maiden, MA: Polity Press.

– 2007. *Weltrisikogesellschaft: Auf der Suche nach der verlorenen Sicherheit*. Bonn: Bundeszantrale für politische Bildung.

Berlant, Lauren. 2011a. "Austerity, Precarity, Awkwardness." Supervalentthought.Files.Wordpress.Com. Viewed 20 July 2015. https://supervalentthought.files.wordpress.com/2011/12/berlant-aaa-2011final.pdf.

– 2011b. *Cruel Optimism*. Durham, NC: Duke University Press.

Berlant, Lauren, and Lee Edelman. 2014. *Sex, or the Unbearable*. Durham, NC: Duke University Press.

Berlant, Lauren, and Dana Luciano. 2013. "Cruel Optimism: Conversation: Lauren Berlant with Dana Luciano," *Social Text*, 13 January. http://socialtextjournal.org/periscope_article/conversation-lauren-berlant-with-dana-luciano/.

Berlant, Lauren, and Michael Warner. 1998. "Sex in Public." *Critical Inquiry* 24 (2): 547-66. doi:10.1086/448884.

Beyoncé. 2014a. "Gender Equality Is a Myth." Shriver Report, 12 January. http://shriverreport.org/gender-equality-is-a-myth-beyonce/.

– 2014b. "Yours and Mine." YouTube. 12 December. Viewed 6 January 2015. https://www.youtube.com/watch?v=x4pPNxUzGvc.

Biendarra, Anke S. 2012. *Germans Going Global: Contemporary Literature and Cultural Globalization*. Berlin: De Gruyter.

Bliss, Karen. 2012. "Shooting of Peaches Video 'Free Pussy Riot' in Berlin." *Rolling Stone*, 15 August. http://www.rollingstone.com/music/videos/peaches-shoots-guerrilla-video-in-support-of-pussy-riot-20120815.

Bohnet, Thomas. 2000. "Das Lied vom süßen Nichts. Münchens 'Chicks on Speed' erobern London." *Süddeutsche Zeitung*, 26 April, 18.

Braun, Christoph. 2007. "Lady Bitch Ray." *Spex Magazin*, 27 December. http://www.spex.de/2007/12/27/Lady-Bitch-Ray/?search=lady+bitch+ray.

Breger, Claudia. 2014a. "Configuring Affect: Complex World Making in Fatih Akin's Auf der anderen Seite (The Edge of Heaven)." *Cinema Journal* 54 1: 65–87.

– 2014b. *Nach dem Sex? Sexualwissenschaft und Affect Studies*. Göttingen: Wallstein Verlag.

Brinkman, Rolf Dieter. 1982. *Der Film in Worten: Prosa, Erzählungen, Essays, Hörspiele, Fotos, Collagen, 1965–1974*. Reinbeck bei Hamburg: Rowohlt.

Bruhm, Steven, and Natasha Hurley, eds. 2004. "Introduction." *Curiouser: On the Queerness of Children*, ix–xxxviii. Minneapolis: University of Minnesota Press.

Burt, Stephen. 2007. *The Forms of Youth Twentieth-Century Poetry and Adolescence*. New York: Columbia University Press.

Buß, Christian. 2011. "Schwarzer attackiert Roche: Häschen im Bett, Oma im Kopf." *Spiegel Online*, 15 August. http://www.spiegel.de/kultur/literatur/schwarzer-attackiert-roche-haeschen-im-bett-oma-im-kopf-a-780345.html.

Butler, Judith. 1990. *Gender Trouble: Feminism and the Subversion of Identity*. New York: Routledge.

– 1997. *Excitable Speech: A Politics of the Performative*. New York: Routledge.

– 2009. "Performativity, Precarity and Sexual Politics." *aibr: Revista de Antropología Iberoamericana* 4 (3): i–xiii.

Carrière, Marie. 2014. "Current Metafeminist Practices in France and Québec." Paper given at the Women in French session at MLA Convention, Chicago, 9 January.

Caspari, Lisa. 2014. "Sexismus-Debatte: Der #aufschrei Und Seine Folgen." *Zeit Online*, 23 January. http://www.zeit.de/politik/deutschland/2014-01/sexismus-debatte-folgen.

Cazdyn, Eric M., and Imre Szeman. 2011. *After Globalization*. Malden, MA: Wiley-Blackwell.

Chicks on Speed. 2010. *Cultural Workshop Now! The Zine*. Publication for the exhibition at the Kunstraum Bethanian Berlin.

Chicks on Speed. 2013. "UTOPIA." *Vimeo*. 16 September. Viewed 13 August 2015. https://vimeo.com/74614251. –, featuring Peaches. 2015. "We Don't Play Guitars." YouTube. Viewed 6 August. https://www.youtube.com/watch?v=pO8MvjiIGko.

Chicks on Speed and Thomas Düllo. 2005. *Cultural Hacking: Kunst des strategischen Handlens*. Vienna: Springer.

Chicks on Speed and Walter Schönauer. 2004. *It's a Project*. London: Booth-Clibborn.

Chicks on Speed, Melissa Logan, Alex Murray-Leslie, Glenn Adamson, Edward Booth-Clibborn, Sandra De Ryeker, and Judith Winter. 2010. ~~Don't~~ *Art Fashion Music*. London: Booth-Clibborn.

Chun, Wendy Hui Kyong. 2009. "Introduction: Race and/as Technology; Or, How to Do Things to Race." *Camera Obscura* 24 (70): 7–35. doi:10.1215/02705346-2008-013.

Citygallerywgtn. 2013. "Chicks on Speed Perform at City Gallery Wellington." YouTube. 9 April. Viewed 13 August 2015. https://www.youtube.com/watch?v=-f8wJVnzv7Q.

Clark, Robert. 2010. "The Guide: Exhibitions: Chicks on Speed Dundee." *Guardian*, 5 June, 39.

Clough, Patricia Ticineto. 2007. "Introduction." In *The Affective Turn: Theorizing the Social*, ed. Patricia Ticineto Clough and Jean O'Malley Halley, 1–33. Durham, NC: Duke University Press.

– 2010. "The Affective Turn: Political Economy, Biomedia, and Bodies." In *The Affect Theory Reader*, ed. Melissa Gregg and Gregory J. Seigworth, 206–26. Durham, NC: Duke University Press.

Coleman, Beth. 2009. "Race as Technology." *Camera Obscura* 24 (70): 176–207.

Connor, Michael. 2013. "Hito Steyerl's 'How Not to Be Seen: A Fucking Didactic Educational .MOV File.'" Rhizome.org, 31 May. http://rhizome.org/editorial/2013/may/31/hito-steyerl-how-not-to-be-seen/.

de Lauretis, Teresa. 1987. *Technologies of Gender: Essays on Theory, Film, and Fiction*. Bloomington: Indiana University Press.

Dean, Will. 2015. "Pussy Riot at Glastonbury: 'The Toilets Aren't So Bad. At Least They Have Doors' Music." *Guardian*, 28 June. http://www.theguardian.com/music/2015/jun/28/pussy-riot-glastonbury-toilets-peoples-republic-putin.

Delius, Mara. 2010. "Helene Hegemann: *Axolotl Roadkill*: Mir Zerfallen Die Worte Im Mund Wie Schlechte Pillen – Belletristik – FAZ." *Faz.net*, 22 January. http://www.faz.net/aktuell/feuilleton/beucher/rezensionen/

belletristik/helene-hegemann-axolotl-roadkill-mir-zerfallen-die-worte-im-mund-wie-schlechte-pillen-1913572.html.

Detje, Robin. 2014. "Gender-Debatte: Anschwellender Ekelfaktor." *Zeit Online*, 24 November. http://www.zeit.de/kultur/2014-11/lann-hornscheidt-feminismus-gender-maenner-polemik.

Dicker, Rory Cooke, and Alison Piepmeier. 2003. *Catching a Wave: Reclaiming Feminism for the 21st Century*. Boston: Northeastern University Press.

Diskussion bei Slutwalk Berlin: "Umgedrehter Sexismus"? 2011. Flyer distributed at SlutWalk Berlin, De.Indymedia.org, 13 August. Viewed 13 August 2015. http://de.indymedia.org/2011/08/313935.shtml.

Dobson, Kit, and Áine McGlynn. 2013. "Introduction." In *Transnationalism, Activism, Art*, 3– 18. Toronto: University of Toronto Press.

Donath, Orna. 2015. "Regretting Regretting Motherhood: A Sociopolitical Analysis." *Signs* 40 2: 343–67. doi:10.1086/678145.

Dreher, Thomas. 2001. *Performance Art nach 1945: Aktionstheater und Intermedia*. München: W. Fink.

Drüecke, Ricarda, and Elke Zobel. 2015. "Online Feminist Protest against Sexism: The German-language hashtag #aufschrei." In *Feminist Media Studies: Digital Feminisms – Transnational Activism in German Protest Cultures*, ed. Christina Scharff, Carrie Smith-Prei, and Maria Stehle. Special issue of *Feminist Media Studies* 16 (1). New York: Routledge.

Edwards, Stassa. 2014. "Carry That Weight: The Revival of Feminist Performance Art." *Hairpin*, 29 September. http://thehairpin.com/2014/09/carry-that-weight-the-revival-of-feminist-performance-art/.

Eismann, Sonja. 2007a. "Feminismus ist Pop!" *Taz: Die Tageszeitung*, 10 November. http://www.taz.de/!5191963/.

– 2007b. *Hot Topic: Popfeminismus heute*. Mainz: Ventil.

– 2008. "Bewegung vortäuschen." jungle-world.com, 15 April. http://jungle-world.com/artikel/2008/15/21547.html.

– 2011. "Musizierende Nähmaschinen." *Taz: Die Tageszeitung*, 17 January. http://www.taz.de/!5128560/.

Elgot, Jessica. 2014. "Topless Femen Protesters Storm Crimean Parliament to Protest 'Putin's War.'" *Huffington Post UK*, 6 March. Updated 7 March 2014. http://www.huffingtonpost.co.uk/2014/03/06/topless-protesters-femen_n_4910812.html.

Emspunk. 2007. "Heiter Bis Wolkig-Hey Rote Zora." YouTube. 8 January. Viewed 13 August 2015. http://www.youtube.com/watch?v=beLokKMK1g8.

Fales Library and Special Collections. 2015. "The Riot Grrrl Collection." New York University. Viewed 13 August. http://www.nyu.edu/library/bobst/research/fales/riotgrrrltest.html.

Femen. 2015. "About." femen.org. Viewed 23 January 2015. http://femen.org/about.

"Feministmum: Fragen und Antworten zu Feminismus und Muttersein." 2015. *Feministmum*. Wordpress Blog. 30 March. Viewed 13 August 2015. https://feministmum.wordpress.com.

Ferree, Myra Marx. 2012. *Varieties of Feminisms: German Gender Politics in Global Perspective*. Stanford: Stanford University Press.

First Supper Symposium. 2014. "Pussy Riot Meets Judith Butler and Rosi Braidotti." YouTube. 21 May. https://www.youtube.com/watch?v=BXbx_P7UVtE.

Fischer-Lichte, Erika. 2004. *Ästhetik des Performativen*. Frankfurt am Main: Suhrkamp.

Fleig, Anne. 2000. "Körper-Inszenierungen: Begriff, Geschichte, Kulturelle Praxis." In *Körper- Inszenierungen: Präsenz und kultureller Wandel*, ed. Erika Fischer-Lichte and Anne Fleig, 7–17. Tübingen: Attempto.

Florida, Richard L. 2002. *The Rise of the Creative Class: And How It's Transforming Work, Leisure, Community and Everyday Life*. New York: Basic Books.

Foucault, Michel. 1980. *The History of Sexuality*. Vol. 1. Trans. Robert J. Hurley. New York: Vintage.

Fox, Oriana. 2010. "Once More with Feeling: An Abbreviated History of Feminist Performance Art." *Feminist Review* 96: 107–21. doi:10.1057/fr.2010.11.

Free to Fight. 1995. "Free to Fight! An Interactive Self Defense Project." *Candy Ass Records*. Distributed by Revolver USA. Booklet and CD. http://web.archive.org/web/20071012180014/http://www.freetofight.org/.

Freedom Requires Wings. 2012. "Pussy Riot – Punk Prayer 'Virgin Mary, Put Putin Away' (English Subtitles)." YouTube. 17 August. Viewed 13 August 2015. https://www.youtube.com/watch?v=lPDkJbTQRCY.

Frevert, Ute. 1990. *Women in German History: From Bourgeois Emancipation to Sexual Liberation*. Trans. Terry Bond, Stuart McKinnon-Evans, and Barbara Norden. Oxford: Berg.

Fuckermothers. 2015. "Fuckermothers: Feministische Perspektiven auf Mutterschaft." WordPress. Viewed 13 August 2015. https://fuckermothers.wordpress.com.

Gansel, Carsten. 2003. "Adoleszenz, Ritual und Inszenierung in der Pop-Literatur." In *Pop- Literatur*, ed. Heinz Ludwig Arnold, 234–57. München: Edition Text + Kritik.

Garrison, Ednie K. 2005. "Are We on a Wavelength Yet? On Feminist Oceanography, Radios, and Third Wave Feminism." In *Different Wavelengths: Studies of the Contemporary Women's Movement*, ed. Jo Reger, 237–56. New York: Routledge.

Georgiou, Myria. 2012. "Introduction: Gender, Migration and the Media." *Ethnic and Racial Studies* 35 (5): 791–99.

"Germany Passes Japan to Have World's Lowest Birth Rate – Study." 2015. BBC News, 29 May. http://www.bbc.com/news/world-europe-32929962.

Gessen, Masha. 2014. *Words Will Break Cement: The Passion of Pussy Riot.* New York: Riverhead Trade.

Gilbert, Sandra M., and Susan Gubar. 2000. *The Madwoman in the Attic: The Woman Writer and the Nineteenth-Century Literary Imagination.* New Haven: Yale University Press.

Gill, Rosalind. 2007. "Postfeminist Media Culture: Elements of a Sensibility." *European Journal of Cultural Studies* 10 (2): 147–66.

Gill, Rosalind, and Christina Scharff. 2011. *New Femininities: Postfeminism, Neoliberalism, and Subjectivity.* New York: Palgrave Macmillan.

Giroux, Henry A. 2013. "Public Intellectuals against the Neoliberal University." *Truthout,* 29 October. http://www.truth-out.org/opinion/item/19654-public-intellectuals-against-the-neoliberal-university.

Gleba, Kerstin, and Eckhard Schumacher. 2007. "Vorwort." In *Pop seit 1964,* 11–14. Köln: Kiepenheuer and Witsch.

Göbel, Esther. 2015. "Unglückliche Mütter - Sie wollen ihr Leben zurück." *Süddeutsche.de,* 5 April. http://www.sueddeutsche.de/gesundheit/unglueckliche-muetter-sie-wollen-ihr-leben-zurueck-1.2419449.

Gottschalk, Katrin. 2014. "Kampagne bei Twitter #EMMAistfürmich: 'Emma' kriegt ordentlich was ab." *Spiegel Online,* 6 November. http://www.spiegel.de/netzwelt/web/emmaistfuermich-debatte-unter-feministinnen-im-netz-a-1001384.html.

Gradskova, Yulia. 2013. "Pussy Riot: Reflections on Receptions: Some Questions Concerning Public Reactions in Russia to the Pussy Riot Intervention." *Baltic World* 6 (1): 56–78.

Griffin, Gabriele. 2012. "More Trans Than National? Re-Thinking Transnational Feminism through Affective Orders." *Women: A Cultural Review* 23 (1): 13–25.

Groeneveld, Elizabeth. 2009. "'Be a Feminist or Just Dress Like One': BUST, Fashion and Feminism as Lifestyle." *Journal of Gender Studies* 18 (2): 179–90.

Groll, Tina. 2014. "Gleichberechtigung: Der #Aufschrei Wird Zum Manifest." *Zeit Online,* 29 September. http://www.zeit.de/karriere/2014-09/aufschrei-buch-rezension/komplettansicht.

Groß, Melanie. 2006. "Das Internet als Platform politischer Interventionen: Ladyfest im Netz." *kommunikation @ gesellschaft* 7 (4): 1–16. http://www.ssoar.info/ssoar/bitstream/handle/document/12784/B4_2006_Gross.pdf.

Gümüsay, Kübra. 2013. "Femen und die muslimische Frau: Gut gemeint." taz.de, 9 April. http://www.taz.de/!114255/.

Guthrey, Molly. 2014. "Barbie Dreamhouse: Pink and Frothy, Techie and Tempting." TwinCities.com, 11 February. Viewed 13 August 2015. http://www.twincities.com/family/ci_25113226/ barbie-dreamhouse-sneak-peek-pink-and-frothy-techie.

Haaf, Meredith, Susanne Klingner, and Barbara Streidl. 2008. *Wir Alphamädchen: Warum Feminismus das Leben schöner macht*. Hamburg: Hoffmann und Campe.

Halberstam, Jack. 2012. *Gaga Feminism: Sex, Gender, and the End of Normal*. Boston: Beacon Press.

Halberstam, Judith. 2005. *In a Queer Time and Place: Transgender Bodies, Subcultural Lives*. New York: New York University Press.

– 2011. *The Queer Art of Failure*. Durham, NC: Duke University Press. Hall, Stuart. 1992. "The West and the Rest: Discourse and Power." In *Formations of Modernity*, ed. Stuart Hall and Bram Gieben, 275–320. Cambridge: Polity.

– 2011. "The Neo-Liberal Revolution." *Cultural Studies* 25 (6): 705– 28. Hammelehle, Sebastian. 2010. "Hegemanns Quellenliste: Axololita Overkill." *Spiegel Online*, 18 February. http://www.spiegel.de/kultur/ literatur/hegemanns-quellenliste-axololita-overkill-a-678708.html.

Hanna, Kathleen. 1991. "Riot Grrrl Manifesto." *One War Art*. Viewed 7 January 2015. http://onewarart.org/riot_grrrl_manifesto.htm.

Haraway, Donna. 1991. *Simians, Cyborgs, and Women: The Reinvention of Nature*. New York: Routledge.

– 2003. "A Cyborg Manifesto: Science, Technology, and Socialist-Feminism in the Late Twentieth Century." In *The Feminism and Visual Culture Reader*, ed. Amelia Jones, 475–97. New York: Routledge.

– 2014. "SF: String Figures, Multispecies Muddles, Staying with the Trouble." Keynote Lecture presented at the University of Alberta, Edmonton. 24 March. https://www.youtube.com/watch?v=Z1uTVnhIHS8.

Hardt, Michael. 2007. "Foreword: What Affects Are Good For." In *The Affective Turn: Theorizing the Social*, ed. Patricia Ticineto Clough and Jean O'Malley Halley, ix–xiii. Durham, NC: Duke University Press.

– 2014. "The Power to Be Affected." *International Journal of Politics, Culture, and Society* (28): 215–22.

Harris, Anita. 2008. "Introduction." In *Next Wave Cultures: Feminism, Subcultures, Activism*, Ed. Anita Harris, 1–13. New York: Routledge.

Harris, Jenn, and Jimmy Gribbin. 2013. *The Julie Ruin – Girls Like Us* (Official Lyric Video). YouTube. 25 September. Viewed 13 August 2015. https://www.youtube.com/watch?v=5wmL97Ape7o.

Harvey, David. 2005. *A Brief History of Neoliberalism*. Oxford: Oxford University Press.

Heffernan, Valerie. 2015. "#RegrettingMotherhood: Between Maternal Taboo and Feminist Protest." Paper presented at the Motherhood and Culture:

International and Interdisciplinary Conference, Maynooth University, Ireland, 17 June.

Hegemann, Helene, dir. 2008. *Torpedo*. Credo Film.

– 2010. *Axolotl Roadkill Roman*. Berlin: Ullstein. Heine, Matthias. 2014. "Sprachlenkung : Professx Statt Professor? So Irre Ist Das Nicht!" *Die Welt*, 5 January. http://www.welt.de/kultur/article127502626/Professx-statt-Professor-So-irre-ist-das-nicht.html.

Heinrich, Hanna, and Jacqueline Segschneider. 2013. "Pussy Riot: Feministische und anarchistische Performance-Kunst." *Pop-Zeitschrift*, 21 July. http://www.pop-zeitschrift.de/2013/07/21/pussy-riotfeministische-und-anarchistische-performance-kunstvon-jacqueline-segschneider-und-hanna-heinrich21-7-2013/.

Henry, Astrid. 2004. *Not My Mother's Sister: Generational Conflict and Third-Wave Feminism*. Bloomington: Indiana University Press.

Hensel, Jana, and Elisabeth Raether. 2008. *Neue deutsche Mädchen*. Reinbek: Rowohlt.

Herman, Barbara. 2014. "Catfight at the Anti-Feminist Corral: Felines Join the Anti-Feminist Debate." *Newsweek: ibt Media*, 30 July. http://www.newsweek.com/catfight-anti-feminist-corral-felines-join-anti-feminist-debate-262138.

Heywood, Leslie. 2006. *The Women's Movement Today: An Encyclopedia of Third-Wave Feminism*. Westport: Greenwood Press, 2006.

Heywood, Leslie, and Jennifer Drake. 1997. *Third Wave Agenda: Being Feminist, Doing Feminism*. Minneapolis: University of Minnesota Press.

Highmore, Ben. 2010. "Bitter After Taste: Affect, Food, and Social Aesthetics." In *The Affect Theory Reader*, ed. Melissa Gregg and Gregory J. Seigworth, 118–37. Durham, NC: Duke University Press.

– 2011. *Ordinary Lives*. New York: Routledge.

Hill Collins, Patricia. 2004. *Black Sexual Politics: African Americans, Gender, and the New Racism*. New York: Routledge.

Hoofd, Ingrid M. 2012. *Ambiguities of Activism: Alter-Globalism and the Imperatives of Speed*. New York: Routledge.

Horak, Gabi, Saskya Rudiger, and Lea Susemichel. 2008. *Feministische Medien: Öffentlichkeitein jenseits des Mainstream*. Königstein: Helmer.

Hornscheidt, Lann. 2015. "Professorx." University website. Viewed 9 August 2015. http://www.lannhornscheidt.com/professorx/.

Horst, Hansa. 2008. "Lady Bitch Ray Bei Schmidt Und Pocher Am 24.04.2008 Teil 1." YouTube. 26 April. Viewed 7 January 2015. http://www.youtube.com/watch?v=8d-40FC3488&translated=1.

– 2008. "Lady Bitch Ray bei Schmidt und Pocher am 24.04.2008 Teil 2." YouTube. 26 April. Viewed 7 January 2015. http://www.youtube.com/watch?v=uwWBIXNyfqA&feature=related.

Horst, Heather, and Daniel Miller. 2012. "Normativity and Materiality: A View from Digital Anthropology." *Media International Australia* 145 (November): 103–11.

Huffington Post. 2013. "10 Celebrities Who Say They Aren't Feminists." *Huffington Post*, Last modified 17 December 2013. http://www. huffingtonpost.com/2013/12/17/feminist-celebrities_n_4460416.html.

Hughes, Caelan. 2013. "Is Lady Gaga a Feminist? A Discussion." *Thought Catalog*. 22 November. http://thoughtcatalog.com/caelan-hughes/2013/11/is-lady-gaga-a-feminist-a-discussion/.

Ingram, Susan, and Katrina Sark. 2011. *Berliner Chic: A Locational History of Berlin Fashion*. Bristol, UK: Intellect Ltd.

Irler, Klaus. 2006. "Keine ist so krass wie ich." taz.de. 2 March. http://www. taz.de/index.php?id=archivseite&dig=2006/07/03/a0108.

Irwin, William. 2004. "Against Intertextuality." *Philosophy and Literature* 28 (2): 227–42. doi:10.1353/phl.2004.0030.

Jagger, Gill. 2008. *Judith Butler: Sexual Politics, Social Change and the Power of the Performative*. London: Routledge.

Jelinek, Elfriede, and Michael Hulse. 1989. *Lust*. Reinbeck bei Hamburg: Rowohlt.

Jenkins, Henry, Tara McPherson, and Jane Shattuc. 2002. "Defining Popular Culture." In *Hop on Pop: The Politics and Pleasures of Popular Culture*, ed. Henry Jenkins, Tara McPherson, and Jane Shattuc, 26–42. Durham, NC: Duke University Press.

Jeremiah, Emily. 2013. "The Case of Helene Hegemann: Queerness, Failure, and the German Girl." *Seminar: A Journal of Germanic Studies* 49 (4): 400–13.

Kämper, Verena. 2014. "Twitter-Debatte über Alltagssexismus: Was wurde eigentlich aus dem #Aufschrei?" *Spiegel Online*, 23 September. http://www. spiegel.de/netzwelt/netzpolitik/aufschrei-was-wurde-aus-der-debatte-ueber-sexismus-a-993233.html.

Kaplan, Ann E. 2003. "Feminist Futures: Trauma, the Post-9/11 World and a Fourth Feminism?" *Journal of International Women's Studies* 4 (2): 46–59. http://vc.bridgew.edu/jiws/vol4/iss2/5.

Karcher, Katharina. 2015. "How (Not) to 'Hollaback': Towards a Transnational Debate on the 'Red Zora' and Militant Tactics in the feminist Struggle against Gender-Based Violence." In *Feminist Media Studies. Digital Feminisms: Transnational Activism in German Protest Cultures*, ed. Christina Scharff, Carrie Smith-Prei, and Maria Stehle. Special issue of *Feminist Media Studies* 16 (1). New York: Routledge. doi:10.1080/14680777.2015.1093099.

Kates, Glenn, and Robert Mackey. 2012. "Russian Riot Grrrls Jailed for 'Punk Prayer.'" *New York Times*, 7 March. http://thelede.blogs.nytimes. com/2012/03/07/russian-riot-grrrls-jailed-for-punk-prayer/?_r=0.

Kauer, Katja. 2009. *Popfeminismus! Fragezeichen! Eine Einführung*. Berlin: Frank and Timme.

Kendzior, Sarah. 2012. "Manic Pixie Dream Dissidents: How the World Misunderstands Pussy Riot." *Atlantic*, 20 August. http://www.theatlantic. com/international/archive/2012/08/manic-pixie-dream-dissidents-how-the-world-misunderstands-pussy-riot/261309/.

Klimke, Martin. 2011. *The Other Alliance: Student Protest in West Germany and the United States in the Global Sixties*. Princeton, NJ: Princeton University Press.

Kotsko, Adam. 2010. *Awkwardness: An Essay*. London: Zero Books.

Kristeva, Julia. 2003. "'Nous Deux' Or a (Hi)story of Intertextuality." *Romanic Review* 93 (12): 7–13.

Kuni, Verena. 2007. "Cyberpopfeminismus." In *Hot topic: Popfeminismus heute*, ed. Sonja Eismann, 120–33. Mainz: Ventil.

La Hengst, Bernadette. 2008. "Pop-Feminismus. Sex, Schweiß und Selbstironie." *Spiegel Online*, 29 April. http://www.spiegel.de/kultur/ gesellschaft/pop-feminismus-sex-schweiss-und-selbstironie-a-546449.html.

LaBelle, Charles. 2001. "Review of Action Pants: Genital Panic, by Valie Export." *Friese Magazine*, July/August. http://www.frieze.com/issue/review/ valie_export/.

Lady Bitch Ray. 2008. "Interview with Çiğdem Akyol. Ich stehe für Vaginale Selbstbestimmung." *Taz*, April 1. http://www.taz.de/1/archiv/digitaz/artikel/ ?ressort=tz&dig=2008%2F04%2F01%2Fa0060&cHash=d1aa58cdb3a9b 1eb5440c8fd94f820f1.

– 2012a. "Die Aufklärung." YouTube, 23 June. Viewed 14 August 2015. https://www.youtube.com/watch?v=q7r6q4K5Nac.

– 2012b. *Bitchsm – Emanzipation. Integration. Masturbation*. Stuttgart: Panini Verlags.

Lentin, Alana. 2011. "Racism in a Post-Racial Europe." *Eurozine*, 24 November. http://www.eurozine.com/articles/2011-11-24-lentin-en. html.

Lerner, Mike, and Maxim Pozdorovkin, dir. *Pussy Riot: A Punk Prayer*. 2013. HBO, film.

Leurs, Rainer. 2013. "Protesting Pink: Dreamhouse Gets Fiery Welcome in Berlin." *Spiegel Online*, 17 May. http://www.spiegel.de/international/ zeitgeist/protests-mar-opening-of-barbie-dreamhouse-in-berlin-a-900430. html.

Little, Anita. 2014. "Beyoncé at the VMAs: Feminist and Flawless." *Ms. Magazine*, 24 August. http://msmagazine.com/blog/2014/08/25/ beyonce-at-the-vmas-feminist-and-flawless/.

Mahrouse, Gada. 2014. *Conflicted Commitments: Race, Privilege, and Power in Transnational Solidarity Activism*. Montreal and Kingston: McGill-Queen's University Press.

Maier, Anja. 2011. "Die Weiber denken, sie wären besser." taz.de, 9 October. http://www.taz.de/!5110280/.

Mansfield, Susan. 2010. "Can't Sing, Can't Play, Can Create an Interesting Show." *Scotsman*, 13 July, 34.

Marcus, Sara. 2010. *Girls to the Front: The True Story of the Riot Grrrl Revolution*. New York: HarperPerennial.

Marcuse, Herbert. 1991. "Cultural Revolution." In *Toward a Critical Theory of Society: Collected Papers of Herbert Marcuse*, vol. 2, ed. Douglas Kellner, 121–62. London: Routledge.

Massumi, Brian. 2002. *Parables for the Virtual: Movement, Affect, Sensation*. Durham, NC: Duke University Press.

Matteoni, Frederica. 2011. "Es ist der Beginn einer neuen Bewegung." jungle-world.com, 23 June. http://jungle-world.com/artikel/2011/25/43438.html.

Матвеева, Гараджа [Matveieva, Garadzha]. "Pussy Riot –Акция! Акция! Пусси Райот ликвидация! Пусси Райот из дэд!" [Pussy Riot – Aktsiia! Aktsiia! Pussy Riot liquidation! Pussy Riot is dead!]. YouTube. Undefined. n.d. viewed 14 August 2015. https://www.youtube.com/watch?v=qmuZwBuEIyI.

McCallum, E. L., and Mikko Tuhkanen. 2011. *Queer Times, Queer Becomings*. Albany: State University of New York Press.

McCarthy, Margaret. 2011. "Feminism and Generational Conflicts in Alexa Hennig von Lange's Relax, Elke Nater's Lügen, and Charlotte Roche's Feuchtgebiete." Special issue of *Studies in 20th and 21st Century Literature* 35 (1): 56-73.

– 2015. *German Pop Literature: A Companion*. Berlin: De Gruyter.

– n.d. "Mad Mädchen: Popfeminism and Generational Conflicts in Recent German Literature and Film." Unpublished ms.

McDonough, Katie. 2013. "I'm Not a Feminist, But...." salon.com, 6 April. http://www.salon.com/2013/04/06/im_not_a_feminist_but/.

McLennan, Rachael. 2009. *Adolescence, America, and Postwar Fiction: Developing Figures*. New York: Palgrave Macmillan.

McLeod, Dayna, Jasmine Rault, and T.L. Cowan. 2014. "Speculative Praxis towards a Queer Feminist Digital Archive: A Collaborative Research-Creation Project." *Ada: A Journal of Gender, New Media, and Technology*, 5: n.p. http://adanewmedia.org/2014/07/issue5-cowanetal/. doi: 10.7264/N3PZ573Z.

McRobbie, Angela. 2009. *The Aftermath of Feminism: Gender, Culture and Social Change*. London: Sage.

Meier, Anja. 2011. *Lassen Sie mich durch, ich bin Mutter: Von Edel-Eltern und ihren Bestimmkindern*. Cologne: Bastei Lübbe.

Meltzer, Marisa. 2010. *Girl Power: The Nineties Revolution in Music*. New York: Faber and Faber.

Miller, Andrew. 2012. "Perfect Opposition: On Putin and Pussy Riot." *Public Policy Research* 19 (2): 205–7.

Missy Redaktion. Varying dates. "Eltern ABC. Missy Magazine." *Missy Magazine.* http://missy-magazine.de/category/eltern-abc/.

Mitchell, W.J.T., Bernard E. Harcourt, and Michael T. Taussig. 2013. *Occupy: Three Inquiries in Disobedience.* Chicago: University of Chicago Press.

Mountz, Alison, Anne Bonds, Becky Mansfield, Jenna Loyd, Jennifer Hyndman, Margaret Walton-Roberts, Ranu Basu, et al. Forthcoming. "For Slow Scholarship: A Feminist Politics of Rersistance through Collective Action in the Neoliberal University." *acme: International E-journal for Critical Geographies* 1 (2015). http://acme-journal.org/index. php/acme.

Mueller, Agnes C. 2004. *German Pop Culture: How "American" Is It?* Ann Arbor: University of Michigan Press.

Murphy, Meghan. 2012. "There Is a Wrong Way to Do Feminism. And Femen Is Doing It Wrong." *Feminist Current*, 31 October. http://feministcurrent. com/6619/there-is-a-wrong-way-to-do-feminism-and-femen-is-doing-it-wrong/.

Nagatajan, Chitra. 2013. "Femen's Obsession with Nudity Feeds a Racist Colonial Feminism." *Guardian*, 11 April. http://www.theguardian.com/ commentisfree/2013/apr/11/femen-nudity-racist-colonial-feminism.

Najumi, Mohadesa. 2013. "Where Femen Has Gone Wrong." *Feminist Wire*, 7 April. http://thefeministwire.com/2013/04/ op-ed-where-femen-have-gone-wrong/.

Nakamura, Lisa. 2002. *Cybertypes: Race, Ethnicity, and Identity on the Internet.* New York: Routledge.

– 2008. *Digitizing Race Visual Cultures of the Internet.* Minneapolis: University of Minnesota Press.

Nasman, Carl. 2014. "Women's Rights Activists Stage Flash Mobs across Germany." *Deutsche Welle*, 17 February. http://www.dw.de/ womens-rights-activists-stage-flash-mobs-across-germany/a-17436887.

Nussbaum, Emily. 2011. "The Rebirth of the Feminist Manifesto: Come for the Lady Gaga, Stay for the Empowerment." http://nymag.com/news/ features/feminist-blogs-2011-11/.

Nutter, Abigail. 2014. "Now Is THE TIME to Be a Feminist: The Media, Patriarchy and You." *Bust*, 27 May. http://bust.com/now-is-the-time-to-be-a-feminist-the-media-patriarchy-and-you.html.

O'Keeffe, Alice. 2013. "Wrecked by Charlotte Roche – Review." *Guardian*, 8 May. http://www.guardian.co.uk/books/2013/may/08/ wrecked-charlotte-roche-review.

O'Reilly, Andrea. 2008. *Feminist Mothering.* Albany: State University of New York Press.

– 2010. *Twenty-First-Century Motherhood: Experience, Identity, Policy, Agency.* New York: Columbia University Press.

O'Reilly, Andrea, ed. 2014. *Mothers, Mothering, and Motherhood across Cultural Differences: A Reader.* Bradford, ON: Demeter Press.

Occupy Barbie-Dreamhouse. 2013. "Die Bagger rollen schon und Brunnen gibt es bereits nicht mehr. Tschüss Barbiehaus." Facebook. Viewed 17 January 2015. https://www.facebook.com/occupybarbiedreamhouse/ photos/ a.440130382739938.1073741831.424632290956414/501822276 570748/ ?type=1&permPage=1.

Oguntoye, Katharina, May Ayim, and Dagmar Schultz. 1986. *Farbe bekennen: Afro-deutsche Frauen auf den Spuren ihrer Geschichte.* Berlin: Orlanda Frauenverlag.

Paech, Joachim. 1997. "Paradoxien der Auflösung und Intermedialität." In *HyperKult: Geschichte, Theorie und Kontext digitaler Medien,* ed. Martin Warnke, Wolfgang Coy, and Georg Christoph Tholen, 331–68. Basel and Frankfurt: Stroemfeld. http://www.medientheorie.com/doc/paech_paradoxien.pdf.

Pape, Ulf. 2013. "Musliminnen wehren sich gegen Femen-Nacktprotest." *Spiegel Online,* 8 April. http://www.spiegel.de/netzwelt/web/musliminnen-gegen-femen-a-893163.html.

Parkin, Simon. 2014. "Gamergate: A Scandal Erupts in the Video-Game Community." *New Yorker,* 17 October. http://www.newyorker.com/tech/elements/gamergate-scandal-erupts-video-game-community.

Paul, Kari. 2014. "New Documentary *Ukraine Is Not a Brothel* Reveals Femen's Core Problems." *Bitch Media,* 11 March. http://bitchmagazine.org/post/new-documentary-ukraine-is-not-a-brothel- reveals-femens-core-problems.

Peaches. 2006. "You Love It." *Impeach My Bush.* XL Recordings. CD.

Peaches TV. 2012. "Free Pussy Riot! #freepussyriot." YouTube, 15 August. Viewed 16 January 2015. https://www.youtube.com/watch?v=SaJ7GzPvJKw.

Peck, Elizabeth G., and JoAnna Stephens Mink, eds. 1998. *Common Ground: Feminist Collaboration in the Academy.* Albany: State University of New York Press.

Pelligrini, Ann, and Jasbir Puar. 2009. "Affect." *Social Text* 27 (3): 35–58.

Pelly, Jenn. 2014. "Nadia Tolokonnikova and Masha Alyokhina No Longer Members of Pussy Riot." *Pitchfork,* 6 February. http://pitchfork.com/news/53860-nadia-tolokonnikova-and-masha-alyokhina-no-longer-members-of-pussy-riot/.

Pham, Minh-Ha T. 2011. "Blog Ambition: Fashion, Feelings, and the Political Economy of the Digital Raced Body." *Camera Obscura: Feminism, Culture, and Media Studies* 26 (1): 1–37.

– 2014. "Fashion's Cultural-Appropriation Debate: Pointless." *Atlantic,* 15 May. http://www.theatlantic.com/entertainment/archive/2014/05/cultural-appropriation-in-fashion-stop-talking-about-it/370826/.

Pilkington, Ed. 2011. "SlutWalking Gets Rolling after Cop's Loose Talk about Provocative Clothing." *Guardian,* 6 May. http://www.theguardian.com/world/2011/may/06/slutwalking-policeman-talk-clothing.

Pirmasens, Deef. 2010. "*Axolotl Roadkill*: Alles Nur Geklaut?" *Die Gefühlskonserve*, 5 February. http://www.gefuehlskonserve.de/axolotl-roadkill-alles-nur-geklaut-05022010.html#more-4775.

Plant, Sadie. 1997. "Babes in the Net." *New Statesman and Society*, 28 January8.

Pollock, Griselda. 1996. *Generations and Geographies in the Visual Arts: Feminist Readings*. London: Routledge.

Porter, Meredith, and Hannah Reid. 2015. "I'm a Feminist Because …" tumblr.com. Viewed January 16. http://feministbecause.tumblr.com.

Potkin, Helen. 2000. "Performance Art." In *Feminist Visual Culture*, ed. Fiona Carson and Claire Pajaczkowska, 75–88. Edinburgh: Edinburgh University Press.

Puar, Jasbir K. 2007. *Terrorist Assemblages: Homonationalism in Queer Times*. Durham, NC: Duke University Press.

– 2009. "Prognosis Time: Towards a Geopolitics of Affect, Debility and Capacity." *Women and Performance: A Journal of Feminist Theory* 19 (2): 161–72. doi:10.1080/07407700903034147.

– 2013. "Homonationalism as Assemblage: Viral Travels, Affective Sexualities." *Jindal Global Law Review* 4 (2): 23–43.

Pussy Riot. 2014. "We Wish Nadia and Masha Well – But They're No Longer Part of Pussy Riot." *Guardian*, 6 February. http://www.theguardian.com/commentisfree/2014/feb/06/nadia-masha-pussy-riot-collective-no-longer.

Radisch, Iris. 2010. "Helene Hegemann: Die alten Männer und das junge Mädchen." *Zeit Online*, 10 February. http://www.zeit.de/2010/08/Helene-Hegemann-Medien.

Rancière, Jacques. 2004. *The Politics of Aesthetics: The Distribution of the Sensible*. Trans. Gabriel Rockhill. London: Continuum, 2004.

– 2009. *Aesthetics and Its discontents*. Trans. Steven Corcoran. Cambridge: Polity Press.

Ray, Lady Bitch. 2007. "Mein Name Steht für Pussy Power." *Antiberliner* 14: 8.

Redfern, Catherine, and Kristin Aune. 2010. *Reclaiming the F Word: The New Feminist Movement*. New York: Zed Books.

Reger, Jo, ed. 2005. *Different Wavelengths: Studies of the Contemporary Women's Movement*. New York: Routledge.

Reinbold, Fabian. 2013. "Sexismus-Debatte: Aufschrei Gegen Gauck." *Spiegel Online*, 6 March. http://www.spiegel.de/politik/deutschland/sexismus-debatte-aufschrei-gegen-gauck-a-887170.html.

Riot Grrrl Berlin. 2012. "This Is a Call to All Pussy Riot Supporters." Facebook. 6 August. Viewed 13 August 2015. https://www.facebook.com/riotgrrrlberlin/posts/338488709569676.

Roche, Charlotte. 2008. *Feuchtgebiete*. Köln: DuMont.

– 2011. *Schoßgebete*. München: Piper.

Roesenblatt, Hannah. 2012. "Mütter sollten ihre Möpse bedecken – Jedenfalls wenn sie rechnen können." Maedchenmannschaft.net. 2 January.

Viewed 17 January 2015. http://maedchenmannschaft.net/muetter-sollten-ihre-moepse-bedecken-jedenfalls-wenn-sie-rechnen-koennen/.

Röggla, Kathrin. 2013. *Besser wäre: Keine: Essays und Theater.* Frankfurt am Main: S. Fischer.

Sadowski, Helga. 2015. "From #aufschrei to Hatr.org: Digital-material Entanglements in the Context of German Digital Feminist Activisms." In *Feminist Media Studies. Digital Feminisms: Transnational Activism in German Protest Cultures*, ed. Christina Scharff, Carrie Smith-Prei, and Maria Stehle. Special issue of *Feminist Media Studies* 16 (1). New York: Routledge. doi:10.1080/14680777.2015.1093090.

Şahin, Reyhan. 2014. *Die Bedeutung des muslimischen Kopftuchs: Eine kleidungssemiotische Untersuchung Kopftuch tragender Musliminnen in der Bundesrepublik Deutschland.* Münster: Lit-Verlag.

– 2015. "Riot Grrrls, Bitchsm, and Pussy Power – Interview with Reyhan Sahin/Lady Bitch Ray." In *Feminist Media Studies. Digital Feminisms: Transnational Activism in German Protest Cultures*, ed. Christina Scharff, Carrie Smith-Prei, and Maria Stehle. Special issue of *Feminist Media Studies* 16 (1). New York: Routledge. doi:10.1080/14680777.201 5.1093136.

Sarrazin, Thilo. 2010. *Deutschland schafft sich ab: Wie wir unser Land aufs Spiel setzen.* München: DVA.

Scharff, Christina. 2011. "The New German Feminisms: Of Wetlands and Alpha-Girls." In *New Femininities: Postfeminism, Neoliberalism, and Subjectivity*, ed. Rosalind Gill and Christina Scharff, 265–78. New York: Palgrave Macmillan.

– 2014a. "Schröder versus Schwarzer? Analysing the Discursive Terrain of Media Debates about Feminism." *Feminist Media Studies* 14 (5): 837–52. http://www.tandfonline.com/doi/full/10.1080/14680777.2013.805157.

– 2014b. "Starting the Debate: Framing Contemporary Engagements with Feminism." Presentation given at the Feminisms in the online lecture series Digital Age: Transnational Activism in Germany and Beyond, 4 November.

Scharff, Christina, Carrie Smith-Prei, and Maria Stehle. 2015. "Introduction." In *Digital Feminisms: Transnational Activism in German Protest Cultures*, ed. Christina Scharff, Carrie Smith-Prei, and Maria Stehle. Special issue of *Feminist Media Studies* 16 (1). New York: Routledge. doi:10.1080/146807 77.2015.1093069.

Schaschek, Sarah. 2014. "Brutale Drohungen Im Internet: Hass Und Hetze Gegen Geschlechterforscher." *Zeit Online*, 12 August. http://www.zeit.de/studium/2014-08/geschlechterforschung-bedrohung-internet.

Schlaffer, Hannelore. 2011. "Die Göre – Karriere einer literarischen Figur." *Merkur: Deutsche Zeitschrift für europäisches Denken* 742 (3): 274–9.

Schubert, Kai. 2013. "Peaches ohne Musik." jungle-world.com, 16 August. http://jungle-world.com/artikel/2012/33/46062.html.

Schuler, Catherine. 2013. "Reinventing the Show Trial: Putin and Pussy Riot." *Drama Review* 57 (1): 7–17.

Schulze, Gerhard. 2005. *Die Erlebnisgesellschaft: Kultursoziologie Der Gegenwart*. Frankfurt am Mein: Campus Verlag.

Schumacher, Eckhard. 2011. "Das Ende der Popliteratur: Eine Fortsetzungsgeschichte (Teil 2)." In *Poetik der Oberfläche: Die deutschsprachige Popliteratur der 1990er Jahre*, ed. Olaf Grabienski, Till Huber, and Jan-Noël Thon, 53–70. Berlin: De Gruyter.

Schwarzer, Alice. 2007. *Die Antwort*. Köln: Kiepenheuer and Witsch.

Scott, Joan Wallach. 2002. "Feminist Reverberation." *Difference: A Journal of Feminist Cultural Studies* 13 (2): 1–22.

Sedgwick, Eve Kosofsky. 2003. *Touching Feeling: Affect, Pedagogy, Performativity*. Durham, NC: Duke University Press.

Seidel, Anna. 2015. "Es gibt keinen wahren Po im falschen." *Berliner Republik*, no. 3. http://www.b-republik.de/aktuelle-ausgabe/es-gibt-keinen-wahren-po-im-falschen

Sherman, Cindy. 2012. *Museum of Modern Art*. Viewed 16 January 2015. http://www.moma.org/interactives/exhibitions/2012/cindysherman/#/6/.

Sky News. 2014. "Pussy Riot 'Whipped' by Cossacks Patrolling Sochi Winter Olympics." YouTube. 19 February. Viewed 14 August 2015. https://www.youtube.com/watch?v=eiwofw_sJOk.

Slaughter, Anne-Marie. 2012. "Why Women Still Can't Have It All." *Atlantic*, July/August. http://www.theatlantic.com/magazine/archive/2012/07/why-women-still-cant-have-it-all/309020/3/.

SlutWalk Berlin. 2012. "Stellungnahme Des SlutWalk Berlin Teams 2012: Zu den sexualisierten Übergriffen auf der SlutWalk Berlin Soli-Party." SlutWalkBerlin.de. 15 September. Viewed 13 August 2015. http://slutwalkberlin.de/post/28192926636/stellungnahme-des-slutwalk-berlin-teams-2012.

Smith-Prei, Carrie. 2009. "Satirizing the Private as Political: 1968 and Postmillennial Family Narratives." *Women in German Yearbook* 25: 76–99. doi:10.1353/wgy.0.0026.

– 2011. "'Knaller-Sex für alle': Popfeminist Body Politics in Lady Bitch Ray, Charlotte Roche, and Sarah Kuttner." In *Wonder Girls to Alpha Females: Contemporary Women's Writing in German and the Return of Feminism*. Special issue of *Studies in 20th and 21st Century Literature* 35 (1): 18–39.

– 2013. *Revolting Families: Toxic Intimacy, Private Politics, and Literary Realisms in the German Sixties*. Toronto: University of Toronto Press, 2013.

– 2015. "Affect, Aesthetics, Biopower, and Technology: Political Interventions into Transnationalism." In *Transnationalism in Contemporary German-Language Literature*, ed. Elisabeth Herrmann, Carrie Smith-Prei, and Stuart Taberner, 65–85. Rochester: Camden House.

Smith-Prei, and Maria Stehle. 2013. "Awkwardness als Provokation: Gedankenspiele zu Popfeminismus, Körperpolitik und der Vermarktung literarischer Frauen." In *Fiktionen und Realitäten: Schriftstellerinnen im deutschsprachigen Literaturbetrieb*, ed. Brigitte E. Jirku and Marion Schulz, 215–30. Frankfurt/Main: Peter Lang, 2013.

– 2014. "WiG Trouble: Awkwardness and Feminist Politics." *Women in German Yearbook Anniversary Volume* 30: 209–24.

– 2015. "The Awkward Politics of Popfeminist Literary Events: Helene Hegemann, Charlotte Roche, and Lady Bitch Ray." In *German Women's Writing in the Twenty-First Century*, ed. Hester Baer and Alexandra Merley Hill. 132–53. Rochester, NY: Camden House.

Solnit, Rebecca. 2014. "Listen Up, Women Are Telling Their Story Now." *Guardian*, 30 December. www.theguardian.com/news/2014/dec/30/-sp-rebecca-solnit-listen-up-women-are-telling-their-story-now.

Sona, Zoé. 2012. "Wir werden wütend." jungle-world.com, 16 August. http://jungle-world.com/artikel/2012/33/46068.html.

Spiegel Online International. 2010. "The Man Who Divided Germany: Why Sarrazin's Integration Demagoguery Has Many Followers." *Spiegel*, 6 September. http://www.spiegel.de/international/germany/the-man-who-divided-germany-why-sarrazin-s-integration-demagoguery-has-many-followers-a-715876.html.

Spivak, Gayatri. 1999. *A Critique of Postcolonial Reason: Towards a History of the Vanishing Present.* Cambridge, MA: Harvard University Press.

Springer, Simon. 2010. "Neoliberalism and Geography: Expansions, Variegations, Formations." *Geography Compass* 4 (8): 1025–38. doi:10.1111/j.1749-8198.2010.00358.x.

Spürk, Alexandra. 2015. "Rapperin und Sprachwissenschaftlerin 'Lady Bitch Ray' hält Seminar an der Universität Köln." *Kölner Stadt-Anzeiger*, 12 May. http://www.ksta.de/campus/rapperin-und-sprachwissenschaftlerin--lady-bitch-ray--haelt-seminar-an-der-universitaet-koeln,15189650,30683406.html.

Staiger, Janet, Ann Cvetkovich, and Ann Morris Reynolds. 2010. *Political Emotions.* New York: Routledge.

Stampler, Laura. 2014. "Annie Lennox on Beyoncé's Feminism: 'Twerking Is Not Feminism.'" TIME.com, 21 October. http://time.com/3529403/annie-lennox-twerking-feminism/.

Standing, Guy. 2011. "The Precariat – The New Dangerous Class." *Policy Network*, 24 May. http://www.policy-network.net/pno_detail.aspx?ID=4004&title=%2BThe%2BPrecariat%2B%E2%80%93%2BThe%2Bnew%2Bdangerous%2Bclass.

Stefan, Verena. 1975. *Häutungen: Autobiografische Aufzeichnungen, Gedichte, Träume, Analysen.* München: Verlag Frauenoffensive.

Stehle, Maria. 2012. "Pop, Porn, and Rebellious Speech: Feminist Politics and the Multi-Media Performances of Elfriede Jelinek, Charlotte Roche, and Lady Bitch Ray." *Feminist Media Studies* 12 (2): 229–47.

– 2013. "Pop-Feminist Music in Twenty-First Century Germany: Innovations, Provocations, and Failures." *Contemporary German Pop*. Special issue of *Journal of Popular Music Studies* 25 (2): 222–39.

Stehling, Miriam, and Tanja Thomas. 2015. "The Communicative Construction of FEMEN: Naked Protest in Self-Mediation and German Media Discourse." In *Digital Feminisms: Transnational Activism in German Protest Cultures*, ed. Christina Scharff, Carrie Smith-Prei, and Maria Stehle. Special issue of *Feminist Media Studies* 16 (1). New York: Routledge. doi:10.1080/14680777.2015.1093111.

Steinmetz, Katy. 2014. "Which Word Should Be Banned in 2015?" TIME.com, 12 November. http://time.com/3576870/worst-words-poll-2014/.

Steyerl, Hito. 2009. "In Defense of the Poor Image." *E-flux*, no. 10, November. http://www.e-flux.com/journal/in-defense-of-the-poor-image/.

Stiles, Kristine. 1996. "Performance Art." In *Theories and Documents of Contemporary Art: A Sourcebook of Artists' Writings*, ed. Kristine Stiles and Peter Selz, 679–94. Berkeley: University of California Press.

Stöcker, Mirja, ed. 2007. *Das F-Wort: Feminismus ist sexy*. Königstein im Taunus: Ulrike Helmer Verlag.

Stockton, Kathryn Bond. 2009. *The Queer Child: On Growing Sideways in the Twentieth Century*. Durham, NC: Duke University Press.

Stokowski, Margarete. 2014. "Emanzen, Die Nackt Tanzen." taz.de, 6 November. http://m.taz.de/Kolumne-Luft-und-Liebe/!148990;m/.

Striff, Erin. 1997. "Bodies of Evidence: Feminist Performance Art." *Critical Survey* 9 (1): 1–18. doi:10.3167/001115797782484628.

SuEcideSally. 2009. "Chicks On Speed Feat. Peaches – We Don't Play Guitars." YouTube. 10 May. Viewed 13 August 2015. https://www.youtube.com/watch?v=pO8MvjiIGko.

Sunderland, Mitchell. 2013. "The Barbie Dream House Experience Is the Scariest Place on Earth." *Vice Media llc*, 25 December. http://www.vice.com/read/the-barbie-dream-house-experience-is-the-scariest-place-on-earth.

Tanenbaum, Leora. 2015. *I Am Not a Slut: Slut-Shaming in the Age of the Internet*. New York: Harper Perennial.

Tayler, Jeffrey. 2013. "Topless Jihadis: Inside the World's Most Radical Feminist Movement." *Atlantic*, 19 December. http://www.theatlantic.com/international/archive/2013/12/topless-jihadis-inside-the-worlds-most-radical-feminist-movement/282503/.

Taylor Swift VEVO. 2014. "Shake It Off." YouTube, 18 August. Viewed 13 August 2015. https://www.youtube.com/watch?v=nfWlot6h_JM.

Torloxten, Stephanie. 2011. "Laut, Grell Und Bunt: Chicks on Speed Im FFT." *Rheinische Post*, 31 January. http://www.rp-online.de/nrw/ laut-grell-und-bunt-chicks-on-speed-im-fft-aid-1.329654.

Traister, Rebecca. 2011. "Ladies, We Have a Problem." *New York Times*, July 24. Last modified 7 February 2012. http://www.nytimes.com/2011/07/24/ magazine/clumsy-young-feminists.html?pagewanted=all&_r=0.

Trieba, Eve-Catherine. 2013. "Wirf einen letzten Blick in Barbies Traumhaus!" *Qiez*, 29 August. http://www.qiez.de/mitte/familie/freizeit-mit-kindern/ barbie-in-berlin-the-dreamhouse-experience-am-alexanderplatz/46268162.

Tuzcu, Pinar. 2014. "#feminisms: Decolonizing Solidarity in Cyberspace." Presentation given at the Feminisms in the online lecture series Digital Age: Transnational Activism in Germany and Beyond, 1 December.

– 2015. "'Allow Access to Location?': Digital Feminist Geographies." In *Feminist Media Studies. Digital Feminisms: Transnational Activism in German Protest Cultures*, ed. Christina Scharff, Carrie Smith-Prei, and Maria Stehle. Special issue of *Feminist Media Studies* 16 (1). New York: Routledge. doi:10.1080/14680777.2015.1093153.

Ugurlu, Ebru. 2015. "Vorlesung mit Skandal-Rapperin: Lady Bitch Ray an der Kölner Uni." bild.de, 13 May. http://www.bild.de/regional/koeln/lady-bitch-ray/haelt-vorlesung-an-der-uni-koeln-40933196.bild.html.

Valenti, Jessica. 2011. "SlutWalks and the Future of Feminism." *Wisconsin State Journal*, 8 June. http://host.madison.com/news/opinion/column/ article_bcd1828b-7c59-5115-bee4-a7fddb9482b1.html.

Vincent, Alice. 2014. "How Feminism Conquered Pop Culture." telegraph.co.uk, 30 December. http://www.telegraph.co.uk/culture/ culturenews/11310119/feminism-pop-culture-2014.html.

Voigt, Claudia. 2012. "Emanzipation: Frauen können alles haben." *Spiegel Online*, August 20. http://www.spiegel.de/spiegel/emanzipation-warum-frauen-ihre-kinder-frueher-bekommen-sollten-a-851069.html.

Wark, Jayne. 2006. *Radical Gestures Feminism and Performance Art in North America*. Montreal and Kingston: McGill-Queen's University Press.

Weber, Beverly. 2004. "Cloth on Her Head, Constitution in Hand." *German Politics and Society* 22 (3): 33–64. doi:10.3167/104503004782353122.

– 2015. "Gender, Race, Religion, Faith? Rethinking Intersectionality in German Feminisms." *European Journal of Women's Studies* 22 (1): 1–15.

– 2015b. "Kübra Gümüsay, Muslim Digital Feminism and the Politics of Visuality in Germany." In *Digital Feminisms: Transnational Activism in German Protest Cultures*, ed. Christina Scharff, Carrie Smith-Prei, and Maria Stehle. Special issue of *Feminist Media Studies* 16 (1). New York: Routledge. doi:10.1080/14680777.2015.1093123.

Whelehan, Imelda. 1995. *Modern Feminist Thought: From the Second Wave to "Post- Feminism."* New York: New York University Press.

Wilding, Faith. 1998. "Notes on the Political Condition of Cyber Feminisms." *Art Journal* 57 (2): 46–59.

Williams, N. 2010. "Is Lady Gaga a Feminist or Isn't She?" *Ms. Magazine Online*, 11 March. http://msmagazine.com/blog/2010/03/11/is-lady-gaga-a-feminist-or-isnt-she/.

Williams, Raymond. 1977. *Marxism and Literature*. Oxford: Oxford University Press.

Wingfield, Nick. 2014. "Feminist Critics of Video Games Facing Threats in 'GamerGate' Campaign." *New York Times*, 15 October. http://www.nytimes.com/2014/10/16/technology/gamergate-women-video-game-threats-anita-sarkeesian.html?_r=0.

Wise, Raúl Delgado, Humberto Márquez Covarrubias, and Ruben Puentes. 2013. "Reframing the Debate on Migration, Development and Human Rights." *Population, Space and Place* 19: 430–43.

Wizorek, Anne. 2014. *Weil ein #Aufschrei nicht reicht: Für einen Feminismus von heute*. Frankfurt am Main: Fischer.

Wnendt, David, dir. *Feuchtgebiete*. 2013. Germany: Strand Releasing, film.

Wolfson, Todd. 2014. *Digital Rebellion: The Birth of the Cyber Left*. Chicago: University of Illinois Press.

Wunker, Erin. 2012. "Once More, with Feeling: Why Feminist Methodology is Crucial." *Hook and Eye*. 1 October. Last viewed 13 August 2015. http://www.hookandeye.ca/2012/10/once-more-with-feeling-why-feminist.html.

York, Lorraine M. 2002. *Rethinking Women's Collaborative Writing: Power, Difference, Property*. Toronto: University of Toronto Press.

Yusupova, Marina. 2014. "Pussy Riot: A Feminist Band Lost in History and Translation." *Nationalities Papers: The Journal of Nationalism and Ethnicity* 42 (4): 604–10.

Zeisler, Andi. 2014. "Feminism's Strange 2014: What We Want to See Happen Next Year." salon.com, 23 December. http://www.salon.com/2014/12/24no_more_celebrity_feminists_what_we_want_to_see_from_feminism_in_2015/.

ZKM Karlsruhe. 2013. "IMA Lab No. 12 – Chicks On Speed." YouTube, 25 January. Last viewed 13 August 2015. https://www.youtube.com/watch?v=IPkO1WYHBSLk.

Zychowicz, Jessica. 2011. "Two Bad Words: FEMEN and Feminism in Independent Ukraine." *Anthropology of East Europe Review* 29 (2): 215–27.

Index

9/11, 31–5, 46, 76, 101, 110

183, 194–6, 202, 217; as cruel
optimism, 83, 100; cyberfeminism,
9, 179, 214n23; and cynicism,
42, 44, 119, 199, 203–4;
depoliticization of, 53–4, 61;
digital feminism, 8, 13, 17, 80,
146, 176–7, 209n2, 211n12; and
event culture, 10, 17, 39, 151, 170,
175; and feminist futures, 31, 34,
43, 46, 75–8; and reverberations,
13, 32–3, 38, 99, 190, 214n24;
as the f-word, 52–3; generational
feminism, 31–2, 43, 48, 53–4, 56,
62, 74, 105–6, 128, 155, 213n8;
global feminism, 13–14, 33, 66,
126; and intersectionality, 6, 15,
23, 35, 44, 47, 50, 54–7, 62–3,
67–8, 75, 93, 116, 125, 133, 142,
212n34, 213n13, 222n17; and
irony, 8, 34–5, 38–42, 83, 102,
123–4, 133, 145, 171, 177, 200–2;
and joyfulness, 6, 17, 81–3, 89, 92,
99–105, 183–7, 201, 205–7; lifestyle
feminism, 41, 54, 56, 93, 112, 160,
163, 213n12; metafeminism, 32–3;
neofeminism, 48, 51–3, 56, 75, 171;
and neoliberalism, 48, 50–4, 59,
96, 112, 139, 163, 178–9, 214n24;
postfeminism, 53–5, 140, 152, 161,
179, 194; and self-awareness, 44,
200, 203; sex-positivity, 91–2, 102,
175; and transnationalism, 3, 5, 8,
10, 12–13, 33, 47, 50–1, 61, 81,
90, 104, 128, 188; and waves, 15,
21, 24, 26, 30–3, 38–44, 48–56,
59, 63, 66, 68–9, 72–5, 79, 82,
116, 163, 175, 179, 185, 197, 203,
212n3, 213n8. See also circularity;
disturbance; German feminism;
popfeminism; riot grrrl
FemTechNet, 223n20; DOCC, 223n20
Feuchtgebiete (Wetlands). See Roche,
Charlotte

Feuchtgebiete (Wetlands) film, 140,
151, 166–70. See also Roche,
Charlotte
financial crisis. See crisis: economic/
Eurozone
flashmobs, 63–4
Foucault, Michel, 143–4, 146, 158,
219n6; and biopolitics, 143–5; The
History of Sexuality, Vol. I, 143,
219n6
Free to Fight: An Interactive Self-
Defense Project, 29, 211n15
F-Wort, Das: Feminismus ist sexy, 53,
171

gender, 7–9, 21, 23, 26–30, 35–6,
42–4, 46–7, 49–50, 54–6, 63, 65,
68–9, 81, 86, 89, 99, 103, 105–6,
110–111, 115–116, 118, 121, 123,
126, 128, 137, 141, 144, 146–7,
160, 164–5, 172, 186–7, 190, 194–
9, 204, 206–7, 210n5, 213n13,
218n10, 222n10
German feminism, 15, 47, 49, 51,
53, 59, 62, 75, 93, 179, 213n13,
214n24; and Afro-German
feminism, 54–5, 213n13; and
Alice Schwarzer, 52–4, 74, 93,
213n9; history of, 15, 26–8, 45,
47–8, 55–60, 68, 93, 211n25; and
neoliberalism, 50–1, 54, 96, 112,
179, 214n24. See also feminism
German pop, 56–7, 59, 68, 152. See
also Brinkmann, Rolf-Dieter
Germany, 12–13, 15, 21–2, 26–8,
30, 45–76, 79–80, 84–5, 90–3,
103, 122–3, 140, 142, 162, 164,
177, 181, 188, 190–1, 197–8, 207,
211n25, 212n2, 213nn13–14,
213n16, 219n8, 222n10
Gessen, Masha, Words Will Break
Cement: The Passion of Pussy Riot,
209n3. See also Pussy Riot